STATE POLITICS
AND THE
PUBLIC SCHOOLS

An Exploratory Analysis

STATE POLITICS
AND THE
PUBLIC SCHOOLS

AN EXPLORATORY ANALYSIS

BY

Nicholas A. Masters

Robert H. Salisbury

Thomas H. Eliot

New York : *Alfred A. Knopf*

1964

L. C. catalog card number: 63-20402

THIS IS A BORZOI BOOK,
PUBLISHED BY ALFRED A. KNOPF, INC.

FIRST EDITION

Preface

BY THOMAS H. ELIOT

In America, local control of the public schools as an article of political faith flies in the face of the facts. The boundaries of the school districts—indeed, their very existence—depend on *state* action. A substantial proportion of their operating revenues are provided from *state* funds. Teachers are certified by *state* officials in accordance with *state* laws. In short, the caliber of the public schools in any given district is to a considerable extent determined by the constitutional provisions, the statutes, and the administrative decisions of the state of which that school district is a subordinate unit.

Usually, of course, the states have delegated considerable discretionary authority to the school-district governments, and so in a single state there are both very good and very bad school systems. Although political scientists have occasionally examined school district government in its political context, they have not done so very often. Perhaps political scientists, like educators, have been lulled by the myth that public education is a "nonpolitical" subject by which the educators mean, I think, that education *should not be* (whether it is or not) a partisan issue or an area of political patronage. But the political scientist who does study school-district politics may find himself examining a unique local power structure and end up writing a case study that interests the residents of one district, but only one. There are tens of thousands of districts and in each, the political pattern is different. To formulate and test a general theory of school-district politics would demand the examination of an impracticably large number of districts.

In contrast, there are only fifty states, and the politics of education at the state level is a significant subject. Moreover, it is a manageable subject for research which can develop workable hypotheses of general applicability. This book is only a beginning. It examines the politics of three states in terms of governmental decisions affecting the public schools, and its conclusions are tentative and far from earth-shaking. But it is a start. I hope that many other states will be examined in a similar context, for the quality of education in this country may well depend, in the long run, on a deeper understanding of the realities of state politics—especially among educators.

This volume was made possible by the Carnegie Corporation of New York, which gave a generous grant to Washington University to finance the two years of research preceding its publication. Its chief author is Professor Nicholas A. Masters, of Pennsylvania State University. When I moved into a major administrative post at Washington University in 1961, Dr. Masters took responsibility for directing the research, as well as doing much of it himself in Michigan and Illinois. Professor Robert H. Salisbury of Washington University's Department of Political Science is mainly responsible for the material on Missouri, and contributed substantially to planning the research and the book itself. I have read the several drafts of every chapter and have sought to contribute chiefly by means of an editorial pencil tipped with acid.

This study had its genesis while I was a Visiting Research Professor at Princeton, when John Honey, then with Carnegie, took an interest in my work in public school politics. I am most grateful to him as I am to Princeton University for the opportunity of spending a year there, and especially to Professors Harold Stein, Marver H. Bernstein, and John F. Sly, all of Princeton University.

All the authors deeply appreciate the help of Professor Carl A. McCandless of Washington University, who did a substantial amount of basic research on administrative decisions at the state level before his work was interrupted by an appointment to the chairmanship of the Department of Political Science, where he succeeded me. Among the graduate students who assisted on the project, we specially want to mention Dr. Donald Flesche, now of Kalamazoo College, who studied the School Problems Commission in Illinois; Lattie F. Coor, Jr., and Lawrence K. Pettit, who did field research in Michigan and Missouri, respectively; and Dr. Margaret Soderberg, now of Eastern Illinois University. The critical judgments and insights of Professor Merle Borrowman of the University of Wisconsin were helpful in interpreting and synthesizing our data. Our gratitude goes, too, to Professor Lawrence A. Cremin of Columbia Teachers' College, to the academicians who advised us at an early conference in St. Louis in May, 1960, to the legislators, administrators, educators, and educational spokesmen in three states who were generous with their time and frank in their statements, and to the Carnegie Corporation of New York.

Washington University
St. Louis, Missouri

Contents

STATE POLITICS
AND THE
PUBLIC SCHOOLS

An Exploratory Analysis

CHAPTER I

❀ ❀ ❀ ❀

Education and Politics

THE NATURE OF THE PROBLEM

Decisions affecting public schools, even those made by a state legislature, are seldom considered political decisions. In fact, many educators seem to abhor the term "politics" and probably with good reason, for "whole school systems have been blighted by the intrusion of certain aspects of politics, especially the use of patronage in appointments and contracts in apparent disregard of the need to give children the best possible education." [1] As a result, the dogma has evolved that public education must occupy a position above the political conflicts that are waged over other public services, and educators are supposed to abide by the maxim that politics and education do not mix. In the eyes of the public, schools and their operations are removed, or should be removed, from the arenas where other governmental decisions are made. A candidate for a position on the local district school board, for example, often escapes the stigma of a politician. Instead he is viewed as a good citizen who is serving his community. True, if elected, he becomes a part of a local governmental agency, but he be-

---

[1] Thomas H. Eliot: "Toward an Understanding of Public School Politics," *American Political Science Review* LIII (December, 1959), p. 1032.

comes a part of an agency set apart or perhaps set above other political units.

In contrast to almost all other areas of public policy, there is no anti-school lobby. Virtually no one opposes public education, at least openly. On the whole, those groups which are ideologically opposed to spending or to increasing the service functions of state government do not consider public schools suitable targets. Even those who vigorously oppose federal aid to the public schools usually base their argument on the theory that public education is essentially a state or local responsibility. Education's special position in the eyes of the public has made some wonder whether we may even speak of the "politics" of education.

Yet the belief that politics and public education are separate, or even separable, could not be further from the truth. A strong commitment to the position that education is essentially a *public* responsibility, coupled with the fact that a public school system is a costly and complicated operation, has placed considerable burdens upon those who decide how to allocate scarce resources. Those concerned with changing the pattern of education or with introducing major innovations (which normally involve increased expenditures) are compelled to negotiate with political officials who are pressured by other interests that desire other goals— such as increased expenditures for mental health or reductions in taxation. In recent years the support of public education has become one of the states' largest expenditures.[2]

Despite the obviously increasing role of government in education, relatively little scholarly attention has been devoted to the many political considerations involved. A major goal of this study is to eliminate at least some of the confusion that surrounds the governmental action in education —whether federal, state, or local. Perhaps this confusion

[2] According to a research report of the National Education Association, for the 1960-61 school year, public school revenue accounted for 33.9 percent of the total revenue of state and local governments: 44.2 percent in Utah was the highest and 24.9 percent in Massachusetts was the lowest.

stems from too ready an assumption that a legalistic examination of formal institutional structure, functions, and problems can adequately define the role of government. Such
analyses are necessary, but they fail to account for the
human behavior that is indeed guided and limited by these
institutional contexts. In brief, the textbook approach which
both political scientists and professional educators frequently employ when discussing this area of public policy
conceals the fact that education is a dynamic thing. It is
sensitive to political conflicts and changes not directly related to educational considerations. A mere cataloguing of
the functions and structure of governmental entities, then,
*pays too little attention to the substantive content of deci-
sion-making.* Although this study is not aimed at the entire
range of governmental activity that pertains to education,
there are some lessons of power for those who care enough
to listen.

Understanding a subject as vast and complex as the political decision-making that affects public schools requires a
careful shaping of the areas to be investigated and the limits
to be observed. A widespread public education system designed "to give every child a free, straight, solid pathway
by which he can walk directly up from the ignorance of an
infant to knowledge of the primary duties of man" has
always seemed to epitomize what the great experiment in
democracy could produce. Every state has its own public
educational system, and the great majority of the people—
excepting some of the belligerents of the recent integration
conflicts in the South—are firmly committed to the concept
of education at the public expense.

Since the responsibility for establishing an American educational system rests almost exclusively with the fifty state
governments, the task of determining how public school
policies are made is indeed a formidable one. Research on
a specific phase or part of a total process as diffused as the
American educational system will inevitably be haunted by

the disquieting doubt that the effort will lead not to viable generalizations but rather to a mere cataloguing of unrelated facts. We assume that some of the forces affecting public school decisions can be examined at close range at the state level and that, as a result, some tentative general propositions may be put forward to bring order to this mass of data.

Although many vital decisions concerning public school policy are made at the local district level, even these rest on delegated authority of the state government. Constitutionally many of the powers of local governments could be rescinded; but the developing pattern of public education has forced state governments to assume a more positive role in areas which were once the exclusive domain of the local districts. Finance, organization of school districts, teacher welfare, teacher certification, and responsibility for raising educational standards of the public schools to a desirable level have all become significant matters requiring state action.

The costs of erecting and maintaining physical plants, libraries, and laboratory facilities have increased to a point where very few school districts can meet their needs out of local resources, under present legal and constitutional restrictions. Sharp increases in property taxes for city, county, and school purposes have brought great pressure to shift part of the educational costs to other forms of taxation.[3] This is generally accomplished by transferring some of the burden to the state, where nonproperty taxes supply the largest portion of income. Moreover, the financial resources of school districts in terms of ability to support public schools vary so widely that action at the state level has been required to produce greater equality of educational opportunity. Some districts which are extremely wealthy can

[3] A state school official in Illinois noted: "The local taxpayer is being taxed to death. The local tax rates cannot be pushed any higher; the taxpayers just won't take it. The result is obvious: only the state can help. I don't know where the school standards would be today if it weren't for the state aid given to education."

support local schools along the lines suggested by leading educators.[4] Others find it totally impossible to operate without state assistance. Some districts are frankly more interested in good education than others and willing to exert the necessary effort to insure good schools.

In addition to the fiscal problems, the increased mobility of population within and among the states has increased the demand for more uniform standards of education in all districts, since the students in even the poorest districts often become the students or citizens of other districts. Factories and other business enterprises are continually relocating in new areas, and the influx of workers and managers creates pressures on small school districts. A growing professional consciousness among teachers has been accompanied by greater pressure to standardize and raise formal qualifications for certification on a state-wide basis. Finally, federal aid to education, particularly for vocational training in high schools, has increased the responsibilities of the state governments, since by federal law the chief state school agency must insure the maintenance of prescribed standards at the local level—as well as distribute the money.

Clearly then, education is one of the major functions of state government today. In fact, much of state politics is politics concerned with public schools. But the ways in which each state is involved in education vary and so do the political processes. Therefore, a study of *each* state is necessary in order to understand the many aspects of public school politics, as well as to provide a basis for meaningful comparisons and generalizations.

[4] These recommendations include, for example, paying higher salaries to the school's administrators and teachers, improving the plant facilities in which the school operates, providing a more extensive and better balanced curriculum, and maintaining a reasonable size school district. For a discussion of such recommendations, see James B. Conant: *The American High School Today* (New York: McGraw-Hill; 1959).

THE CRITERIA OF RELEVANCE

In this study we have selected three states for analysis: Illinois, Michigan, and Missouri. The researchers' *access* to influential political and educational leaders in the states under consideration was the principal reason for selecting them.

Each of the three states differed in one or more fundamental ways from the other two. For example, Missouri does not have the variety or spontaneity of group activity surrounding public school issues that exists in both Michigan and Illinois. Although both Michigan and Illinois have elected chief state school officers who play active political roles, they differ significantly in their respective responsibilities as well as in their perception of their offices. In Missouri, on the other hand, the appointed chief officer carefully avoids, as far as possible, any type of political role or any entanglement with elected officials. In terms of structure, in Illinois the salient feature of the state educational decision-making apparatus is a quasi-legislative, quasi-executive commission which has enjoyed unprecedented support since its inception. Neither Michigan nor Missouri has any comparable governmental agency to carry the educational load.

As V. O. Key, Jr., found variations in the politics of Southern states,[5] we also found considerable variations in the patterns of political activity of the three Midwestern states we examined—variations which have had a profound impact on education issues. Illinois and Missouri have no powerful labor organizations as identified or integrated with the Democratic party, as the United Automobile Workers Union in Michigan. In Missouri state politics, the Democrats have been the dominant party; in Illinois and Michigan, partisan politics has been more competitive. Patronage is a significantly more powerful weapon in Illinois than in either Michigan or Missouri.

Empirical studies should reflect the criteria by which it

[5] V. O. Key, Jr.: *Southern Politics* (New York: Alfred A. Knopf; 1953).

is decided what data are relevant and what are not. Our basic research strategy was to look first at the groups, individuals, and governmental agencies that have a direct and tangible stake in the outcome of education decisions or have the formal responsibility for them. Our assumption was that this would lead us to the sources of power and help us to unmask the realities of political processes in this policy area. In essence, our criteria of relevance in this study are implied in the following questions:

1. From an examination of state political processes at a particular point in time (1961-62), is it possible to make any generalized statements about how those concerned with or involved in education policies make their decisions?

2. To what extent are education policy decisions made in response to general public pressure as opposed to proposals articulated by particular organized interests?

3. In the formation of education policy does the power to determine who gets what, when, and how lie in the hands of an identifiable power structure, or is power fragmented, indicating that influence relationships vary in terms of particular issues?

4. Do the interests concerned with public school policy display any distinctive political style that significantly affects the way in which decisions are reached as well as their content? [6]

5. To what extent are education policies shaped by factors operative in the larger state political system?

6. What factors produce consensus on education policies; which ones generate controversy?

We have attempted in this study to raise questions that might be tested in future inquiries. It should be made clear, however, that our study yields no *scientifically* predictive

[6] The term "interest" refers to that "mass of activity [or behavior] operating in a given direction." Charles B. Hagan, "The Group in a Political Science," in Roland Young (ed.): *Approaches to the Study of Politics* (Evanston: Northwestern University Press; 1958), p. 45.

generalizations and avoids normative judgments, including judgments as to whether teachers individually or collectively should be involved in politics. On the whole, our choice of supporting observation and interview data has been a *free one;* we followed no standard set of techniques and methods and had no precisely defined puzzles to solve. In brief, our fact-gathering was not undertaken to articulate a particular decision-making paradigm. Yet our study was not conducted in a conceptual vacuum. Each state was viewed as a separate political system having its own patterns of actions and behavior. Our "units" of analysis were groups and the role individuals play within them. The major part of our analysis was directed to the active participants at the strategic points of education policy-making in the legislatures of our three states. The images and perceptions these participants had of themselves and other individuals and groups involved in or concerned with education policies constituted a large part of our "raw materials." Ideologies and symbols, as well as formal-legal arrangements, were treated in terms of their effect or impact on the behavior of political groups. Finally, we attempted to identify and describe the patterns of inter-action that link the active participants in the decisions about education policies with other interests and individuals in society.

We fully recognize and appreciate the interdependence of theory and empirical findings. Our approach was not, however, to posit testable propositions at the outset. Current paradigms for studying decision-making (e.g., community power structure models) did not seem to fit well the situations we examined; we concluded that a more fruitful approach would be to present our findings as *a posteriori* hypotheses for further research. It was hoped that if and when our hypotheses are integrated with the findings from other studies, they will take us a little further down that rough-hewn path that leads to a more general theory of politics, or that stage in scientific development where research is conducted within a conceptual scheme or model that, for research purposes, is widely accepted within the community of scholars.

We should comment on the limitations of this study before proceeding to a discussion of public school decision-making in each of our three states. First, the most obvious limitation is the study's exclusive concern with three states. The study would have been improved if it had included six, or twelve, or fifty. This was impossible, however, and we rest our case on the defense that the study is largely *exploratory*. Second, education is a big item in state politics and, like other policy areas, involves many interests. To account for all the interests and to analyze all of the issues in each state would have been an impossible task. So we concluded that it would be more profitable to focus attention on a few of the major policy issues and decision-making structures that produce the major policy decisions and reserve detailed treatment of specific phases for subsequent studies. We hope that our study will lay the groundwork for formulating some broad generalizations about public school politics and bring the relationship between politics and education to the attention of political scientists, professional educators, and any other people concerned about public schools.

CHAPTER II

❀ ❀ ❀ ❀

Missouri:
Low-Pressure Politics

If you ask an insider how public school policy is made in Missouri, the answer will go something like this: there isn't much conflict on school questions. In the legislature nobody can be against the schools. Besides, the school people have one of the strongest lobbies in the state. They can get most anything they ask for—provided there's enough money to pay for it. The speaker may feel that he has described the process fully enough to satisfy any reasonable inquiry. But although the statement is accurate as far as it goes, it requires much elaboration to provide a full picture of how education policy is made in Missouri. Who are "the school people"? Why are they so influential? Indeed, how influential are they, if they must work within the limitations of the available money?

In 1959, Missouri ranked forty-ninth in public school revenue from state and local sources as a percentage of personal income. The state ranked eighteenth in per capita income but thirty-eighth in per capita expenditure for local schools (see Appendix I, p. 286). Missouri has no state-wide teacher tenure protection. The politics of public schools includes what is not done as well as what is.

The following analysis attempts to demonstrate that an apparent paradox is nevertheless a valid picture of education policy-making; that the Missouri school men are indeed influential, though their achievements seem unimpressive when compared with Michigan and many other states.

In Missouri, the school men are organized in one major group, the Missouri State Teachers Association (MSTA), which defines Missouri's school needs and presents them to the state legislature. However, the proposals MSTA makes to the legislature are adjusted to the state's political traditions. The Missouri political system militates against large state expenditures and high service levels. It is what we shall call a low-pressure system. Within such a system, the MSTA can get what it asks for only if it does not ask for too much. This chapter describes the MSTA and its operations, explores the political system within which MSTA functions, and finally considers some specific cases involving education issues both of local and state-wide importance.

THE SCHOOL MEN IN MISSOURI

The Missouri State Teachers Association holds a virtual monopoly over the process of articulating the policy demands of the public school professionals. This group alone presents demands to the state legislature and presses for their passage. For example, in Missouri, teachers colleges do not play as direct or prominent a role as they do in some other states, notably New Jersey. The University of Missouri's College of Education, the several state colleges, and the private universities of the state rarely become involved in legislative struggles over elementary and secondary school policy. Whatever influence these professional educators have on school policy is exerted through their contacts with MSTA, which we discuss below. Moreover, the process of seeking legislative support for higher education in the state is quite different from that in which the public schools are involved; different interests are active and different legislators are concerned.

School administrators and school board officials do not constitute *major* separate interests in Missouri as they do in Michigan and Illinois. The administrators belong to MSTA, which represents them and in effect controls them. The officials have their own association, but rarely try to change policy through independent action. Instead they devote most of their efforts to supporting MSTA proposals.[1] Nor do the various lay groups interested in education—such as the PTA's[2] or the League of Women Voters—act as innovators.[3] Finally, the State Board of Education and the Department of Education it governs carefully avoid *direct* contact with the legislature's pending policy matters.

The teachers union is not as yet a significant participant in the state political arena. Since 1961, however, it has gained membership, particularly in St. Louis. MSTA leadership is concerned about the growing union strength and the possible threat it poses to MSTA hegemony. Nevertheless, since most state education decisions still are directed primarily at outstate school systems, where MSTA remains strong, the challenge of the union is minor. Perhaps its prin-

[1] The Missouri Association of School Boards was organized in 1936, and since 1953 has employed a full-time secretary. The association attempts to provide services—handbooks, in-service training, conferences, etc.—for school boards. It has not attempted to influence policy except as a supportive group for MSTA proposals.

[2] The Missouri Congress of Parents and Teachers consists of over 2,000 units with a membership of nearly 200,000. Its office is located in the MSTA building in Columbia, and its political efforts are similarly linked.

[3] Private citizens' groups were very instrumental in generating enthusiasm for a state-supported junior college program in 1961. This program did not attract much direct interest from existing school groups, however, and so an unusual citizen effort was required in order to make any political headway. In other words, there were no important professional teacher groups with a stake in developing a junior college program. If the program was to get support, it had to come from lay groups. Public elementary and secondary school programs *do* attract constant and intense interest from professional school men, and this leaves little opportunity for lay groups to exercise influence.

cipal effect is to nudge MSTA leaders into more vigorous action in behalf of state aid.

To some extent, all these groups may be important in feeding information into the policy-making system. The University of Missouri College of Education conducts studies that may eventually be translated into policy demands. School men in the various localities do not ignore laymen's interest in the schools. They are important as supportive interests, backing up MSTA demands and giving them a broader base. MSTA sometimes adjusts its demands to assure this broad support, too, but there is no discernible pattern of overt influence leading from these groups to the MSTA and thence to the legislature. Rather, the MSTA serves as *the* agency which articulates the policy demands of the school people *ab initio* and presents these demands to governmental policy-makers. Insofar as a separate role in the process can be identified for other groups, it consists of contributing to the climate of education opinion—within which MSTA develops specific policy demands. Thus any discussion of the "school men" in Missouri state politics leads almost exclusively to a discussion of the MSTA.

The MSTA and Its Strategy

The Missouri State Teachers Association was founded in 1856. Its first constitution proclaimed its purposes "to promote the sacred interests of education by uniting the different members, advancing their mutual improvement, and elevating the profession to its just intellectual and moral influence in the community." This organization grew slowly until after the turn of the century, but between 1907 and 1923 the membership jumped from 667 to 21,303. In recent years, virtually all public school teachers and professional school administrators in the state have joined, and it now has more than 30,000 members.

From the beginning, the MSTA has sought to influence legislation and to work for constitutional amendments of advantage to public school development. The short official centennial history of MSTA points with pride to and claims at least partial credit for a substantial list of accomplishments.[4] Some of the principal items may be noted:

the establishment and support of state normal schools and of the College of Education at the University of Missouri;

the establishment and improvement of certification requirements for teachers;

the development of compulsory school attendance legislation and lengthening of the school year; the extension of kindergarten, junior college, and adult education programs; programs for physically and mentally handicapped; and free textbook legislation;

the reëstablishment of the office of county superintendent after its abolition in 1874 and the raising of its standards of performances;

the development of legislation to encourage larger school district units;

the establishment of an appointed bipartisan state board of education, replacing the elected state superintendent of schools;

increased financial support for education at the state level and support for measures making it easier to finance schools at the local level; provision for retirement benefits for teachers; provision for continuing contract law to give some degree of job security to teachers.

Some of these programs may not owe their approval solely to the efforts of the MSTA, but the organization, except perhaps in the area of teacher welfare, has had an impressive record of legislative accomplishment.

MSTA influence in Missouri stems partly from the organization's ability to adapt its demands and its tactics to the political context in which it operates. (This context will be examined in detail at a later point.) In addition, however,

[4] See *A Brief History of the Missouri State Teachers Association, Issued on the Occasion of its Centennial Anniversary, 1856-1956*, n.d.

the organization's effectiveness results in part from internal cohesion. Its internal structure and operation are therefore significant.

The basic units of MSTA are the 278 community associations composed of groups of 25 or more teachers and administrators in particular districts or groups of districts throughout the state. These community associations attempt to maintain cohesion among the various groups associated with public school problems at the local level and are the basis for sending delegates (one for each 25 members or major fraction thereof) to the state Assembly of Delegates.

The Asssembly of Delegates is the official policy-making body of the MSTA. As with any large group, however, a relatively small nucleus of members makes policy decisions and exerts influence. A part of this nucleus is the Executive Committee, which is composed of the annually elected president and vice-president plus one representative from each of ten districts. The district members are nominated by district associations, of which five are organized around the state teachers colleges, with St. Louis, St. Louis County, Kansas City, St. Joseph, and South Central Missouri forming the other five. The district associations are otherwise autonomous from the state organization but their activities are coördinated through the state office of MSTA.

The Executive Committee is the administrative agency of MSTA, issuing publications, controlling expenditures and membership, assisting local community associations, serving as a committee on teacher welfare, appointing all other standing and special committees, receiving their reports and passing them on to the Assembly of Delegates. The Executive Committee thus occupies a crucial position in shaping the MSTA's policy recommendations. Through its appointment of a legislative committee and special committees for major public policy questions such as the foundation program, it helps to energize the campaigns of the MSTA.

A substantial portion of the concrete recommendations

for legislative action emerge from the work of the committees which the Executive Committee appoints. They reflect the diverse local experience of the members and work closely with the Executive Committee, the MSTA staff, and educators in the state colleges and universities. These committees are the formal mechanism through which more or less standard professional education recommendations, adapted to the Missouri scene, are prepared.

The Executive Committee also appoints the staff of the MSTA. The staff is another major locus of influence within the organization. Four professional staff members plus an office staff occupy the MSTA headquarters across from the University of Missouri campus in Columbia. The professionals are all products of Missouri, taking their formal training at Missouri universities and acquiring teaching and school administrative experience entirely in outstate—or rural—Missouri. All four have long experience in their present positions, ranging from fourteen to twenty-three years of service. Indeed, since 1915 when the first full-time executive secretary of MSTA was appointed, only three men have held that position. The present incumbent has served in this capacity since 1941.

Continuity in office and the completeness of identification with Missouri contribute greatly to the success of the MSTA staff in getting legislative results. For while the Executive Committee and the MSTA membership generally participate in formulating policy demands, it is inevitably the full-time professional staff that carries on the day to day legislative work. That the legislators regard the MSTA as the most effective lobby in the state is due in no small measure to their feeling that Everett Keith, Executive Secretary of the MSTA, is the most skillful lobbyist.

What are the bases of Keith's and the MSTA's influence? What is his role; how is it defined? What are its limits? Certainly one basis is the considerable influence the school people are able to muster with respect to individual legislators. The MSTA officials are well situated to contact the teachers and administrators, school boards, PTA's and others interested in education in each county of the state, alert them to school issues, and successfully exhort them to contact their representatives. Members and friends of MSTA are typically persons of prominence and influence in their local communities and legislators naturally treat their views with respect. The deference given their views on education issues is partly that accorded to leading citizens actively concerned with the issues before the legislature. MSTA's supporters are not simply composed of leading citizens, however. The school people have a special tactical advantage which most lay education interest groups do not possess. They have a direct interest in school legislation, not merely an altruistic concern. Accordingly, they are given a more respectful hearing by legislators. It is an observable fact that legislators are usually more sympathetic to "realistic" (i.e., self-interested) claimants to public funds than to groups which they regard as do-gooders.

More than that, the school people are professionals, and their claims for legislative support are made in a context of professional expertise. Over the years MSTA has worked to develop a professional reputation for teachers and public school officials, and consequently, MSTA legislative recommendations are regarded as based on expert opinion in the public school field. The MSTA staff works closely with the University of Missouri College of Education, the State Department of Education, and other professionals to assure that MSTA proposals embody the common thinking of all the professional educators. MSTA is a part of the National Education Association, and its proposals usually follow the national pattern of professional educators' views, thus reinforcing the appearance of expertise.

Nothing would be as damaging to MSTA's standing as an expert than to have rival experts appear on the legislative scene. Therefore, unity among the various educational groups—school boards, county superintendents, PTA's, etc. —is a high priority objective for the MSTA. MSTA leaders take great care to avoid actions that will result in divisions in the education lobby. As we shall see later, in 1961 MSTA shied away from taking stands that might alienate school boards or county superintendents. Indeed it seems fair to say that a major reason Missouri has no teacher tenure or minimum salary laws is that MSTA has not wished to alienate its school board supporters in behalf of its classroom teacher constituency by recommending such proposals to the legislature. Unity strengthens MSTA's bargaining position, but also imposes limits on its objectives.

Avoiding local issues and local quarrels is another rule which governs MSTA's legislative objectives. We shall explore below the process of resolving local education issues in the state arena. We should note here, however, that MSTA stays away from these issues as much as possible. MSTA has adopted the position that local issues may involve local factional quarrels, and if the organization were to take a position, siding with one faction against another, it might jeopardize its state-wide activities. The quest for unity among educational interests thus requires MSTA to confine itself to state-wide issues only. Unity enables the MSTA to present its recommendations as the products of detached, objective study, supported by all the professional experts in the state, and in addition, supported by a large organization which, if necessary, can mobilize considerable grass-roots pressure on individual legislators.

This strong bargaining position is further reinforced by MSTA's great symbolic advantage: namely, its position as spokesman for improving the public schools. Few legislators feel secure enough to challenge that symbol directly. "Who can be against the schools?" said one legislator. "That's like opposing motherhood or the flag." During the 1961 legislative session, Republicans frequently vied with Democrats in House debate to see which party could establish the

greater reputation as champion of the schools. After one
morning's partisan debate, for instance, one legislator laugh-
ingly expressed it this way: "Well, another hard morning
fighting for the kiddies."

No one opposes schools openly. No one in the legislature
opposes improving them. Thus no one openly resists MSTA.
No one in the legislature opposes the *idea* of increasing state
financial support for public schools. However, public money
is in short supply in Missouri as elsewhere, and its scarcity
constitutes the strongest limitation on MSTA effectiveness.

"Where is the money coming from?" is a frequent negative reaction to many legislative proposals. When public
school issues involve state expenditure, MSTA is faced with
its most demanding legislative task. Broadly, the organization and its leaders respond in two ways to the problem of
money.

First, MSTA scales down its demands for support to
"reasonable" levels, hoping to minimize conflict over school
issues. Keith and his associates are fully conscious of the gap
between the Missouri school aid level and that of, say,
neighboring Illinois. (Keith also points out that by comparison with other neighboring states—Arkansas, Oklahoma, or
Nebraska, for example—Missouri's record is much more impressive.) Nevertheless, rather than press for state aid at an
abstractly desirable level, MSTA has sought to pitch the
formula for aid at the highest level that present or immediately prospective state revenues will support, assuming no
major shift in existing patterns of allocation of state money.
Missouri's political culture includes a powerful tradition
against asking for more money than the revenue picture
comfortably allows. This means that one agency should not
seek money at the expense of another. It also means that
an agency or interest group should ordinarily wait for additional revenue to be available rather than try to lead its own
campaign for tax-increase proposals.

The two-step increase in the foundation program exemplifies how this norm constrains MSTA, Missouri's most powerful lobby. Having secured authorization for increased state aid in 1959, MSTA attempted to finance the increase through an earmarked boost in the sales tax. This failed, however, and MSTA was forced to wait until 1961 when, from a variety of sources, increased revenue was available to finance the Foundation Program increase.

A second response of MSTA to the problem of money is to support all gubernatorial requests for tax increases. Almost all of the requests for increased taxes that have any serious chance of legislative passage are presented by the governor. MSTA has supported all such proposals in recent years as a matter of policy. As Keith put it, "We'll take any live (tax) program," and the governor's program is the only one "alive." In Keith's judgment, this approach is the best MSTA can do to maximize the chances of having enough revenue to finance an increase in state aid. In 1961, for example, the status of the governor's revenue program was described at the head of each MSTA Legislative Bulletin, and the importance of these tax measures to full financing of the authorized state aid increase was regularly noted. Moreover, MSTA agreed to delay pushing certain other legislative requests until after passage of the governor's revenue measures was assured.

The MSTA's policy of supporting all of the governor's proposals for increased taxes is a critical factor in its relationships with other major interest groups in the state. Whenever MSTA supports a sales or cigarette tax boost, labor groups oppose it. If, as in 1961, MSTA backs a proposal to begin withholding of state income taxes, business groups oppose it. Partly as a result of these variations, MSTA does not have any strong durable alliances with nonschool groups. Keith does not regard these groups as enemies. None of them would or could risk the stigma of being anti-school. But MSTA's dependence upon increasing state revenues by whatever means are most readily available requires the or-

ganization to retain its freedom of action. Hence it forms
no lasting alliances on a *quid pro quo* basis.

The MSTA's self-imposed policy of not attempting to
obtain more money for schools unless it is apparent that increased revenues are forthcoming, does not preclude its seeking objectives that require positive legislative action, which
may eventually cost substantial amounts of money. This
means that Keith and his associates are often trying to buck
the system. Missouri is a low tax, low service state in almost
every area of state activity, and to change this substantially,
in education or any other policy area, requires skillful handling. The policy is to capitalize on any opening the political
system offers for increased appropriations. True, Keith and
the MSTA might choose to fight the inertia and fiscal conservatism of the system in a direct frontal assault, utilizing
the newspapers and the other mass media in an effort to
mobilize such massive public backing that demands for educational policy would be irresistible. But the only time in
recent years that they adopted this strategy was in the campaign for the foundation program in the period from 1952
to 1956. MSTA organized a citizen's committee and under-
took a broad public campaign to mobilize extensive popular
support to increase financial aid for public education.

The situation is different in Missouri when the desired
legislative result involves a more modest change; and resistance, while present perhaps, is not so strong nor so strategically located as it was in 1953, when the governor himself
opposed the MSTA's program. In such circumstances, Keith
and MSTA mobilize their own specialized grass-roots support but do not try to extend that support very far beyond
their own membership. Legislative Bulletins to MSTA members, phone calls to counties whose representatives are
wavering, speech materials to legislators and other political
figures, and other similar tactics are employed for this kind
of campaign. In these circumstances, unity within the school
men constituency is of special importance. MSTA relies

heavily on school administrators, school board members, and county superintendents as contacts in communicating constituency sentiments to individual legislators. In order to maintain these contacts in good order, MSTA must and does avoid exerting itself on behalf of some recommendations which the classroom teachers or college educators might regard as obvious articles of faith. Teacher tenure and proposals to eliminate the office of county superintendent of schools are good examples.

Although MSTA uses both the general public campaign and the more limited grass-roots pressure, the most characteristic way in which Keith and MSTA seek legislative support is by working *with* the Missouri political system rather than against it. "Quietly" is the key to this process. Keith does not usually try to pressure legislators. He does not buttonhole them in the corridors, nor cajole and flatter them in the hotels. He does not testify at committee hearings (although MSTA officers and MSTA-designated experts often do). Instead he uses a more subtle approach. He sits in the back of the committee room, or at the rear of the legislative gallery, or in the offices of the most important legislators, talking with those whom he feels can help the most. He and his staff draft in bill form four or five of their key proposals at each session, and they provide technical data and advice on many other bills. MSTA often serves as an informal staff to the education committees of the legislature.

Keith's contacts with individual legislators are highly selective. He makes no attempt to get broad coverage and rarely tries to persuade the uncommitted or to convert opponents. He relies primarily on the devoted supporters of MSTA objectives, who hold such key positions as chairman of the House Education Committee. Keith's friends are, for the most part, outstate Democrats. The MSTA does not reject Republicans; its key legislation always has bipartisan sponsorship. But in the last several years there have been so few Republicans, relatively, that no group is likely to expend great effort cultivating their support. Moreover, on the whole, Democrats are regarded as somewhat more sympathetic to most MSTA objectives than are Republicans. Such hard-core opposition to public expenditure as there is in Missouri—and this means opposition to MSTA—is largely among outstate Republicans.

Keith makes little effort to cultivate support among metropolitan representatives either. MSTA is less influential in the urban areas and could bring less effective grass-roots pressure on urban legislators. The urban districts have less need of state aid and so give less support to MSTA recommendations. Moreover, there is some degree of suspicion that, if aroused, metropolitan representatives might be more responsive to parochial school interests than to MSTA. We found no evidence of attempts by parochial school groups to influence the legislature on major public school questions, but the high proportion of Catholics and Lutherans in the large cities makes MSTA chary of working up interest in state school issues in St. Louis and Kansas City. Keith is content to prevent serious overt opposition from the cities, while seeking his active proponents outstate.

In this posture and in the quiet tactics employed to implement it, Keith and his colleagues adhere fully to the norms of the Missouri political culture. As we noted earlier, the MSTA staff is entirely drawn from outstate Missouri experience. It is not surprising that they have chosen primarily to try to get what they can with a minimum of agitation or conflict rather than attempt broader public campaigns in behalf of larger objectives. The latter strategy would surely require MSTA to hire new personnel in place of Keith and his associates, for they are as much a part of the culture as the legislature they work with so closely.

"THE INTERESTS" AND PUBLIC SCHOOL POLITICS

We have suggested that the tactics of moderation in behalf of limited objectives characterize MSTA activity in Missouri. This mode of activity seeks to minimize conflict over education issues and thereby get legislative results. *A priori* judgment might seem to indicate that other groups in the state would be embroiled in more severe conflicts. Specifically, an urban and rural cleavage of some sort might be anticipated, since these interests are so often thought to engage in constant battle; rival economic groups, each staking out claims and vigorously competing with each other, would fit the expected pattern. If such conflicts occurred with any frequency in Missouri, they would surely affect public school policy, but the relationships of these putative groups and education issues are not what we might anticipate. Let us consider each of them to see why.

Urban-Rural Splits and the Local Unity Norm

In many states, including Missouri, it is often alleged that rural interests dominate the state arena to the disadvantage of urban interests. Specifically, St. Louis newspapers often attribute the defeat of bills proposed by the St. Louis School Board to unsympathetic rural legislators. Statistical and qualitative analysis alike have shown that this myth does not account for much that occurs or, at most, grossly oversimplifies situations where outward appearances suggest rural domination.[5] The myth assumes that rural interests are substantially united in opposition to equally unified urban interests, whereas in fact neither grouping ordinarily exhibits the

[5] On this point, see R. S. Friedman: "The Urban-Rural Conflict Revisited," *Western Political Quarterly*, XIV (June 1961), pp. 481-495, and references cited therein.

assumed unity.[6] Legislators themselves stoutly deny the validity of the myth. Rather, in Missouri, the norm to which legislators insist they conform calls for legislators to support the request of a local delegation when it unites in support of a legislative proposal affecting only the local area. If the local group is not united, the other legislators will not approve the requested change, refusing to get involved in local quarrels. A variety of local public school issues is dealt with according to the norm of local unity.

Most local proposals emanate from the large urban areas: St. Louis City, St. Louis County, and Kansas City. However, almost any area of the state may have a special problem requiring special treatment of some kind or other, and it is this potential need for reciprocity which gives the norm such force in the legislature. It follows from the norm that all urban problems which are framed into legislative requests by the St. Louis or Kansas City administrations are treated as *local* problems, not *urban* problems. Thus, if the urban delegation agrees on the proposal, outstate legislators will support it. Precisely what "unity of the local delegation" requires is somewhat hazy. It does not require unanimity; the defection of an intransigent representative or two can be ignored. It does not require bipartisan agreement; a Republican dissenter in a predominantly Democratic delegation cannot kill the bill. Local disagreement can sometimes be minimized, too, through an intensive campaign beyond the local area by the proponents of a measure. But the norm does generally govern. Local interests lose when they are divided, win when they are united.

Traditional reliance on the local agreement formula serves to minimize overt urban-rural dichotomies. "If the St. Louis

[6] For discussions of this point with reference to Missouri, see David R. Derge: "Metropolitan and Outstate Alignments in Illinois and Missouri," *American Political Science Review,* LII (December 1958), pp. 1051-1066; Robert H. Salisbury: "Missouri Politics and State Political Systems," *Missouri Political Science Association: Research Papers 1958* (Columbia: Bureau of Governmental Research, University of Missouri; 1959), No. 2, pp. 9-24.

delegation can agree on a bill, we'll pass it," is a sentiment that has been voiced in Jefferson City for nearly a century.[7] It does not, of course, eliminate all country-city conflicts. There remains a distinction in perspective and value between the modal urban legislator and the modal rural legislator. They are concerned with different problems and look to different bases of support. City legislators are regarded, accurately for the most part, as primarily interested in two kinds of questions, those involving labor and those affecting the city's party organizations to which city legislators owe their election. Neither interest is of much concern to outstate representatives. The latter are concerned by the general lack of local resources in outstate Missouri and the consequent dependence upon state programs of aid for highways, schools, welfare services, and the like.

This difference in interests is reinforced by differences in ethnic and religious background—as well as speech patterns and oratorical flourishes. Each grouping views the other with a certain suspicion, a presumption that "the country boys" will not understand city problems and vice versa. For instance, school men inside the legislature and out feel that wealthy St. Louis County has little sympathy for state programs that aid rural schools with funds raised largely in urban areas. St. Louis newspapers, on the other hand, often blame the defeat of local St. Louis bills on rural opposition.

To summarize, it seems fair to say that rural interests practically never unite to oppose united urban interests. Rather, there is a kind of presumptive urban-rural difference which must frequently be negotiated away in order to enact urban legislation. The local unity formula assists this negotiation by providing an automatic basis of alignment for rural interests: pro when there is unity among the affected urban legislators; anti when there is not.

[7] Thomas S. Barclay has described the importance of this formula in connection with the original separation of St. Louis City from St. Louis County in 1875. *The Movement for Municipal Home Rule in St. Louis* (Columbia: University of Missouri; 1943), pp. 37 ff.

We have already noted that MSTA stays out of local issues. The local unity formula also has a conservative effect which reinforces the general Missouri system. If urban legislative proposals require urban unity, then a substantial area of public policy cannot be materially altered except by first achieving broad agreement. If the change is a major one, for example, broad expansion of local financial resources, it will take much time and energy to achieve the necessary local unity. This slows down change in public policy and it may sometimes appear in roll call votes as rural opposition to the programs retards enactment, for the bulk of the votes against the measure will come from outstate. Clearly, rural legislators could have voted for the proposed changes, and greater rural resistance to urban programs cannot entirely be ignored. On the whole, however, in Missouri conservatism or inaction with respect to urban problems is based on intra-urban disputes rather than urban-rural conflicts. The outstaters too have local matters for which they will seek legislative approval and invoke the same local agreement norm.

Thus, although a certain amount of mutual suspicion may be present between urban and rural representatives, this will rarely blossom into overt urban-rural conflict over public school questions. We will consider some examples below.

St. Louis and Kansas City

Most of the "local" school issues that develop in Missouri have to do with two major cities in the state, St. Louis and Kansas City. As we have noted, the internal politics of the local area determines the outcome of these local proposals in the legislature, so we must look briefly at the intra-urban conflicts in the two cities.

Both cities have developed political systems in which the party organizations are largely separated from the policy-making administrative leaders of the city governments.[8]

---

[8] See Robert H. Salisbury: "St. Louis Politics: Relationships Among In-

The local politicians concentrate their attention on the patronage offices of the city, or in the case of Kansas City, the city and county. Their concern with policy matters is marginal. They rarely succeed in controlling the policy-making offices of mayor or, in Kansas City, city manager. Both cities have home rule charters which help insulate the policy-making offices from the pressures of patronage demands by providing for merit system protection of municipal employees and, in Kansas City, by establishing the city manager system. Neither home rule provision, however, controls the so-called "county offices." In St. Louis these offices—recorder, license collector, collector of revenue, etc.—are required and governed by state statute, even though St. Louis is not part of any county. In Kansas City, the county offices are part of the Jackson County governmental structure. In both cases they are the primary sources of patronage for the local party organizations.

In both cities, especially St. Louis, quite different social groupings have come to cluster around the two sets of offices. The policy-making agencies are associated with the daily newspapers, downtown business interests, and the middle-class citizens, while, in keeping with urban political tradition, the ward politicians draw their support from locally active labor groups, Negroes, and other lower income strata.

The politician-party organization grouping in the cities is intensely interested in participating in the state arena, where decisions are made concerning the salaries and other perquisites of the jobs which are their lifeblood. Moreover, the state offers supplements to the meager patronage available locally, including the legislative seats themselves. On the other hand, the policy-making agencies of the cities are less interested in state affairs. They decide locally, under their own charter authority, many of the issues which concern them most. The federal authorities make other substantial decisions.

For example, the state makes few decisions as important to the city of St. Louis as those which Washington makes on urban renewal. To be sure, on occasion a city administration has important policy objectives that can only be achieved with state legislative help, and both city administrations present legislative programs embracing both major and minor items to each session of the legislature. When they approach the legislature, however, the city administrations are in the position of any other respectable interest-group claimant. They cannot assume the support of the city legislative delegation and must bargain for whatever support they receive. With greater interest in the arena and control over the machinery of nomination and election, the politicians dominate the selection of state legislators, and the latter have a primary obligation to represent the party organization interests in Jefferson City. In the same way, state executive officials pay closer heed to party groups with votes than to policy-oriented city officials who have no direct control over blocs of votes in primary contests. Of course, policy-makers and politicians do not inevitably disagree with each other. On many issues harmony prevails. Yet there are always differences: in interest, in base of support, and in personal values; and these differences must be negotiated away before urban unity can be achieved.

Thus it is relatively unusual to have an urban interest that really unites the city delegation with the city administration. The latter can usually get city representatives to introduce and speak for its measures, but it is likely to find indifference at best and often resistance emanating from local interests that oppose the request. Even opposition of modest local strength, provided it has contact with the politician grouping, may be able to kill the measure by splitting the city delegation and thereby evoking outstate opposition—in keeping with the local unity norm. The local unity norm is the standard mechanism on which the legislature relies to resolve local issues requiring state legislative action. This category includes a considerable number of public schools issues, especially issues affecting St. Louis or Kansas City. Let us look at some examples from the 1961 session.

A relatively simple example of the local unity rule in relation to education occurred in 1961 with House Bill 671 and Senate Bill 197. Both bills revised the procedures for annexing territory to the Kansas City school district. The first specified that territory to be annexed must be adjacent to the Kansas City district. The second specified "adjoining," not "adjacent." The latter bill would have permitted somewhat easier annexation. The two versions reflected a controversy between the Kansas City school district and one nearby. House Bill 671 was sponsored by a representative whose district included an area adjacent to Kansas City, and he hoped to forestall Senate Bill 197 with his bill. This demonstration of disagreement among Jackson County Democrats was enough to kill both bills.

Senate Bill 96 was designed to improve the St. Louis City public school retirement system as recommended by the St. Louis Public School Retirement Board. It had no opposition within the city and the city legislators all supported it. It passed both houses unanimously.

A group of bills and constitutional amendments affecting both St. Louis City and St. Louis County also received unanimous approval eventually. The major one of these proposals authorized St. Louis County to levy a tax of $1 per $100 assessed valuation, with the revenues to be apportioned among the county's 27 school districts on the basis of number of students in average daily attendance. This equalization tax was regarded as a step toward boosting the resources available to the poorer and more crowded suburban districts. The legislators from St. Louis County had met several times before and during the early stages of the session and were all in agreement. They all accepted the equalization tax as a way of helping poor or overcrowded suburban districts without giving up local school-district autonomy. Some of the outstate legislators who were especially cognizant of school problems resented the proposed tax measure. One said:

These rich St. Louis County people never want to help rural Missouri, and here when they could go ahead and reorganize [into fewer, larger districts] and get the same result, the way we have outstate, they won't do it. Hell, we wanted to keep our little districts too but we combined. Why can't they? Then they wouldn't need this tax and it would be cheaper all around. But it's their money, I guess.

So the norm of local unity prevailed. The resolution calling for a vote on the constitutional amendment required for equalization passed the House unanimously.

In the Senate two other amendments were added to make a package. One of these raised the levy which the St. Louis City Board of Education could raise without a referendum from $.89 to $1, thus placing the city on a par with other districts in the state. St. Louis City legislators were not enthusiastic about combining their proposal with those of the county, but they finally agreed. A second proposal provided for an increase from $.35 to $.50 in the basic levy which St. Louis County might raise for general operating purposes. County representatives had developed the required agreement on this measure early in the session and had no objection to combining it with the school tax. The final package won unanimous approval in both the Senate and the House.

Several bills affecting the St. Louis City school system illustrate the relationship among the school board there, the political divisions in the city, and the state legislative arena. We have spoken of the division in St. Louis between the policy-making offices and the political offices and the socioeconomic groups associated with the offices. Some of the potential for more direct conflict which this division of interest contains has been realized with respect to control of the St. Louis Board of Education. The St. Louis school system, like that in Kansas City, is governed directly by state law rather than under home rule charter provisions. This has meant that through state legislative influence, the politicians in St. Louis could use the school system as a source of patronage. They did so by keeping the building and maintenance department separate from the instruction program and using the former for patronage purposes, leaving educational policy decisions largely to the professional staff. Control of the school board was essential to maintain the patronage control, but until recently the ward organization had had little trouble in dominating the nonpartisan, at-large election of board members.

Periodically during the past decade, the metropolitan papers and other policy-oriented interests have agitated against politician control of the school board. The central theme of this agitation has been unit control, placing building and maintenance functions under control of a single superintendent, thus eliminating the administrative separation that was viewed as the major protective covering of the patronage opportunities.

With unit control as the battle cry, blue ribbon tickets were formed on several occasions to compete with the politician slate for board of education posts. After several defeats, the blue ribbon group won enough seats so that by April 1961, they controlled a majority of the board and it was, for the first time, actively committed to unit control. The board hired a lobbyist, himself a former legislator, and sought more eagerly than in other years to get favorable action on its proposed bill.

The board had another advantage over former times. Many of the city ward leaders had concluded that whatever patronage had been gained in the building and maintenance department was not worth the effort. The concentrated fire of the newspapers, grand jury investigations of board members (one member was convicted for exploiting school employees for private purposes), and otherwise tarnished reputations had convinced many political leaders in the city that for them the administrative independence of the building and maintenance division was a wasting asset.

The bill for unit control was sent to the House Committee on Governmental Organization rather than the House Education Committee. Three influential St. Louis representatives served on this committee, whereas only one city member was on the Education Committee, and he was completely inactive. Thus local unity could be tested more accurately in the former committee's action. The committee voted 5-4 to recommend that the bill not pass, with the three St. Louisans joining two other Democrats against it. The reasons for rejecting the bill were more than the traditional desire to protect patronage. As we have noted, the legislators were losing enthusiasm for the jobs involved. They did fear, however, that the blue ribbon board would drastically change the present non-teaching personnel. The board was characterized as "Republican." It might attempt to oust all Democrats and replace them with deserving Republicans. Actually the recently elected school board, though chosen as a nonpartisan ticket, contained one acknowledged Republican and some others whose political affiliation was held suspect by Democratic leaders.

This fear was reinforced by the proposed unit control bill which affirmed the principle of merit system protection for nonteaching employees but did not spell out the procedures for implementing it. The city legislators and the public school employees union wanted the tenure of these employees protected by legislation, not left up to the "Republican" board. Consequently, they opposed the unit control bill. Instead they backed a separate bill to provide merit protection for nonteaching personnel similar to the tenure law for teachers in St. Louis. After differences between the union and the school board had been compromised, this bill passed the legislature almost unanimously. A last-ditch effort was made to get the reorganization bill through by introducing it in the Senate. This bill did come out of committee successfully, but not until June 9, much too late to get through the rest of the legislative process by the constitutional deadline of June 30, even if the St. Louis legislators had all supported it.[9]

These examples illustrate something of the nature of urban interests in the state legislature as they are related to public school questions and suggest the ways in which other legislators respond. Urban residents do not present a united grouping with the voting potential to exert substantial power in the state arena. Instead, they are divided into two distinct groupings with different sets of interests. Sometimes they are in direct conflict, but even when there is no incompatibility, they must negotiate and renegotiate whatever agreement they may reach on any given issue. The other legislators wait for an "agreed bill"[1] to be presented to them, and in the absence of local agreement, they say "No!"

ECONOMIC INTERESTS

Missouri is often characterized as a conservative state. The principal evidence of conservatism cited is the relatively low level of taxes and services in the state. This evidence is often accompanied by charges that a rather generalized "they"—a combination of economic interests—run things for their own benefit and prevent the enactment of desirable programs. Conspiratorial theories of this kind are difficult

[9] After losing the legislative battle over unit control, the St. Louis Board of Education decided they could achieve most of their intent by administrative action. The board designated the superintendent of instruction as the chief officer of the school system and required other officials, including the head of the building and maintenance department, to report to him. This action, combined with the act providing tenure and merit system protection for nonteaching personnel, may be expected to eliminate most of the remaining political controversy (involving the ward organizations) from the St. Louis school system.

[1] The "agreed bill"—one which, as a matter of accepted practice, all interested groups approve before the legislature acts—is described as it works in Illinois by Gilbert Y. Steiner: *Legislation by Collective Bargaining* (Urbana: University of Illinois, Institute of Labor and Industrial Relations; 1951).

to prove or disprove. However, our inquiry leads us to the conclusion that no pervasive conspiracy or alliance can be said to dominate the political process in Missouri and that, as is often the case, conspiratorial theories are of little use in explaining how policy is made.

Missouri may be a low tax, low service state, but it also has been relatively free of anti-labor legislation, agitation of rightist fringe groups, and other phenomena often associated with conservatism. There is no state minimum wage law, but neither is there a right to work law. Missouri legislators do not investigate "un-American activities." A state with a considerable Southern tradition, Missouri has nevertheless established an active Human Rights Commission and in 1961 passed an FEPC law. Rather than conservative, it might better be described as low-pressure. We have said that MSTA's activities are adapted to the low-pressure norms and expectations. So are the activities of the major economic interest groups in the state. Each group tends to seek a narrowly defined program calling for marginal adjustments in policy with as little fuss as possible.

Missouri presents no particularly unique combination of economic groups. Railroads and trucking companies, oil companies and highway contractors, Farm Bureau and Missouri Farmers Association, utilities, small loan companies, banks, insurance companies, and a host of other business and economic groups have stakes at issue in the state political arena. Similarly, a wide variety of labor unions participate vigorously in efforts to improve job security through state legislation. Two related generalizations apply to all these groups. None of them is large enough or, if large, sufficiently concerned to dominate the others. Secondly, none of these groups is actively interested in more than a few issues among all those under consideration at any given time.

When it considers matters of importance to these groups, the legislature may face a situation in which two rival economic interests are competing directly over a legislative proposal. Thus, oil interests battle contractors over gasoline tax increases, or railroads fight truckers over truck weight and height limitations. A second type of situation will find a particular economic group—for instance, dairy farmers— seeking legislative assistance and facing no particular opposition. Still a third pattern, and far rarer than the first two, would involve a broader alliance of groups in conflict with a rival alliance. Thus, when labor unions joined together in support of minimum wage legislation, they were opposed by a combination of farm and business groups. This kind of situation calls for expressions of the traditional liberal versus conservative sentiments, and the political speeches as well as the final votes reveal the broad political convictions of the legislators and their constituencies.

But such issues are rare, and, being rare, do not govern the tone of the legislature. Neither the rhetoric nor the voting alignments on one issue will necessarily carry over to the next. Whatever alliances are formed are apt to be *ad hoc* rather than all-purpose. The broad-based economic groups—the Chamber of Commerce, the Associated Industries of Missouri, or the State Labor Council—find that their influence varies in some inverse proportion to the number of issues in which they interest themselves, so they tend to concentrate their attention on the bread and butter issues.[2]

One must *never* assume that economic interest groups have no significant influence on legislation. They do, and a large portion of the specific actions of the legislature may be viewed as responsive to *some* economic group. But the focus is on specific and incremental adjustments accompanied by a rationale which emphasizes job or investment protection against the impersonal forces of the larger world. No one seeks to depart from existing conditions in any dramatic, drastic, or rapid way, but rather to preserve things as they

[2] See George D. Young: "The Role of Political Parties in the Missouri House of Representatives," unpublished Ph.D. dissertation (University of Missouri; 1958), p. 85.

are, as far as possible. In this sense, labor groups are as conservative as business groups in the state, differing only in the
specific objects of their conservative desire. Again, this
emphasis reinforces the norms of the system, minimizes conflict, and encourages group spokesmen to employ the legislative tactics of quiet persuasion without ideological ferment.

An important consequence of this pattern for education
policy is that MSTA rarely comes into direct conflict—or
indeed contact—with the broad business, labor, or farm
groups. Officially, MSTA regards all the big economic interest organizations as friends. "We get along fine with all of
them. They all support better schools." But MSTA has so
successfully defined the means to secure "better schools" in
Missouri that there is little room left for argument from
other groups. Indeed, MSTA has little need to call on its
friends for overt demonstrations of support and prefers not
to do so.

Finance is the one area of occasional conflict between
MSTA and economic interests. MSTA supports all of the
gubernatorial recommendations for increased taxes. These
recommendations have included several to which labor
unions take particular exception, notably, the sales tax and
the cigarette tax. Union spokesmen outside and inside the
legislature have expressed their objections to taxes which
"bear heavily upon the workingmen" but as we shall see
later, this does not affect many votes. MSTA leaders do not
think this disagreement constitutes any basic antagonism
and labor spokesmen agree. The same may be said of the opposition of some business groups to income tax withholding.
The principal effect of such opposition is to reinforce MSTA's
wariness, discussed earlier, of forming alliances with noneducational groups. Thus, on school issues, the major economic interests are, at most, of marginal importance to the
outcome.

THE POLICY-MAKING PROCESS

In the previous section, we described the principal groups that seek public school policy decisions in Missouri and indicated the relationships between these groups and other groups that make demands of the decision-making process. Let us now examine the process itself. We shall focus our attention on the institutions of Missouri government, and, conceiving of them as arenas within which rival claimants seek advantageous decisions, consider how education policy is formulated.

THE PARTY BALANCE

First, however, we might indicate briefly the relative strength and differential support of the two political parties in the state, for the character of the party struggle vitally affects the decision-making process. Missouri is usually classified as a "politically marginal state, leaning Democratic." [3] This designation is not only ambiguous, but misleading. In presidential elections, to be sure, Missouri has a long tradition of swinging back and forth in support of whichever party captured the presidency.[4] Moreover, in recent presidential races the Missouri results have shown extremely narrow margins indeed.[5] But the political uncertainty of the presidential campaigns has not been reflected at the state level. Democratic candidates for state-wide office have won handily during most of the past three decades. Republicans controlled the governorship from 1941 to 1945 and organized at least one house of the General Assembly in 1943, 1945, 1947, and 1953. Since then, however, Republican strength has

[3] For a summary of Missouri's political complexion compared to other states, see Austin Ranney and Willmoore Kendall: *Democracy and the American Party System* (New York: Harcourt, Brace & Co.; 1956), p. 162 ff.

[4] The 1956 election provides the only exception to this rule since 1900.

[5] Stevenson carried the state in 1956 by less than 5,000 votes; Kennedy won by less than 10,000.

dwindled. In the legislature, for instance, Democratic margins have been as follows:

	House		Senate	
	D	R	D	R
1955	97	60	19	15
1957	93	64	21	13
1959	112	45	26	8
1961	100	57	28	6

No Republican has won a state-wide elective office since the 1940's and against well-known candidates like United States Senator Stuart Symington, the Republicans have had difficulty finding someone to run on the party ticket.[6]

This means that when the MSTA seeks support from Missouri office-holders they must deal primarily with Democrats. Unless their support can be won for MSTA demands, the desired legislation cannot pass. Republican support is welcome, of course, but it is not a major object of MSTA's political attention, since Republicans cannot muster even close to a majority.

In the legislature, Republican strength is heavily concentrated among representatives from rural districts, including a substantial number from the Ozarks. Although the metropolitan areas supplied Mr. Nixon with a large number of votes in 1960, they were not so generous to Republicans running for state office. In 1961 there were no Republicans from St. Louis City in the legislature; there were two from Jackson County (Kansas City) and three from St. Louis County—a total of five Republicans out of fifty-two senators and representatives from the big centers of population in the state. Urban Democrats are much more numerous, of course, but they too are outnumbered by outstate representatives. The legislative leadership among the Democrats is largely

[6] The leading hotel in Jefferson City has portraits in its lobby of notable politicians, both state and national. Only Democrats are included.

drawn from the rural sections of the state, and in recent years governors have come from these areas also.

Party balance is important to public school issues. MSTA, to the great satisfaction of its leaders, does not get caught up in severe partisan wrangling. Its demands are not joined together with other policy issues into the broad ideological platforms of two competing parties. In state politics, the Republicans are not powerful enough to force meaningful alternatives, and the Democrats are sufficiently secure in power and diverse in interests to discourage programmatic politics. So public school issues are not the object of partisan rhetoric. Conflict is minimized, and the unity of the school men is not challenged by sharply competitive party forces.

THE GOVERNOR

The office of governor in Missouri has traditionally been regarded as weak. That is, Missouri governors have not been expected to furnish vigorous leadership in behalf of policy objectives. They have not been thought to possess much power over party affairs. And interest groups with legislative demands to make do not often look to them for assistance. Yet the formal instruments of authority which Missouri's governor possesses are great enough to permit him to exercise a larger role than he does. Indeed, the two recent incumbents, James T. Blair and John M. Dalton, have been more active than their predecessors were in seeking legislation. Nevertheless, they too have sought only limited objectives and have met with only limited success.

The Missouri governor's instruments of power cannot be ignored. For example, he has the item veto, which Governor Donnelly used in 1953 to block a public school appropriation in excess of the constitutionally required minimum.[7] Governor Dalton exercised his veto power 35 times in 1961, but it cannot be said that he thereby controlled the legislative process. He did not use the vetoes as a club to pressure the

[7] See below in discussion of foundation program.

legislature to pass his program. In fact, his vetoes were often unanticipated, and generally came after the legislature had adjourned.

The governor's control over revenue is more important. We have already described the importance of "the available revenue" as an effective limit to the demands pressed upon the legislature. The governor largely dominates the decision as to the amount of revenue that will be available through his recommended tax program. Very rarely indeed will legislative leaders attempt to push for tax increases on their own. Instead they rely on the governor to present them with a budget that balances expenditure and revenue and that specifies whatever tax boosts may be necessary to pay for any increased expenditures. Whatever unpopularity results from tax increases is thereby passed on to the governor. ("The cat is on his back," as one legislator put it.) At the same time, however, the legislature is thereby limited in seeking to expand state services. Legislators cannot hope to expand particular state programs unless the governor is willing to recommend the necessary taxes.

The governor's fiscal recommendations constitute the heart of his program in each legislative session. Legislative leaders feel most committed to push these measures and give them their first attention. Nonfiscal recommendations of the governor may or may not be seriously considered, but in any case they will be taken up later in the session.

Gubernatorial domination of the fiscal picture has been reinforced by the more general influence which the executive exerts over the allocation of funds among the various state agencies and functions. One facet of the increasing leadership which Governors Blair and Dalton assumed has been the development since 1956 of an effective budget office. This office has given the governor the tools to develop and present to the legislature a more fully detailed and tightly controlled budget than he could formerly.

For our present purposes, we may note two related effects

of the executive budget. First, by presenting a detailed budgetary agenda to the legislature, the governor presumes that they will accept his allocations. To alter this allocation in a material way, the legislators would either have to find additional revenue from tax increases not recommended by the governor or would have to cut one agency's appropriation in order to add to another. Neither course of action is likely to prove attractive to the legislature. Secondly, the agenda-setting power of the governor forces interest groups with a stake in appropriations to come to him more than they did in the past. Thus MSTA must get the governor's approval for increases in the foundation program. Without this approval, as we shall see, MSTA has come fairly close to success in getting increased appropriations, but even the strongest lobby in the state has not won its financial appeals without gubernatorial endorsement.

One other factor that contributes to the governor's influence is his control over the subject matter of special sessions of the legislature. In such sessions legislators may consider only those items he puts before them. Thus he can concentrate public attention on a smaller agenda and often, as a consequence, get a larger proportion of his recommendations passed than is possible in the more diffuse regular session. Governors Donnelly in 1956 and Blair in 1958 used special sessions with considerable effectiveness.[8]

Despite these elements of influence, however, gubernatorial leadership of the legislative process is limited. The traditions associated with the Missouri governorship emphasize weakness rather than strength. Some of these weaknesses are institutional, but others, perhaps more important, stem from the fact that no influential groups in Missouri, including MSTA, make sufficiently large demands for state action to encourage a governor to break with tradition and seek to

---

[8] Public school interests, however, have worked well enough with the legislature so as not to need any particular attention in the recent special sessions.

exercise broad programmatic leadership. In a low-pressure
system, the powers of an office are exercised in a low-pressure
way.

The institutional limitations are considerable, however.
The governor of Missouri may not succeed himself, and,
once elected, his political future is frequently dim. "The
woods are full of ex-governors," is a common expression in
Missouri. Almost as soon as the governor takes office, the
state political leaders begin to think about his successor, and
in the latter half of his four-year term, the governor often
finds himself consigned to relative insignificance so far as
legislative influence is concerned. The governor has limited
patronage, and can use little party pressure to advance his
legislative recommendations. As a former representative
writes:

There are few patronage jobs in the state government anyway,
so the number of applicants a representative could succeed in appointing (by virtue of supporting the governor) would be limited.
An official of the governor's budget staff estimated that only about
2,500 of the approximately 22,500 state employees were appointed
under the patronage system.[9]

As a result, Missouri governors have been relatively
passive, accepting or rejecting most legislative actions without attempting to guide them. Outside of the budget, "there
has not been much of an effort to formulate a program which
is known as the governor's and which representatives are
urged to follow." [1] Even the relatively active Blair and Dalton concentrated their efforts on getting their revenue measures passed, and they acquired much of their influence
informally, by cajoling and bargaining with individual legislators. They had few effective formal sanctions to give them
leverage.

Another aspect of the governor's relationship to the system
should be mentioned. As we have seen, Democratic candi-

[9] Young, *op. cit.*, p. 63.
[1] *Ibid.*

dates dominate the election picture in Missouri. Insofar as
political office is worth competing for, we might assume
that fairly sharp competition would appear in the Democratic primaries. Yet, in fact, most recent Democratic nomi-
nees have been chosen without serious opposition. No
Democratic gubernatorial or senatorial candidates have
faced serious primary challenges since 1952. This absence
of competition for what is almost certain victory may be
due partly to the comparative unattractiveness of Missouri's
political world to ambitious men. The modest perquisites
and power attached to public office may not be great enough
to evoke sharp competition. In addition, through an informal
process of quiet negotiation among persons of political influence in various parts of the state, a "succession" of Democratic hopefuls is often arranged, and, when necessary,
rearranged. This helps further to reduce overt conflict. Potential candidates are "assigned" places on the waiting lists
and given appropriate rewards for waiting their turn pa-
tiently. The succession is backed up by few sanctions, but
in the absence of counter-pressures from groups not represented in the negotiations, it is generally adhered to. In
turn, such informal mechanisms help maintain the traditional
norms of politics in Missouri, reinforcing the low-pressure
character of the system.

MSTA leaders would welcome stronger executive leadership in Missouri. They are pleased that Blair and Dalton
have taken a more active role. They feel that this expansion
of gubernatorial influence helped to accomplish MSTA's major objective of 1959 and 1961—increased state aid for public schools. MSTA anticipates that more forceful governors
will press for general expansion of state services, including
public schools. MSTA has been able to get along well both
with Blair and Dalton and sees no reason to believe that a
still more vigorous governor would not be sympathetic to
MSTA desires. Indeed, the most recent experience with
an "unsympathetic" governor, Governor Donnelly (1945-49

and 1953-57), reinforces this view. Donnelly epitomized the judicious governor. He remained aloof from the legislative process and then vetoed the bills he didn't like, including increased state aid to schools. MSTA fully recognizes the limitations which the state constitution and the Missouri political culture place on executive leadership. But even though the organization has adjusted so successfully to low-pressure politics, MSTA is not content with the limits such a system imposes on them. Accordingly, they hope that vigorous, perhaps ambitious, men will enlarge the governor's role in the future.

THE LEGISLATURE

In any political system where power is diffused and fragmented, the legislative body is of special importance in the policy-making process. Whenever public policy decisions are to be made (or blocked), the legislature cannot be by-passed, and if no structures of power outside its halls can control legislative choices, the dynamics of the legislature itself will be of critical significance in shaping the policy outcome. So it is in Missouri. The MSTA, along with most other interest groups in the state, must give its principal political attention to the legislature.

The Missouri legislature, like any other legislature, is a complex institution. With a House composed of 157 members and a Senate of 34 members, the legislature presents a differentiated structure of roles and sub-systems for the performance of its many and diverse legislative tasks. We shall examine those elements most important to public school policy-making.

How does the legislature structure its deliberations? How do the legislators get things done? A number of possibilities suggest themselves, several of which we have already considered. We have found that decisions are not made along urban versus rural lines. Large-scale economic groupings do not impose their will on any large segment of the legislative output. Ideological cohesion—liberals against conservatives, for example—rarely emerges in meaningful fashion.[2] Party programs are not well enough articulated and party loyalty is not usually dependable enough to encourage the structuring of legislative issues along party lines.

Gubernatorial pressure is considerable on budgetary questions, and on these important issues it constitutes the principal basis, together with the related party pressure, for the legislators' decisions. But as we have seen, executive leadership is weak on nonbudgetary issues. The local unity norm is an important means for resolving a considerable range of questions with a minimum of conflict.

What other possibilities are there for structuring the legislative process? Certain leaders in each house might have enough prestige and/or power to enable them to control the process of decision-making. These might be the formal leaders—the speaker and majority floor leader in the House, the president pro tem in the Senate. Or they might operate in a more specialized fashion: the legislators might defer to certain of their colleagues in particular areas where the latter were regarded as expert or powerful. Conceivably, a version of the local unity rule might be extended to a host of apparently state-wide issues, granting each legislator a kind of *liberum veto* on all questions having a major impact on his district.

Presumably, such a system would act to block most legislation, but it might work in a very low-pressure system. Or the legislature might not organize its business in any enduring way. In this case each issue would be fought out from scratch. Then not only the resolution but the process of exercising influence to achieve the resolution might vary greatly from one day to the next.

It can be argued that this last type of situation is intolerable, that no legislature can function at all in such a context of uncertainty. In any event, the Missouri General As-

[2] See Young, *op. cit., passim.*

sembly does not function that way. The local unity norm
and even the limited executive pressure serve to reduce uncertainty. So, too, on occasion, does party identification: e.g.,
on such issues as salary increases for patronage offices controlled by one party. In some measure, all of the others mentioned—House leadership, committee leadership, specialized
leadership, and even the *liberum veto*—operate as decision-
making guides to the legislators. And there are times when
the Missouri legislature seems to approach each controversy
afresh, debate it along lines that are difficult to anticipate,
and resolve it according to criteria that seem to vary almost
daily.

The structuring of the legislative process cannot be separated from the legislator's relationship to his constituency.
The influence of the "expert legislator" is predicated on
the relative absence of strong, conflicting pressures from
constituents. The local unity norm assumes that there are
substantial constituency pressures from the local area involved. Thus before talking about the Missouri legislative
process, we must say something of the legislator and his relationship to constituents, at least as it affects public school
issues.

Representation. How does a Missouri legislator conceive
of his role? What does he think he is supposed to do? Our
data suggest little agreement on this question among legislators. One representative said: "I'm here to represent my
county. I usually agree with their views, but whether I do or
not, they send me here to vote *their* way, not mine."

Another said just the opposite: "I don't pay much attention
to the mail. I look at the *Post-Dispatch* because I think they
often are right, but I get very little pressure to do one thing
or another and I generally ignore that. I make up my own
mind."

Most legislators—even, perhaps, the two just quoted—
really fall between these two extremes. In actual operation,
the direct constituency pressure referred to by the first

legislator occurs on only a fraction of the bills acted upon. Not many people in his county have views on most matters affecting St. Louis or Springfield, or for that matter on many issues of state-wide application. So our first speaker above has a substantial number of free votes on which no district pressure or interest is expressed. On the other hand, the legislator who says he disregards pressure has often internalized certain political norms and values which are widely shared in his district. As a result he may vote their way without being conscious of responding to pressure at all.

We might essay the following generalization about representational style in Missouri. Missouri legislators are committed by their constituency on certain votes, with the proportion varying in some rough inverse relation to the size and diversity of their districts.[3] Thus a Senator is less apt to be committed than a House member, an outstater more committed to a delegate role than a suburban representative. A St. Louis City representative will be committed by his district on matters affecting the local party organization and, usually, on labor issues. Otherwise, he is apt to have a free vote to cast with his party, his friends, or his logrolling allies. Indeed, he may not cast it at all. Many St. Louis legislators have had high absentee records.

St. Louis citizens are usually rather indifferent on questions of state-wide public school policy. The high proportion of parochial school students in the city, the lesser dependence of city schools on state aid, and the special status of the

[3] This conclusion is based on less systematically collected data than those of Heinz Eulau, John C. Wahlke, William Buchanan, and Leroy C. Ferguson, "The Role of the Representative: Some Empirical Observations of the Theory of Edmund Burke," *American Political Science Review*, LIII (September 1959), pp. 742-756. Eulau, *et al.*, suggest, albeit tentatively, that the delegate role may be more often required in politically competitive areas. Such areas would be apt to be more than less heterogeneous. Eulau's findings are not directly contradictory to the conclusion presented here, but they point up the complexities involved in any generalized analysis of representative roles.

St. Louis school system, with its unique administrative structure and tenure law, all contribute to reducing interest in
state-wide school problems. In addition, MSTA has much less
influence in the city than outstate. In outstate Missouri MSTA
can count on one county superintendent, and at least one and
usually more school boards and district superintendents to
express MSTA views to each representative. In St. Louis, on
the other hand, one board and one superintendent must reach
eighteen members of the House and seven senators. Coupled
with relative indifference of the metropolitan public toward
state school policy, the greater difficulty of exerting influence
through the city school people on city legislators has led
MSTA to concentrate their efforts on the outstate legislators
and leave the city boys alone.

As a result, a city legislator is likely to agree that MSTA
is very powerful and hasten to add, a bit perplexedly, "I
never see anything of them. They don't contact me." Although the city legislators are relatively indifferent on public school issues, they are certainly not enemies of the MSTA.
MSTA leaders are slightly suspicious that the orientation of
city representatives will tempt them to oppose tax increases
for state aid to schools. With its basic strategy of avoiding
conflict over education issues, MSTA finds in this suspicion
further reason to leave the cities alone.

Thus MSTA looks for committed support primarily among
outstate legislators whose constituencies contain a larger
proportion of school men than is the case in the city. This
same consideration makes representatives easier to work with
and rely on than senators. Since an outstate senator represents several counties, the pressure on him may be somewhat
diluted. But a House member from a single county can
hardly ignore the clamor of the school men's opinion, since
mobilization of school superintendents is easier in small
areas, or so it is alleged by MSTA officials.

The smaller size and more homogeneous character of their

districts contribute to the fact that representatives of out-state counties are likely to be more firmly committed to MSTA demands than are city legislators. For both, however, the dynamics of the free vote are illuminating. When the constituency does not control them directly, how do the legislators make up their minds? Executive pressure is one factor, but we have already noted the limitations on this type of influence. Another potential factor is leadership within the legislature itself.

Leadership. Formal leadership in the Missouri legislature has three salient characteristics: it is held by relatively young persons, it changes considerably from one session to the next, and it is weak. This pattern was not always the case, or at least not so much so. Some veterans complain that the leaders of today cannot control things the way their predecessors did. In the not too distant past, the legislature was a normal stepping stone for ambitious political careerists. A decade or two of apprenticeship in the House and Senate could groom one for the governorship, for example, as it did Donnelly and Blair. The legislature is still sometimes a stepping stone, but the stopover is brief and the apprenticeship short. Thus the three main formal leaders of the House in 1959, speaker, speaker pro tem, and majority floor leader were serving their fourth, second, and fifth two-year terms respectively. Their ages were 33, 38, and 36. In 1961, all three had moved on to higher office. Their successors were serving their sixth, third, and third terms, and two of them were less than 35 years old. The leadership in the Senate is substantially older in years and, usually, in legislative service. Even here, however, the turnover is considerable. The president pro tem and majority leader of the 1959 session did not hold those offices in 1961.

The legislators explain the rapid turnover and youthfulness of the leadership this way. Formal leadership of the House or Senate is a task requiring the skills of lawyers.

The technical problems of the legislative process contain mysteries which the legislator with legal training can grasp and utilize more effectively than the layman. In recent years, however, legislative service has not been sufficiently attractive to lawyers to hold them for more than a few terms. The low pay,[4] the difficulty of maintaining a private practice, and the unpromising character of the careers possible in the Missouri political arena generally are all cited as reasons why relatively few lawyers occupy legislative seats in Missouri. Those lawyers who are there are likely to be young, and there is felt to be a certain inverse correlation between personal skill and competence, on the one hand, and age. The more likely prospects do not remain long in the legislative arena. Again, these remarks apply more to the House than to the Senate. Leadership has the greatest potential impact on decision-making in the House. Youth, inexperience, and short-term commitment to a legislative career all tend to reduce the leaders' ability to control their colleagues, as well as their inclination to exercise such power as they might possess.

The formal sanctions of the leadership are impressive. In the House, the speaker possesses powers of recognition and referral, and, as in the case of the St. Louis unit control bill, referral can be of critical importance. The speaker makes all committee assignments and designates the chairmen. Assignments are made, in part, according to the preferences of the members and since each member sits on several committees in each session, the speaker rarely tries to exercise much selectivity in making assignments. Somewhat greater influence may be exerted through the choices of chairman. Seniority, in the House or on the committee, is *not* the only criterion for selection. Support of the speaker's candidacy

[4] In 1961 the legislator's salary was increased from $1,500 per year to $4,800 per year, but it is, of course, too early to determine what effect there may be on legislative turnover.

in the party caucus may be a factor and was in 1961. Preferences of the members will have considerable effect. And there are so many committees and so much turnover of membership that virtually any third-termer and many two-term representatives will head some committee. Thus the speaker's powers are limited in practice to a point that gives him only occasional leverage over legislation.

Much the same may be said of the floor leader. The floor leader controls the calendars, deciding which calendar of bills will be taken up at a given point. This gives him some degree of choice. For example, he can decide whether to call up a bill when a small attendance may prevent its getting the required constitutional majority for passage, or hold it over until the absentees return the next week.

The speaker and floor leader together serve as the principal links between the governor and members of his party in the legislature. They communicate his desires to the caucus and indicate to the executive what the representatives will take. Again, however, this kind of communication is limited primarily to fiscal issues and appropriations. The leaders feel the greatest responsibility for these and they utilize their full strength to shepherd these bills through.

Yet just as the governor tends to confine his legislative leadership to his revenue program, so the legislative leaders tend to husband their influence for that same program. On other questions, including most public school issues, the leadership plays a relatively passive role, largely confining themselves to keeping the legislature moving along at a reasonably productive pace. They make little effort to control committee work. In 1961, for example, committees were thought to be reporting too many bills with "do pass" recommendations, thus clogging the calendars. The leadership called a conference with the chairmen to get them to ease up, but no marked change resulted. Floor procedure permits anyone to speak once on any bill and to interrogate a speaker whenever he will yield. As a result, extended debate, particularly at the perfection (amendment) stage, is common, and if the bill is controversial, discussion may last for a very long time. The leadership rarely tries to intervene or control debate, and the legislators take a certain pride in occasionally reversing positions taken by the leadership, though usually only on bills not included in the governor's program. The leadership frequently is uncertain about the outcome of controversial bills, but again, is content to keep things moving and let those legislators with more interest in the particular legislation count the noses and worry about the way debate is handled.

Such a limited conception of the role of the formal leaders means that on specialized subjects such as public school legislation, the floor leader and the speaker remain on the sidelines. Sponsors of the bills in question and/or the chairmen of the committees reporting the school bills are given full opportunity to organize their own majorities, guiding the debate and rounding up support as best they can. Consequently, MSTA has had little need to make a special effort to establish its influence with the official leadership of the House.

Leadership in the Senate is a different matter. The Senate is so small that the modest formal sanctions available to the floor leader (president pro tem) are not very important in affecting the legislative outcome. Influence is highly personal in the Senate, and on education issues as well as most others, the necessary support is garnered through informal procedures of interpersonal negotiation.

Since it helps account for the action taken on some school bills in 1961, we should recall here the veteran legislators' complaint that the present leaders are less effective than their predecessors. They cite former leaders with nostalgia, pointing out their greater tenure and experience and alleging their greater ability to control the House. By greater ability they seem to mean the ability and determination first of all to control a broader range of legislative business than the present-day leadership is concerned with, and secondly, to exercise this control through bipartisan majorities put together through quiet negotiation and compromises between majority and minority. Now, it is said, the majority leadership encourages the legislators to react to issues on a partisan basis. The leaders allegedly ignore Republican requests for consideration in committee or on the floor, "steal" Republican bills by reintroducing them under Democratic sponsorship, and so on. Rather than minimize conflict over issues, they welcome party conflict as an easy way to get the votes for bills proposed by Democratic sponsors or against Republican measures. There is no necessary ideological content to the partisan controversy. As Young points out: "No matter how trivial a Democratic bill might be, if a Republican takes the floor to challenge it, there is a good chance the two parties will find themselves opposing each other."[5]

It is very difficult to document these charges except by pointing out that legislators on both sides of the aisle generally agree that partisanship is more marked now than it once was. Roll call analysis does not give very convincing evidence of increased partisanship, however,[6] and how much allegedly lazy or ineffective leadership may be responsible for any changes is surely debatable. It is true that on some issues, including some school bills, Republicans sought to make a record, and in some of these cases[7] the Democrats seemed to be reminding the Republicans that there was a solid Democratic majority in the House, without much regard for the contents of the bill. In 1961, this tendency did not affect bills sponsored by the MSTA itself, but we should point out that a legislature acting along partisan lines would be most

[5] *Op. cit.*, p. 80.

[6] Young found 7.5 percent of the total 1957 House roll calls pitting 80 percent of the voting Democrats against 80 percent of the voting Republicans. Two thirds of one party opposed two thirds of the other on about one third of the roll calls. *Ibid.*, p. 176. For the period 1949-1957, Derge classified 8 percent of the rolls as party votes. *Op. cit.*, p. 1060.

[7] See the discussion of H.B. 367 below.

undesirable from MSTA's point of view. MSTA's strategy is based on the premise that everyone supports better schools and that professional educators are in the best position to determine the means of improvement. If school questions were generally to become caught up in partisan debate, MSTA strategy would require substantial alteration and MSTA objectives would perhaps be jeopardized.[8] Thus MSTA must look with favor upon legislative leadership which minimizes conflict, and cast a disapproving eye upon any trend toward increased partisanship in the legislative process.

The Committee System.   The committees of the Missouri legislature are crucial arenas for the policy-making process. In part, they are important because in a legislature, important decisions are typically made in committee. In addition, in Missouri the principal legislative leadership for the particular segment of policy with which a given committee deals is likely to emerge from the committee. We have already noted the relative indifference of the formal House leadership to questions outside the core of gubernatorial or party program. Most public school questions other than financing state aid *are* outside this area of interest to the leadership. They are left to whatever specialized leadership may exist in the legislature, and the "experts" on school questions tend, naturally, to be associated with the education committees.

In several sessions prior to 1961, Senate members exercised substantial leadership on public school questions, especially the late C. R. (Ted) Hawkins, a Republican from central Missouri. The other legislators regarded Hawkins as more knowledgeable and more interested than they in school matters, and they looked to him for guidance. He worked closely with MSTA leaders and generally was acknowledged as *the* leader on school issues. Hawkins' death in 1960 left a considerable vacuum. He had no obvious successor.

---

[8] Young concluded that the only ideological issue that divided the parties in 1955 was a resolution endorsing federal aid to public schools. *Op. cit.,* p. 131.

The chairmen of the education committees of both House and Senate took other assignments in 1961, further extending the leadership void. Into this gap MSTA thrust its perennial and most reliable strength—influence with individual House members. With MSTA backing, the principal education experts emerged in the House, primarily on the basis of Education Committee service. There was no Ted Hawkins around in 1961, but his role was increasingly being filled by the new House Education Committee Chairman, V. M. Baltz. We shall examine Mr. Baltz's activities in a moment, but first let us look at the committee system generally.

For all the considerable importance of committees in the Missouri legislature, the committee system is still remarkably unstructured when compared, let us say, with Congress. Each legislator serves on many committees, averaging about five in the House and seven or eight in the Senate. Obviously, legislators cannot give concentrated attention to all their assignments. Moreover, legislators of the majority party may have greater responsibilities than simple membership. Almost all second-termers in the House hold at least a vice-chairmanship, and usually every majority party senator chairs a committee. Again, the result is to reduce the attention legislators can give to particular subjects. Put another way, it may reduce the number of legislators who can concentrate their attention sufficiently on any one subject to gain any great familiarity with it. In either case, the acknowledged specialist has a great potential influence over his colleagues, but the legislator must choose to make the effort to develop the specialized knowledge required. It will not develop automatically.

Specialized familiarity of legislators with policy issues may develop as a result of long service on a particular committee. Yet in Missouri, committee assignments change considerably from one session to the next. Even among ranking members there is a good deal of switching. Most changes result from the desire of individual legislators to get different assignments. Some are a consequence of the speaker giving his supporters the choice positions. Some changes result from the leadership's recognizing particular competence on the part of a legislator. Seniority is not ignored entirely, but it is a relatively minor factor either in making committee assignments or in designating chairmen. The result is considerable turnover of committee members. While turnover militates against the development of specialized expertise among legislators, it permits even greater influence to be exerted by any experts who do emerge.

The Education Committees. In the Missouri House of Representatives, there are two committees that handle most education matters. The Education Committee is the larger of the two and by far the more important. The Public Schools Committee was created in 1951 and is supposed to handle school finance bills. Its workload is usually light, and in 1961 it was virtually inactive.[9] Our discussion will focus on the House Education Committee and its counterpart, the Senate Education Committee.

From 1953 through 1961 the rankings of both Democrats and Republicans on the House Education Committee changed almost every session. The House Public Schools Committee had five different ranking Democrats and three Republicans in the same period. Taking the period 1955 through 1961, 42.3 per cent of the members of the House Education Committee continued in service at least one term; 51.25 per cent of those who returned to the House held on to their assignment. Only 23.3 per cent of the House Public Schools Committee members continued in service; 36.9 per cent of those who remained in the legislature stayed on the committee, indicating the lower preference given to the less active Public Schools Committee. The figures for the Senate Education Committee are 57.7 per cent and 73.2 per cent,

[9] From 1951 through 1959, 78 House bills were referred to the Education Committee and 38 to the Public Schools Committee. In 1961, however, 18 bills of interest to us were sent to Education and only 4, all minor, went to Public Schools.

suggesting the greater continuity in that body. (Illinois figures are: House Education Committee, 64.3 per cent and 67.9 per cent; Senate Education Committee, 65.7 per cent and 82.1 per cent.) Committees like Appropriations and Ways and Means will attract transfers from Education, while the latter has more appeal and is a busier committee than many others.[1]

The figures given above suggest the considerable degree of discontinuity of service that characterizes most committees in the Missouri General Assembly, particularly in the House. What role does the committee play in the legislative process that might be affected by discontinuity of membership and leadership? All bills are referred to committee by the speaker or lieutenant governor. Under the rules, committees are supposed to report back all bills to the floor, but in fact a good many bills die in committees. From 1951 to 1961, fifteen bills out of seventy-eight referred to the House Education Committee received no report. An additional eleven received a report recommending that the bill not pass. Except in extraordinary cases an unfavorable report kills the bill, and these eleven were not extraordinary. Thus the committees in the period screened out one third of the bills proposed. Committee amendments and substitutes are fairly common, and certainly many of the informal arrangements and compromises that characterize the legislative process anywhere are made in the committee stage. As noted earlier, there were some complaints in 1961 that the committees were not screening out enough bills, that they were favorably reporting anything anyone asked for. Committees of the Missouri legislature do not often kill bills for which there will be any very substantial support in the floor, but they are still important in the process.

[1] In his thorough discussion of the Missouri committee system, Robert F. Karsch finds that the House Education Committee ranked twelfth among the 54 House committees in total work load. *The Standing Committees of the Missouri General Assembly* (Columbia: Bureau of Government Research, University of Missouri), No. 1, 1959, pp. 22 ff.

Granting the importance of their role, how do the committees function? They have no research staffs, so that for expert assistance they must depend on the legislative research committee, members of the executive branch, representatives of interest groups, and the legislators' own individual expertise.[2] With reference to educational questions, the latter two sources of information are much the most important. The MSTA draws a good deal of its effectiveness from the fact that it is virtually the only source of information to which committee leaders turn. The State Department of Education plays a role here also, but its role is relatively minor.

The experienced and informed legislator has great influence. On questions of concern to a particular local area, the representatives of that area are deferred to, but even on bills designed for state-wide application, the experiences related by the legislators regarding their particular local situations are accorded considerable weight. The lawyer with competence at examining a proposed statute for technical flaws will have influence in committee deliberations. And special attention will be given the views of the legislator who is regarded as an expert in a particular subject. The latter's influence depends both on his knowledge and his ability to use it without offending the sensibilities of other legislators. Frequently, but not always, the legislator who best combines expertise and skill at interpersonal negotiation will also be the committee chairman. When this is the case the chairman will, of course, carry great weight in committee deliberations.

On some committees there are no effective experts. In such cases the committee is likely to do little but report back the bills referred to it, or in some cases, do the bidding of

[2] A good discussion of the significance of the expert legislator may be found in William Buchanan, Heinz Eulau, LeRoy C. Ferguson, and John C. Wahlke, "The Legislator as Specialist," *Western Political Quarterly,* XIII (September, 1960), pp. 636-651. Buchanan, et al., find that education is one of the areas in which legislators most frequently specialize, ranking behind only law and finance, p. 641.

the leadership or of an interest group and kill the bill. The committee as a distinctive entity will not much affect the legislation it considers if there are no members on it with some degree of specialized knowledge and interest.

A committee has relatively little power simply as an institutional mechanism apart from its members. An influential man as chairman can be powerful; an uninterested or inept man as chairman will have little impact.

There is one significant difference between the House and the Senate in the role played by the committees. The Senate is so small that committees are much less important as agencies for the division of labor. Each senator serves on about one third of the Senate committees; each committee has at least one third of the membership serving on it. Consequently, a committee is more often another name for the Senate, or at least for its dominant leaders, and committee action tends to be Senate action under another name. A particularly influential expert in the Senate may choose to work through his committee rather than on the floor. A recalcitrant chairman may try, though rarely with success, to block action desired by the Senate leadership. But the committee is usually an alter ego of the Senate rather than a distinct arena where a balance of forces prevails that is different from that on the floor.

The committees dealing with public school questions during the 1961 session varied considerably in their composition, leadership, and outlook. In the House, the primary committee was the Education Committee, but the Public Schools Committee played a supporting role and a number of other committees handled legislation of concern to some school interests. Of the bills we concerned ourselves with, the House Education Committee initially considered eighteen; Public Schools, four; and other committees, nine. In the Senate the Education Committee dealt with eleven proposals, Judiciary with two. Based on the 1961 session, the House Education Committee is clearly the most impor-

tant, not merely by volume of bills considered but in terms
of the importance of the bills. Thus all but one of the Senate
bills were primarily of local concern, affecting only one part
of the state.

We have already noted the frequency with which the
House Education Committee kills bills, 26 out of 78 from
1951 through 1959. Of the eighteen referrals with which we
have dealt in the 1961 session, five were killed.[3] Figures on
committee actions in the form of amendments to or substitutes for House bills referred to it are not available for the
whole period, but in 1959 and 1961 seven bills were revised
in committee out of a total of thirty-three. Sixteen bills were
reported favorably in the same form in which they had been
introduced. The committee obviously plays a role of some
substantive significance, and we shall examine its operations
with reference to the most recent period.

The size of the committee has varied somewhat from
year to year, but generally there are twenty-odd members,
twenty-three in 1961. The party balance very roughly reflects the division in the House, but fluctuations of interest in
certain subjects will result in some unevenness in party ratios
on various committees. In 1961 fifteen of the twenty-three
members were Democrats. Ten of the twenty-three members had served on the committee in 1959, and one other
had seen earlier service on the committee. Five Democrats
and two Republicans had more than two terms of committee
service. Continuity of service and influence on the committee
bore some relation to one another, but there were two or
three new members who were active, and at least one three-
term member was entirely inactive.

The speaker selects committee members, consulting to
some degree with the representative he has designated to

[3] The figures for 1961 are not comparable with those of previous years.
The latter are drawn from Karsch, *op. cit.*, 1961 figures include only House
bills. Senate bills are not included, nor are a few House bills which we
have excluded as too peripheral in their subject matter to our interests. See
below, for examples.

be chairman. A considerable portion of the members welcome the assignment, since Education is one of the most active committees in the House. Representatives of districts in which state colleges are located often have a special constituency interest, though in 1961 only one of these had a seat on Education. Background in school work is sometimes a basis for selection; five of the most active members had been teachers at some time in their lives.

The chairman seeks some rough balance of group and area interests on the committee but tends, by design, to limit the representation of the metropolitan areas. St. Louis City representatives are not thought to have much interest in education questions. From 1953 through 1961, only 8 of 131 committee members came from St. Louis, about half the proportion that St. Louis representatives have in the House as a whole. Jackson County members are apparently more interested. They held 9 seats during this period, and more important, controlled the chairmanship for most of two terms. St. Louis County representatives are regarded as interested in school matters but difficult to deal with. As an outstate representative said, "They have wealthy districts and don't understand the problems of rural Missouri schools. They don't want to pay (through state revenues) for better schools." Six St. Louis County representatives served on the committee between 1953 and 1957, including three Republicans (all the other urban representatives were Democrats). Since 1957, however, no St. Louis County legislator has been a member.

Overall, the metropolitan areas have held 17.5 per cent of the committee seats while controlling 24.8 per cent of the House since 1953.[4] If anything, this figure overstates the influence of urban representatives on the committee. In 1961, the St. Louis City representative was entirely inactive and rarely attended meetings, and the legislators with the greatest concern for state-wide school policy were clearly

[4] If one adds the seats held on the Public Schools Committee, the total urban share is 15.1 percent.

those from outstate, both on the committee and in the House.

Influence in the Education Committee is an amalgam of experience with and knowledge of public policy questions affecting schools, experience and knowledge concerning the actual operations of the schools toward which policy is directed, persuasiveness of style in dealing with other members, and access to nonlegislative sources of influence such as the governor or the MSTA. These sources of influence are to some extent mutually reinforcing, but some members are persuasive though inexperienced while others have considerable background and are ineffectual. Only about half a dozen of the members can muster enough of the sources of influence to make a continuing impact on committee actions. One member, a lawyer, may be effective regarding the technicalities of bill drafting. Another, a former county superintendent, may influence reorganization proposals by drawing on his knowledge of the details of school district organization. A third, having served several terms on the committee, will recall the intentions and maneuverings involved in earlier legislative efforts in an effort to maintain some continuity of action. In the unhurried, low-pressure atmosphere of the Missouri legislature, the influential members are prepared to make haste slowly, working over the course of two or three sessions sometimes to develop the consensus which will keep education policy "nonpolitical."

In committee, party considerations are rarely in evidence, partly because those who might emphasize partisan views are not welcomed on the committee. The predominance of outstate representatives of both parties, concerned to defend the interests of schools and teachers in the poorer counties of rural Missouri, promotes consensus. These are the counties for which state aid is more important and, as is so often the case, intensity of concern is a major component of influence.

These observations about influence within the committee apply with particular force to the chairman, at least in the 1961 session. V.M. Baltz represents Shannon County, which is one of the least populous and poorest counties in the Ozarks. Baltz, who attended Southwest Missouri State College and taught public school for some years, identifies himself fully with the school people. He has been actively engaged in Democratic politics for many years, has held county office, and has been elected to five nonconsecutive legislative terms. In his last four terms he has always been on either the Education Committee or the Public Schools Committee, and in 1959 he was a member of both, holding the chairmanship of Public Schools. He sought the chairmanship of Education in 1961, and he was regarded as the logical choice, since, even in 1959, he had been one of the more active and influential members.

Baltz is quiet and unassuming in demeanor, rarely raising his voice and indeed speaking infrequently on the floor. He speaks quietly to those from whom he expects support, but rarely gains much publicity outside the legislature. In committee and corridor negotiation, however, Baltz is very important. Everett Keith of the MSTA comes directly to him to discuss public schools legislation and the Keith-Baltz relationship is often a principal means of communicating MSTA's desire and expert opinion to the committee. Keith talks directly to some other members of the committee from time to time, but Baltz is his main contact. As chairman, Baltz has access to the governor and is in the best position to know how the Governor thinks on public school questions whenever he is involved in the issue. Baltz works closely with his counterpart in the Senate to iron out differences whenever possible without the cumbersome machinery of a conference committee. He assists in promoting the governor's revenue program to assure maximum revenue from which to finance aid to the schools. Baltz serves on the Appropriations Committee and is thereby in a position to protect school funds there.

In committee sessions, Baltz may say very little about local bills, preferring to avoid involvement in any controversy that might adversely affect his ability to get his bills through later on. He is very conscious of taking a "state-wide benefit" viewpoint; this precludes getting mixed up in local quarrels. He is often quiet concerning bills pushed by other legislators which do not have the sanction of expert testimony of professional education groups behind them. Such bills frequently are inspired by particular local situations but are drawn so as to apply to the whole state. If there is objection to such a bill—for example, growing out of differing local circumstances in other parts of the state—Baltz is confident that the objection will be expressed without his getting involved. He lets the sponsor handle the presentation to the committee and on the floor as well, not wishing to dilute his influence by using it too often. He concentrates his personal attention and sponsorship on the few bills that are of special importance to him and usually this means to the MSTA as well. MSTA bills are normally sponsored by Baltz and one of two or three other legislators who are regarded as specially conversant with education matters.

Baltz has a good deal of patience with his colleagues, in committee and on the floor. It does not dismay him that a bill he favors does not pass the first session it is offered. He, and the MSTA, are willing to work over a longer time span to secure their legislative goals, and since most legislators are not interested enough in school matters to give them such sustained attention, Baltz's influence grows with time. Again, his quiet, almost self-effacing tactics serve him well.

Baltz's deep commitment to the MSTA program sometimes takes him into positions he does not entirely approve. Thus in 1959 he co-sponsored the earmarked cigarette tax increase and handled the proposed sales tax increase designed to finance the increase in the foundation program, even though he disapproved of earmarked taxes. He has a strong commitment to increase state support for rural area schools, especially those in reorganized districts. Baltz has little patience with the protests of wealthier urban and suburban districts against increased equalization payments, and anticipates cutting the flat grant portion of state aid. He looks on metropolitan delegations with a kind of guarded suspicion. Like many outstate legislators of both parties, he regards them as beholden to labor and unsympathetic to the needs of rural Missouri. He argues that since outstate supplies much of the cities' labor force and market, it is in the interests of the urban area to help finance education in the hinterlands.

Baltz does not have the kind of reputation as an education specialist that would automatically mobilize majority support whenever he indicated his position. He has little formal authority to control policy, and he prefers to husband the resources he has rather than use them at every opportunity. Nevertheless, his influence is substantial on those few issues which are regarded as most important to the school people in a given legislative session. On those questions he comes closer than anyone else to being *the* key figure in the legislature. Moreover, his influence and accompanying reputation for expertise on public school issues is steadily growing. Although he has not yet fully achieved the stature of recognized expert, Baltz is surely the most likely candidate to succeed the late Senator Hawkins as the man to whom large numbers of legislators look for guidance on education policy.

Action on the Floor. The process of considering bills on the floor of the House or Senate reflects the factors already identified as important in other respects. The limited strength of interest groups outside the legislature, the relative weakness of gubernatorial and legislative leadership, the uncertain character of party identification—hardly visible at all on one occasion and flaring up decisively on another—the influence of legislators with technical knowledge who can communicate it inoffensively, and the representational perspectives that legislators bring with them are all evident during floor action. We shall focus our attention on the House where, especially in 1961, those factors were significant in affecting the legislative outcome. (In this session, and probably as a general rule, the small size of the Senate so increased the importance of interpersonal relations on all levels that it is extremely difficult to distinguish the various components.) Also, in 1961 the House was the crucial arena for most public school issues.

Floor action in the House occurs in two stages: the perfection or amendment stage, and the third reading and final passage. Passage requires a majority of the whole membership. During the perfection stage, amendments and perfection require only a majority of those voting. In both stages the rules of debate, *as observed,* permit any member to speak or to interrogate another member. Members use these opportunities liberally, and bills that raise any degree of controversy at all will often be debated for several hours or even days. Although the majority members, at least, have ample office space,[5] the bulk of the membership attends the floor sessions, and a considerable portion listens to the debate even when they do not participate. There is a certain amount of inattention and occasional horseplay, but the general tone of proceedings is decorous and serious. The quality of debate is not always impressive, but its impact is considerable.

A substantial number of legislators expect to decide how to vote on the basis of floor proceedings. What one's friends say, the individual bargains that are struck quietly while discussion is going on, and the logic of the arguments presented are all factors. As one legislator said following an extended debate: "We were beaten until 'Mr. X' got up and spoke. A lot of these country boys will listen to him, and he saved the bill."

The sponsor of a controversial bill knows that his floor performance will affect the outcome, often decisively, and

[5] The minority members must make do with one bullpen plus an office for the minority leadership. Consequently many Republicans use their desks on the floor as offices. All senators have office suites.

the outcome is often in doubt until the debate is concluded and the voting boards light up. Again, this would not be true if power relationships within or outside the legislature were clear enough to indicate more definitely how the legislators should decide. But the legislators are frequently without such instructions and must make up their minds on an *ad hoc* basis. For this process, floor consideration is of crucial importance. Rarely, therefore, do members orate for outside consumption. No premium is put on declamatory skill. Members speak primarily to each other and, *mirabile dictu,* listen.

Since legislators do listen to one another, it is often during debate that an issue develops into a partisan controversy. As we have noted above, a Republican may get up to oppose a bill, a Democrat responds, and soon the issue has been defined in party terms. The importance of floor debate and its uncertainty may be seen in the fate of H.B. 720, described below, where a relatively noncontroversial bill became a rhetorical plaything. MSTA has enough reliable supporters in the House so that floor debate holds few dangers for its bills. But on other bills affecting the schools, the largely unstructured character of the discussion can lead to many dangers that are hard to anticipate.

The perfection stage is ordinarily the critical point for a bill. Although it requires a smaller total vote than final passage, it is here that amendments may undermine a bill and make it unpalatable to its sponsors. Roll calls are not always required, and since this is only a preliminary stage, public attention is less sharply focused on the bill. If and when a bill reaches the third reading stage, even though it may have been controversial at an earlier point, the disagreements have often been ironed out, and it may go through more easily than it did at the perfection stage.

A substantial number of bills die on the calendars at each session. Many of these casualties do not have any substantial opposition (though, of course, some casualties do and are such that opponents prefer to remain covert). The leisurely and detailed floor consideration of bills, even at the end of the session, makes it impossible for many bills that are introduced late or reported late from committee to get through the full legislative process. The Missouri legislature usually puts in three days a week for the first two or three months of its sessions and four and five days a week from then on. Sessions may last for four to six hours a day in May and even longer in June. But the lack of strong leadership or extensive interest group influence makes it difficult to rush controversial bills, or even bills about which there is uncertainty as to their merits, through the mill. The operative presumption of the legislative area is "When in doubt, say no." We have seen how this is consciously applied to local measures and the system of considering on the floor of the Missouri House has just that effect.

We have attempted in the foregoing discussion to identify and explain the principal factors that influence the Missouri General Assembly as it makes decisions affecting the public schools of the state. Although such generalized statements are the primary objective of our inquiry, they may often seem formal and empty without the richness and variety of instances in which these forces were at work. Accordingly, we shall turn our attention to several specific issues: first, the sequence of legislative actions over several years by which the foundation program of state aid to local school districts was developed, and second, the whole range of bills introduced in the 1961 legislative session dealing with education.

THE SCHOOL FOUNDATION PROGRAM

Until 1955, state aid to Missouri public schools was based on the constitutional guarantee that one third of the general revenue be allocated to the schools, plus whatever additional money could be pried loose by virtue of MSTA's legislative influence. Although MSTA made some progress in the late 1940's and early 1950's, it required a substantial political effort in each legislative session, leaving little energy for other programs. Moreover, MSTA and other educational groups were dissatisfied with the levels of support provided under this system, especially for the impoverished areas of rural Missouri. After these areas began to implement the Reorganization Act of 1948, it was easier to urge increased aid without seeming to support inefficient one-room schoolhouses.

The first concrete step to achieve a formula for providing state aid was the appointment of a Citizen's Committee for the Study of Education in 1950, by the state board of education. In 1952, the committee recommended a foundation program and thus began the public campaign which continued through 1961 to establish and finance a foundation formula for state aid to Missouri's public school system.

The 1953 General Assembly appropriated nearly ten million dollars for public school aid, in addition to the traditional appropriation of one third of the general revenue fund. Governor Phil Donnelly, a conservative outstate Democrat, vetoed this additional item, thus irritating and frustrating the large number of legislators who desired to support the public schools more generously.[6]

The 1953 General Assembly also created a Joint Legislative Education Study Committee, with a citizens' advisory committee, to study the public schools and made recommendations to the 1955 session. The resolution provided for the speaker of the House to appoint 6 representatives, the president pro tempore of the Senate to appoint 6 senators, and for the 12 legislators to select 6 citizens to form the advisory committee. (Eventually, 31 citizens, including the state commissioner of education, were selected.)

After eighteen months of study, the joint committee recommended to the 1955 legislature a minimum level of public school support from state and local sources and a greater emphasis on equalization. The committee also recommended

[6] See Young, *op. cit.*, p. 117.

an increase of one percent in the state sales tax as a means of financing the Foundation Program. The program called for about a $22,000,000 annual increase in state grants to elementary and high schools, changing the basis of distribution from classroom units to average daily attendance (ADA). There were to be three major types of payments under the program: equalization grants, to insure every district ample funds to maintain a minimum level of support of $185 per pupil in ADA; flat grants of $75 per pupil in ADA; and teacher incentive payments, based on the number of accredited semester hours a teacher had earned.[7] The last two provisions were added to win the support of the legislators from wealthier districts, particularly St. Louis County, whose local schools had already attained a level of support well beyond the proposed level of $185 per ADA and thus would be ineligible for equalization grants.

Two separate bills were introduced in the 1955 Senate: S.B. 3, calling for the Foundation Program, with the stipulation that it be submitted as a referendum; S.B. 4, calling for an increase in the sales tax, also with a referendum provi-

[7] Average daily attendance is computed by dividing the total number of days attended of pupils in grades 1-12 inclusive and between the ages of 6 and 20 by the actual number of days that the school was in session, including legal holidays and legally authorized teachers' meetings. According to the 1955 Foundation Program formula, the equalization quota was determined by multiplying the ADA of resident pupils by $110 and subtracting from the product the amount received from the local property tax and the income from other school district tax sources. The teacher incentive payment was based on the following table:

Semester Hour Credits	Incentive Payments
150 or more	$300
120-149	200
90-119	100

The flat grant amount was determined by adding the ADA of pupils residing and attending in the school district to the ADA of nonresident pupils, whose tuition the district of residence is required to pay, and multiplying the sum by $75.

Under the provisions of a 1959 amendment, the formula was upgraded substantially for all three types of payments.

See State of Missouri, Department of Education, *Missouri School Laws 1960* (Jefferson City, 1960), *passim*.

sion.[8] The Missouri State Teachers Association, along with the Congress of Parents and Teachers Associations, favored both bills but concentrated on S.B. 3, which it had had a big hand in fashioning. MSTA rallied its forces early and marshalled overflow crowds before the Education Committee to demonstrate support for the foundation bill. The Senate Education Committee acted quickly and reported the bill out with the recommendation that it pass. Thirteen days later the bill passed the Senate unanimously. It was soon to become the first major change since 1931 in Missouri public school finance.

Action in the House followed a significantly different pattern. Strategically placed opposition forces had had time to consolidate. Organized labor, for example, opposed to any regressive tax measures, was fearful that passage of the bill to increase school aid would virtually assure the passage of the sales tax increase. Legislators friendly to labor favored instead an increase in the income tax. Although the bill reached the House on March 16, it was not until April 19 that the speaker assigned it to the Committee on Constitutional Amendments. On May 9, the committee reported out the bill favorably, *but* with a labor-backed committee amendment, inserting a new section to increase the income tax revenue by $27,000,000 a year and to earmark the tax for the public schools. The amendment also called for changing the date of the referendum from October 4, 1955, to the regular election day in November 1956. The reasoning was that the MSTA and other school interests would be more apt to get out the vote in a special election, but those who would

[8] House Democratic leaders chose a different route to increase the state school moneys. They proposed to raise the appropriation, as in 1953, but in order to block another veto, to raise the percentage figure of general revenue rather than the dollar figure. There was an effort by House Republicans to raise the figure still further in order to show their support for education and, by upsetting the state budget, embarrass the Democrats. This was foiled only by some intricate parliamentary maneuvering, a rare occurrence in the Missouri legislature. See Young, *op. cit.*, pp. 117-119.

favor the income tax increase over the sales tax increase could be more readily mobilized on the regular election day.

The school lobby opposed the amendment to include a tax increase plan in the foundation bill itself, fearing that it might bring about its defeat at the polls. MSTA continued to press for its separate sales tax increase proposal to be submitted to the voters to finance the program.

The committee amendment failed by a vote of 25-114. Only 4 Republicans and 21 Democrats voted for the amendment. The bill without the amendment then passed the House 135-11. Of the 11 negative votes—10 Democratic and 1 Republican—7 were from the city of St. Louis. At this point, both House and Senate had approved the idea of a foundation program, but the conflict over the method of financing the proposal remained unresolved.

The bill for a referendum to increase the sales tax (S.B. 4), passed the Senate 22-8, after having been amended to lower the increase from one cent to one-half cent. Seven Democrats and 1 Republican voted against the bill. The Republican was from outstate; of the Democrats, 5 were from St. Louis and 2 were from Kansas City. In the House, the leadership sat on the bill as they awaited the fate of the proposed income tax increase. Although the bill had passed the Senate on April 26 and had been sent to the House, and although the General Assembly was pressing to meet its May 31 deadline, the speaker did not refer the measure to a House committee until May 1, and then he referred it to the Committee on Organization and Related Matters, headed by a Kansas City Democrat who opposed the bill. The chairman announced that the House committee would hear proponents of the bill on May 24 and opponents on May 31, the last day of the session—obviously too late for the House to act.[8a] On May 11, the St. Louis *Post-Dispatch* lamented: "As the matter now

[8a] In 1955 the biennial sessions of the General Assembly still were required to terminate after five months rather than six, as is now the case.

stands . . . the new program will be submitted to the voters without the additional revenue in sight to pay the full state aid guarantees." [9]

The MSTA went into action and on May 18 a motion to take the bill out of committee passed the House 91-27. The following day, however, with 79 votes needed for final passage, S.B. 4 received only 73. Only 15 negative votes were cast, but 40 members were absent and 28 were recorded as "present but not voting." The sales tax increase was dead, and the struggle over financing the Foundation Program continued.

On the day that the Senate had passed the sales tax measure and sent it to the House, a group of six senators had introduced S.B. 351, providing for the levying of a tax of five cents per package on all cigarettes sold in Missouri. On the following day, the bill received a favorable committee recommendation, and on May 9 it passed, 22-10, after it had been amended to lower the tax from five cents to two cents. All seven St. Louis senators voted against the measure. Of the other three negative voters, one was a Kansas City Democrat, one an outstate Democrat, and one an outstate Republican. The bill was intended to be part of a scheme to submit to the voters several propositions (including the sales tax proposal) to increase state taxes $32,000,000 to $34,000,000 a year, not only for increased school aid but also for the operation of mental and penal institutions and possibly increased old-age pensions. It was estimated that the two cent cigarette tax would bring in from 8 to 10 million dollars a year.[1]

Organized labor opposed the cigarette tax measure for the same reason that it opposed the sales tax increase: it would bear more heavily upon the laborer and other lower income persons. As had been the case with the sales tax

[9] St. Louis *Post-Dispatch* (May 11, 1955), p. 10A.
[1] At the time Missouri did not have a cigarette tax, although many cities and towns in the state were levying one.

proposal, the cigarette tax bill was assigned to the House Committee on Organization and Related Matters, headed by a pro-labor Kansas City Democrat. The chairman, in order to avoid hearing the bill, left the state without giving any authorization to his committee to hear the proposal. MSTA mobilized its supporters, however, and by a vote of 79-33, the bill was taken from the committee and placed on the calendar for the third reading. On the same day the House passed by voice vote an amendment to earmark the tax for public schools. On the following day, May 19, the bill passed the House 80-12. Of the 12 negative voters, 2 were outstate Republicans; of the 10 Democrats, 5 were from the city of St. Louis, 1 was from Kansas City, 1 from St. Louis County, and the others from outstate.

The speaker refused to sign the bill, contending that since the original bill was still in the possession of the committee chairman, the House could not legally act on it, and, therefore, the bill that was passed was not valid. The Missouri Supreme Court later upheld the House action, after the Missouri Tobacco Dealers had challenged the legality of the measure.[2]

On the penultimate day of the session, as the MSTA and its allies had begun to breathe more easily over their narrow triumphs in the House, the Senate received a motion that it should not concur in the House amendment to earmark the cigarette tax for public schools. A substitute motion that the Senate should concur lost by two votes. With one exception, the urban Democrats were solidly against concurrence. The next day, as the General Assembly faced its adjournment deadline, the St. Louis *Post-Dispatch,* in reporting the Senate action of the day before, averred: "The powerful state school lobby, which is demanding that additional revenue be raised to finance the $67,000,000-a-year school aid program in full, suffered a setback late yesterday in the Senate."[3] The *Post-*

[2] Young, *op. cit.,* p. 49n.
[3] St. Louis *Post-Dispatch* (May 31, 1955), p. 1A.

Dispatch further reported that the MSTA had put the heat on Senators during the dinner hour to change their minds, and at night session a senator who had earlier voted against concurrence in the House amendment asked the Senate to reconsider the matter.[4] He was forced to withdraw his request, however, as the bill had already been returned to the House.

The school lobby stood ready to revive the sales tax increase if it was necessary, but the House, by a vote of 108-1, refused to recede from its amendment to earmark the cigarette tax for the public schools. Later that night, as the adjournment hour neared, the Senate accepted the House amendment 18-13. One Republican and four outstate Democrats had switched their votes from "Nay" to "Yea"; one Republican switched from "Yea" to "Nay"; and the two Democrats who were absent on the first vote were recorded on the negative side. After having accepted the House amendment, the Senate passed the bill 20-11.

Thus on October 4, 1955, the voters of Missouri were presented with two referenda: one to institute a foundation program for the public schools, and the other to levy a cigarette tax earmarked to help finance the new school program. Not yet able to relax, the MSTA and the Congress of Parents and Teachers Association campaigned vigorously for both proposals. There was no organized opposition to the foundation program, but labor groups, tobacco distributors, and the St. Louis *Post-Dispatch* opposed the cigarette tax.

The foundation referendum carried 247,639 to 75,286, losing only five wards in the city of St. Louis. The cigarette tax proposal carried 230,851 to 95,717 but lost in St. Louis, carrying only three wards. Kansas City, St. Louis County, and the rural areas voted for both proposals.

Only 13 percent of the eligible voters participated. The *Post-Dispatch* editorialized: ". . . except in St. Louis, the voters who could have defeated the cigarette tax stayed at

4 *Ibid.*

home, leaving the field to the school lobby and permitting a new tax to be levied by the lightest vote in any recent Missouri election." [5]

THE 1959 AMENDMENT

At its special session in 1958, the Missouri General Assembly passed a resolution creating a Special Joint Committee on the Foundation Program to report to the 1959 session. The committee of four senators, four representatives, and four members appointed by the governor proposed that the level of state support be increased by approximately $26,000,-000 annually in order to approximate the average level of state support per pupil in ADA that was provided in the nation in 1957-58. The committee bill (S.B. 166) called for increases in equalization grants, flat grants, and teacher incentive payments, bringing the minimum level of support per pupil in ADA up from $185 to $232. The committee made no recommendations as to the financing of the increase.

The strategy of the public school lobby was to secure passage of the increased formula *with or without* a companion bill to raise the necessary revenue. MSTA was, of course, determined to fight to the end for passage of the requisite tax increase, but even without the added revenue it was felt that once the formula was increased, the full financing of it would be in the offing, perhaps at the next legislative session if not at this one.

Thus, as the bill to increase the foundation formula entered the early stages of the legislative process the Senate attached—by voice vote—two qualifying amendments: the first specified explicitly that sufficient state revenues to finance in full the increased amounts called for were not available, unless additional revenue was provided; the second, that if the state school moneys were insufficient to finance the amendment, the moneys for each school district would be calculated according to the original formula, with

[5] St. Louis *Post-Dispatch* (October 5, 1955), p. 2D.

any remaining school moneys to be paid proportionately under the provisions of the amendment. With the above amendments attached, the bill passed the Senate unanimously on March 24. In the House, the bill was favorably reported from the Public Schools Committee the day after it was assigned, and a week later, it passed by a 123-24 vote.

With these preliminaries out of the way—that is, the approval for increasing state aid to schools having been given—the issues relating to finance, which involved real conflict, came to the fore. Senate Bill 200, known as the "MSTA bill," had been introduced as a companion to S.B. 166. It called for a one-half cent increase in the sales tax upon approval in a referendum vote. Although the bill was introduced on February 5, as late as March 24 the St. Louis *Post-Dispatch* reported that the bill "is buried in the Senate Ways and Means Committee and is believed to have little chance of passage.[6] Then on April 27, the Senate Appropriations Committee slashed $26,016, 281 from the operating funds for state agencies, schools, institutions and welfare programs. The committee reductions followed the failure of the legislature to act on three major tax increase bills which had been recommended by the governor in an effort to balance the state budget.

Two days later, on April 29, the Senate Ways and Means Committee reported out the sales tax measure, recommending that it pass, with a committee amendment changing the referendum date from October 6, 1959, to the regular election day in November 1960. On May 13, the bill passed the Senate 21-12. The negative voters were all Democrats; 7 were from St. Louis, 3 from Kansas City and 2 from outstate.

In the House, the bill was referred to the Ways and Means Committee, and within three days the committee reported the bill out with a favorable recommendation. On the floor, the proposal was amended to change the referendum date

[6] St. Louis *Post-Dispatch* (March 24, 1959), p. 3A.

back to October 6, 1959, and to earmark the increase for the
public schools until a cutoff date of July 1, 1961, after which
each succeeding General Assembly would have power to
dispose of the revenue as it preferred. The purpose of the earmarking provision was to assure enough revenue to put the
new foundation formula into immediate effect. Opponents
of earmarking argued that it would establish a level of increased state aid which, realistically, no subsequent legislature could reduce, and that other state functions were equally
in need of more money. MSTA pressure was firm, however.
The earmarking amendment passed 62-60, and the amended
bill was approved 88-29.

On May 29, the Senate passed a motion refusing to concur
in the House amendment and requesting a conference. Many
senators felt that the tax increase should be spent on other
state services besides the public schools. Later that same
day, in an unprecedented action, the House, by voice vote,
refused to recede from its amendment and refused to grant a
conference to the Senate. The Missouri State Teachers Association was adamant in its opposition to a conference. It obviously felt that, with rush hour adjournment imminent, the
school lobby and its friends could effect a coup similar to that
in 1955 when it persuaded the opposition into last-minute,
emergency approval of the cigarette tax proposal.[7]

Neither the House nor the Senate would yield, however.
Thus no increased revenue was provided to finance the increased foundation formula.

Although Missouri ranked eighth among the 50 states in
per capita personal income in 1959,[8] it was only forty-seventh
in both state tax collections per $100 of personal income[9] and

[7] During the course of interviews conducted after the session, several
state senators reminisced about how they had pleaded with MSTA to "release" the House for a conference.

[8] Robert E. Graham, Jr., "General Rise in State Income in 1959," *Survey
of Current Business*, 40: 10-24 (August 1960), 17.

[9] Graham, *loc. cit.* Also U.S. Department of Commerce, Bureau of the
Census, *Governmental Finances in 1959.* G-GF59 No. 2 (Washington, D.C.:
the Bureau of the Census, September 30, 1960), p. 11.

per capita total state expenditures for all purposes.[1] The stalemate in the 1959 General Assembly left the situation substantially the same. Missouri ranked only thirty-sixth in estimated revenue from state sources per pupil in ADA for the 1960-61 academic year. The month before the 1961 session convened, the St. Louis *Post-Dispatch* reported: "Public education in Missouri is facing a crisis. Strong demands are being made on the new legislature and the administration of Governor-elect John M. Dalton for prompt and effective action to build the state's educational standards to at least the national average."[2] A special joint committee on taxation reported to the legislature that, compared with fourteen other midwestern states, Missouri was last in per capita yield from the cigarette tax, ninth in per capita yield from the income tax, last in return from the liquor tax, and seventh in yield from sales tax.[3] In this context, Governor Dalton proposed to boost state revenue by providing for the withholding of the income tax and by increasing the levies on cigarettes and on beer, wine, and liquor.

Even though MSTA had fought hard for earmarked taxes in 1955 and 1959, it much preferred to support the general revenue increase proposed by the Governor. A large proportion of the state school money (78.5 percent in 1958-59, 78.4 percent in 1959-60) comes from the general revenue fund. The earmarked cigarette tax accounted for 13.1 percent in 1958-59 and 13 percent in 1959-60.[4] Therefore, MSTA happily concentrated its legislative influence in the Seventy-first General Assembly on support of the governor's revenue program and on the transfer from general revenue to the state school

[1] U.S. Department of Commerce, Bureau of the Census, *Compendium of State Government Finances in 1959* (Washington, D.C.: Superintendent of Documents, GPO, 1960).

[2] St. Louis *Post-Dispatch* (December 13, 1960), p. 1B.

[3] State of Missouri, *Journal* of the Senate (February 14, 1961), pp. 184-190.

[4] State of Missouri, Office of Education, *One Hundred Tenth Report of the Public Schools* (Jefferson City, June 30, 1959), p. 45.

moneys fund of the amount necessary to finance in full the foundation program.

Throughout the 1961 session, the MSTA legislative committee, through its weekly bulletins, informed the membership that in order to ensure full financing of the foundation program, their legislators must be influenced to pass H.B. 113 to transfer $207,119,798 from general revenue to the state school moneys fund, and to support the governor's revenue program *in toto*. These two points were repeated in each weekly bulletin, with the reminder: "He who takes full financing of the foundation program and does not support revenue measures is of little help." [5]

Early in the session, the MSTA informed its members:

It would seem that anyone who could not support an increase in the cigarette, beer, and liquor taxes when they still would be generally low as compared with other states, could not do anything. Anyone who does not support these gives only lip service to financing the foundation program, higher education, mental health, old age assistance, and other functions of government. It is not what one says but what one does that really counts. Pretense alone will not finance the foundation program or anything else. [6]

As it turned out, full financing was achieved with relative ease. On January 17, H.B. 113, the bill to transfer from general revenue to the state school moneys fund enough to finance the foundation program, was introduced. By April 24, it passed the House unanimously and was sent to the Senate. Meanwhile, the cigarette tax increase bill had passed both the House and Senate on March 13 and April 21 respectively, increasing the tax from 2 to 4 cents a package. In the Senate there were only four negative votes, all from St. Louis Democrats. Of the 5 "No" voters in the House, 3 were St. Louis Democrats and 2 were Democrats from outstate; additionally,

---

[5] Missouri State Teachers Association, Legislative Committee, *Legislative Bulletin*, No. 9 (March 16, 1961), p. 1.

[6] *Ibid.*, No. 6 (February 23, 1961), p. 1.

there were 8 who were recorded "present but not voting." Of the latter, 5 were St. Louis Democrats, 1 was a Kansas City Democrat, 1 a Democrat from St. Louis County, and the other an outstate Republican.

Since the amount of money provided for in H.B. 113 was calculated before passage of the cigarette tax increase, the Senate, on June 21, amended the bill by subtracting the amount that the cigarette tax increase was expected to raise, and then passed H.B. 113 unanimously. The 1961 General Assembly also passed bills to increase that tax on beer, liquor, and wine, and to collect state income tax by withholding.

The history of MSTA's efforts to secure a fully financed foundation program illustrates many of the points made in our earlier discussion. The major role MSTA played is obvious. So is its very considerable influence. So also, however, are the limits of that influence. MSTA's dependence on the governor for revenue recommendations is shown by the failure to achieve full financing in 1959 and by the session in 1961. As we have stressed throughout, the greatest conflict over public school policy in Missouri is over finance. Virtually no one opposed the *idea* of increasing state aid for the public schools, but there was opposition from at least three sources to the financing of this increase. One source of difficulty was the general fiscal conservatism which pervades the state and which resists almost any expenditure proposal. On this ground, for example, Governor Donnelly had vetoed an increase in school money appropriations in 1953, and it was an obstacle for any group wanting a higher level of expenditures to overcome. A second source of opposition lay in the competing demands of other groups for state funds. This underlay much of the opposition to proposals for earmarking tax measures, and part of the reason MSTA has sought to support all gubernatorial revenue-raising proposals is to avoid coming into direct conflict with other groups seeking state support.

A third source of opposition was the labor unions and city legislators. In 1953, the support given by the speaker to

these groups greatly strengthened their ability to resist regressive tax proposals. As we have seen, however, even they
lacked the votes to prevent unfavorable action. Furthermore,
although the city-labor groups were not allies of MSTA, their
opposition was not very deep-seated. In 1955 and thereafter,
the House leadership was not especially pro-labor, and on
public school issues, including the earmarked cigarette tax
increase passed in 1961, the city-labor legislators were content with rather perfunctory opposition.

Although finance is a critical area of education policy, it by
no means exhausts the range of questions involving the public schools that the Missouri legislature considers. Let us
examine a larger collection of issues to illustrate the variety
of factors affecting school legislation.

THE 1961 SESSION AND PUBLIC SCHOOL POLICY

We have selected 44 bills and resolutions introduced in the
1961 session of the Missouri legislature as constituting a reasonably complete list of the education proposals of that session. There is, to be sure, a certain arbitrary quality to the
selection. Because of their rather remote connection with
education issues and interests, we have omitted a bill which
permitted school boards to prohibit fraternities and soror-
ities and another bill increasing the benefits of the state retirement system in which public school teachers participate
along with other state employees. On the other hand, a bill
providing state support for symphony concerts in public
schools is included. The selection, though limited, permits
us to indicate the character of proposals related to public
schools and a rough distribution of those bills by types. In the
total of 44, there are a few instances where similar bills were
introduced in both houses or where a bill is accompanied by
a resolution to submit a constitutional amendment. One
group of bills, originally involving two issues, was combined

into one bill/resolution package by the time it was finally passed. Thus the 44 bills and resolutions we examined involve only 39 separate issues.

Thirty-one of the 44 proposals were introduced in the House, including all 5 of those in which the MSTA took an especially active interest. This reflects the finding that with more members and more numerous direct local pressures operating on representatives as compared to senators, a consistently larger volume of legislation is initiated in the House on most questions. It is also partly due to the larger membership of the House, which presents a more complex legislative task requiring more time to complete the process. Therefore, it must be started earlier. Specifically for education interests, however, the House, in 1961, was perceived as a more receptive and sympathetic arena than the Senate. As we have explained above, the leadership of the House Committee on Education had had longer association with public school issues and a greater personal interest in them than their opposite numbers in the Senate. The previous chairman of the Senate Committee had moved over to Appropriations, and the Republican senator most respected on school matters had recently died, leaving no senator in either party with much experience in the field and no one with much inclination to develop a specialized concern for it. Even in 1959, however, when there were senators more intensely interested in education questions, the Senate had been less receptive than the House to MSTA influence. As we have noted earlier, representatives are more susceptible to MSTA influence than senators. The latter, with longer terms and larger districts, are less responsive to the school people and the MSTA concentrates its efforts on the House as a result.

Proportionately, Senate bills did slightly better in surviving the full legislative course than did those originating in the House. Eighteen of the 31 House bills passed the House and 11 of these passed the Senate. Eight of the 13 Senate bills passed the Senate and 6 of these passed the House. It should be noted, however, that 12 of the 13 Senate bills were of limited consequence. Thus almost all public school policy of state-wide application, drawing the attention of or originating with professional educators in the state, began in the House.

We have classified the 44 bills by types, again on a somewhat arbitrary basis. The first classification is bills of local origin and significance. Twenty-four of the 44 bills may be classified as purely local in application. Eighteen of these involved St. Louis (11), Kansas City (4), or St. Louis County (3). Thirteen (or 15 counting duplications) of the 24 passed at least one house, and 8 (or 11) passed both houses. Six local bills would have had state-wide application if adopted but we classify them as local because they were proposed in response to some clearly localized situation that a single individual legislator was attempting to change. Only 2 of these 6 passed even one chamber, and none became law.

The 20 bills designated nonlocal in origin and significance included 5 that the MSTA sponsored, more or less officially. Four of these passed both Houses. One was the appropriation bill submitted in the governor's budget to finance the foundation program. Another was a tax measure, submitted as part of the governor's revenue program and earmarked for support of public schools. Both of these became law. The remaining 13 proposals (12 House bills and 1 Senate bill) were proposed by individual legislators and/or noneducational groups. The MSTA took an interest in some of these, but not as a particularly active sponsor or opponent. Six of these 12 House bills passed the House, but only one passed the Senate. The one Senate bill became law. Only two of these bills were sponsored by legislators who were in any sense specialists on questions of education.

If these figures have any value other than description they suggest that educational policy in Missouri is not made by legislators acting on their own, outside the informal but dominant, specialized channels devoted to matters affecting the public schools: namely, the MSTA. They suggest, secondly, that MSTA, in part to conserve its influence, concentrates its attention on a relatively small proportion of the total number of issues affecting the schools.

Again by a rather arbitrary procedure, we may say that 9 of the 20 nonlocal bills were somewhat controversial in the sense of having active support *and* substantial opposition, at least at some time while they were being considered. Seven of these passed the House and 3 became law. Only 5 of the local bills were controversial in this sense, and these involved only 3 separate issues. In keeping with the local unity norm, none of these bills became law. In most of the other cases, some of which we examined earlier, the local area representatives had agreed in advance as to what they wanted. On a few local issues the local spokesman was not sufficiently concerned with matters to do more than make the gesture of introducing the bill. And in one or two instances, the sponsor of the bill had second thoughts as the matter was discussed and action was deferred by mutual agreement.

SOME EXAMPLES

As previously mentioned, bills affecting the public schools that were presented in the 1961 legislature dealt with diverse subjects. None of the proposals that would have had statewide application were deeply controversial, and certainly none of them could be regarded as major issues in the session. Still, the types of proposals illustrate the character of state legislative involvement in public school policy. We have already discussed several of the local bills and the financing of the foundation program. Here we shall look briefly at a few of the other proposals made.

MSTA Bills. In 1961, as we have seen, the MSTA devoted its primary effort to assuring the full financing of the foundation program. The appropriation measures and the revenue proposals of the governor received special attention, and MSTA did not seek major legislation on other subjects. Nev-

ertheless, four measures were more or less officially sponsored
by the organization.

House Bill 2.   H.B. 2 amended the continuing contract
law. Except in the city of St. Louis, Missouri teachers do not
have tenure. This bill originally provided that a decision not
to renew a teacher's contract must be approved by a majority
of the school board, that reasons for non-renewal be given
the teacher in writing, and that the teacher have the right to
a hearing before the board. The bill was sponsored by Representative Baltz (Democrat) and Representative Henry (Republican), who had also introduced the bill in 1959. The
sponsorship indicated the bipartisan, official MSTA character
of support. In 1959, the bill had narrowly failed on third
reading in the House. In 1961, however, it quickly emerged
from the House Education Committee and was perfected in
February. The House passed the bill after dropping the provision for a hearing. The Senate amended the bill further by
dropping the requirement of written reasons for non-renewal
and the House concurred on June 19.

The potential for controversy on this bill was indirectly
within the MSTA. The organization was committed to the
principle of strengthening teacher security, and the Assembly
had recommended the bill. The leadership of MSTA was
wary of offending the school boards, however, by forcing
written statements of reasons for non-renewal. MSTA legislative leaders were therefore entirely prepared to accept and
even to encourage the amendments eliminating the provisions that might embarrass the school boards and endanger
the unity of the school people which MSTA regards as essential for success.

House Bill 3.   Sponsored by Baltz and Henry, this bill
would have exempted teacher retirement benefits from state
and local taxation. It was referred to the Ways and Means
Committee which recommended that it not pass. MSTA
sponsored this bill which would have put teachers on the
same basis as highway department and other state employ-

ees. However, there was considerable opposition to the proposal on the grounds that it would open the gates to further exemptions or, perhaps, to the elimination of existing exemptions. MSTA did not put forth much effort for the bill. No representative of the organization testified in committee and no grass-roots support was mobilized.

House Bill 4. Also sponsored by Baltz and Henry, this bill authorized school boards to hold summer schools. It was passed out quickly from committee and passed the House on February 1. Senate consideration was delayed until June and passage there occurred only after an amendment was accepted specifying what was probably clear anyway: that no state funds should be used for summer schools. Little controversy attached to this proposal since it was entirely discretionary so far as local districts were concerned and no state funds were involved. MSTA expended little effort.

House Bills 5 and 214. These bills contained nearly identical provisions permitting the Public School Retirement System to invest the assets of their fund more freely. H.B. 5 also contained provisions affecting membership in the retirement system. This bill was reported favorably from committees and then, due to uncertainty over some of the technical features of the bill, it was stricken from the calendar at the request of the sponsors. H.B. 214, limited to retirement fund investments, passed through all stages of the legislative process without difficulty. Baltz and Henry sponsored both bills and the MSTA supported them. However, their noncontroversial nature required little exertion on MSTA's part.

House Bill 218. This bill provided that the county superintendent offer instruction on the danger of radioactive fallout. Largely a frivolous bill, it was treated as such in committee, where it died. It was, perhaps, a kind of facetious effort to enlarge the county superintendent's functions.

House Bill 282. This bill was sponsored by Baltz and Minority Leader Steelman. It provided that school board elections could be contested by petition of one or more qualified voters. No procedure for contesting school board elections exists under present law. The MSTA was quietly but firmly opposed to this, fearing that potentially endless litigation could tie up school boards indefinitely. The bill was reported out of committee with the recommendation that it not pass. Baltz's sponsorship was at least partly a concession to some Republicans who desired the bill. It maintained maximum bipartisanship on school matters at little real cost.

House Bill 98. In one county of the state, railroad corporations had discovered that certain statutes relating to real property taxes had conflicting provisions, and had escaped some school taxes as a consequence. Utilities elsewhere in the state had not yet discovered this possibility, but presumably would soon. This bill was sponsored by the representative of the county involved and corrected what had been an oversight in earlier legislation. It passed with relative ease, getting unanimous votes in both House and Senate.

House Bill 305. A second bill growing out of a local situation was the proposal to permit residents of a reorganized county—one where all schools are under district superintendents—to vote on whether to abolish the office of county superintendent of schools. The sponsor of the bill came from a reorganized county where the county superintendent was ready to retire and regarded his office as superfluous. The bill would have applied to many other counties, too, however. In committee, a number of objections were raised as to the technical adequacy of the bill's language. Other opponents, notably a former county superintendent on the committee, argued for the continuing importance of the county superintendent. The sponsor had no great wish to become involved in the larger issue of the county superintendent's role in general and was quite willing to hold off on the bill pending further study.

House Concurrent Resolution 2. Passed later in the session by a vote of 82-47, this resolution provided for an interim committee study of the county superintendent's office. This resolution was not looked on with favor by the MSTA, which felt that such a study would be unlikely to produce anything but some agitation against the county superintendents. MSTA works closely with these officials, often using them as intermediate contacts between the MSTA and legislators in grass roots campaigns. MSTA did not try to block the resolution, however. The House Democrats generally supported it (61-19) while Republicans, especially from the Ozarks area, were more strongly opposed (21-28).

House Bill 334. This bill was introduced by the House leadership, the majority leader and speaker pro tem, and sponsored by the Junior Chamber of Commerce. It provided for the compulsory immunization of school children, originally excepting only those whose physical condition or religious beliefs gave objection. MSTA supported the bill but made no special effort for it. There was opposition from the chiropractors, who are an influential group in outstate Missouri, and some general objection to the compulsory feature of the bill. The bill was amended on the floor of the House to extend exemption to any child whose parents objected in writing and to eliminate the provisions of criminal sanctions for noncompliance. The voting alignment showed concentrated opposition in the poorer rural areas of the state, with the Republican Ozarks heavily against the bill. Only one representative from an even moderately urbanized area opposed the bill on perfection, and a considerable party split emerged (Democrats 44-12, Republicans 10-39). Having scraped through the House, the weakened bill passed the Senate easily (25-1) and became law.

House Bills 302 and 489. Both these bills were designed to ease requirements for the small, rural districts, most of which are located in South Central Missouri. H.B. 302 provided for the transfer of seventh and eighth grade students from one elementary district to another. Tuition would be paid by the sending district and state aid given in reimbursement in the same manner as when high school students are sent from small districts to larger ones in lieu of reorganization into larger units. H.B. 489, which unlike H.B. 302 did not become law, would have permitted persons with appropriate experience but who were not certified public accountants to audit school district accounts in six-director (i.e., rural) districts. Many Missouri counties have to bring a C.P.A. from St. Louis at considerable expense while, in Representative Baltz's county (Baltz sponsored the bill), a retired railroad auditor could do the job for less than half as much. The C.P.A.'s opposed the bill, and it was not reported out of committee, but Baltz felt that it might succeed after another session or two of discussion.

House Bill 367. The cutoff birth date for children entering the public schools varies widely in Missouri. This bill would have made September 30 the uniform date; a child entering first grade would have to be six years old by that date. Some objected to the bill because it would have affected accounting procedures in certain minor ways, but the main issue was party. The bill was sponsored by Republicans. On perfection, a Democrat moved to amend the bill to make December 31 the cutoff date. Observers felt that the representative moving the amendment did not really understand its effects, but it passed nevertheless in a sharp party division (Democrats 55-10, Republicans 0-41). The sponsors withdrew the bill, since no one desired it in the amended form. This was one of several instances when a party issue was created in the legislature in part at least to remind the Republicans of their minority status.

House Bill 451. This bill would make Labor Day and Good Friday legal school holidays with the effect that districts which presently do not hold school on these days could still receive credit for a full week of school and get state aid accordingly. Although MSTA had sponsored the bill in previous years, it did not sponsor it in 1961. The benefits of the bill were somewhat greater for urban areas and the strongest opposition came from outstate Republicans, but the voting alignments were not clear-cut. Democrats 64-22, Republicans 17-34, was the final breakdown. As in 1959, the bill passed the House and died in the Senate, more because it was low in priority for everyone than because of any direct and strong opposition. There were some objections to the inclusion of Good Friday as a legal holiday on grounds that it violated the separation of church and state. The effort at serious discussion of this issue "dissolved into laughter when the 'collection plates' (the round metal tops from large ashtrays) went around the floor."[7] This was a relatively rare instance in which the Missouri legislature declined to consider an issue seriously, and the low priority attached to it (as evidenced, for example, by the non-involvement of MSTA in 1961) may account for the departure from the usual pattern.

House Bill 720. Another example of frivolity substituting for deliberation followed the introduction of a bill sponsored by the majority leader to authorize the state board of education to arrange classical music performances for school children throughout the state financed by state revenues. The bill was initiated at the behest of the Kansas City Symphony but would have included the St. Louis Symphony and other artists. It was attacked on the floor for requiring classical music only and an amendment striking "classical" from the bill passed. "For some of us 'Home on the Range' would mean more than any classical music," said a representative from Ozark county.[8] A second amendment eliminating state financial aid also passed, and the sponsor withdrew the bill, "with sincere apologies to the school children of this state and to the people who were interested in a well-rounded education for school children. . . ." When the character and strength of the opposition became clear, supporters of the bill joined in the fun, moving that the House sing "Home on the Range," that any vocalist singing in a foreign language

[7] St. Louis *Globe-Democrat* (May 3, 1961).
[8] Kansas City *Times* (June 2, 1961).

be accompanied by an interpreter, and so on. The opposition was concentrated among rural Republicans with a considerable number of outstate Democrats joining them, especially on the amendment to eliminate state funds. On the striking of "classical," the vote was 67-47: Democrats 24-44, Republicans 43-3. On no other bill in the session did the cultural perspectives and prejudices of the members play so large a role, and the low priority attached to the issue by all concerned helped permit the uninhibited expression of views, serious and otherwise.

House Bills 733 and 734. These two bills were companion measures sponsored by the Missouri Association of Social Welfare. H.B. 734 authorized the state board of education to certify social workers, and H.B. 733 permitted programs for emotionally disturbed children to be included in special education programs with school social workers paid for largely by the state. The MSTA cooperated with MASW on these bills but asked that they be held up until after the financing of the foundation program was assured. H.B. 733 was the more controversial since it involved state expenditure. It barely won approval in the House, with substantial numbers of outstate representatives from both parties voting against perfection (Democrats 38-26, Republicans 21-24). The floor debate was marked by considerable hostility towards social workers whose functions in this program (or generally, for that matter) were not understood by many legislators. Those handling the bill were unable to explain it persuasively, and it appeared that a more articulate presentation would have widened the margin. Actually both bills finally passed the House by wide margins, 118-5, 115-5. In the Senate, however, H.B. 733 was killed by taking it out of the Education Committee and sending it to the Committee on Economics and Major Expenditures. In effect, this action indicated that the issue was defined as primarily budgetary rather than educational. Accordingly, the strength of MSTA and MASW was very much reduced since these groups were not budgetary experts and could exercise no special leverage. Social workers had such a low priority in terms of competing claims for state funds that their hopes were doomed.

H.B. 734 had much less opposition, despite a tendency to suspect social workers as persons whose good intentions were supported by no demonstrable skills such as doctors had. The bill came to the floor on June 20 and, given any opposition at all, its low priority doomed it on the face of more pressing end-of-the-session controversies.

One last case is an appropriate conclusion to our discussion. Prior to the beginning of the 1961 session of the General Assembly, Governor-elect Dalton had been quoted as saying that the present foundation formula was inadequate, giving an undue amount of state aid to wealthier districts and too little stress to equalization. Revision of the formula would raise considerable controversy among school people themselves, and MSTA felt strongly that this should not be undertaken until full financing was assured. During the session, three Senate resolutions were introduced, each calling for an interim committee to study some phase of the public school system. MSTA looked upon them with favor but felt in no position to push for their approval. The three proposals were combined into one substitute providing an interim committee for:

Comprehensive and detailed study of the needs of public elementary and secondary education with particular emphasis on the functioning of the foundation program, the organization of school districts, and the need for revision and codification of the school laws.

The substitute resolution also instructed the committee to explore the needs of higher education. The substitute passed in a voice vote in both houses, and the committee was appointed, to report in 1963. The committee was chaired by Senator Waters (Democrat, St. Joseph) who sponsored the original resolution. Representative Baltz was vice-chairman. Baltz was also chairman of the subcommittee to examine the foundation program, which, for our purposes was the most significant. MSTA had no special formal position from which to influence the committee's deliberations, but friends of MSTA served on it and MSTA expected to "help them with information and advice." [9]

The significant thing about the committee for our purposes, is the mechanism through which they operate. An *ad hoc* committee, appointed by the state board of education, was the device used to begin the campaign for the original foundation program. A legislative interim committee recommended the 1959 increase. Now another interim committee is put to work. Everett Keith believes that such mechanisms are likely to be very helpful in realizing MSTA goals. "We believe they ought to have a standing [interim] committee." This would be but a short step away from the Illinois School Problems Commission, which we examine in Chapter 3. It is entirely possible that Missouri may move toward establishing some arrangement like that in Illinois as a way to insure greater legislative support for school proposals *without increasing the conflicts of interest over them.*

In its main outlines, the politics of public education in Missouri revolves around the MSTA. No education issues emerge that challenge the predominant values or vested interests within the total political system. The state's large urban school districts are "taken care of" through the so-called local unity norm and in return for the bargain are content to let MSTA handle matters of state-wide application, including items affecting them. The MSTA, largely by adopting a strategy of accommodation, has "routinized" the decision-making process. In this way it has been able to gain and hold a predominant or elitist position within the state's

[9] One subcommittee was concerned only with a codification of the school laws, but its composition is interesting. It was chaired by a member of the Legislative Research Council staff. On it sat three MSTA representatives, three from the Missouri Bar Association, two from the Missouri Association of School Boards, and one from the state department of education.

political structure. Although the MSTA through its relations with the official agencies of government provides for Missouri a stable and seemingly durable power structure, forces are emerging that suggest that this arrangement or pattern is not permanent. Everett Keith believes that MSTA has pressed successfully for as much as the Missouri political system would allow, but elements of discontent with the low conflict style of politics are increasingly evident. A growing teachers union in St. Louis constitutes direct competition for MSTA, and growing demands for state services from many sources threaten to open the state's politics to much more conflict than in the past. As a result, MSTA must press harder and seek more in order to maintain its position as spokesman for the education interests.

CHAPTER III

❀ ❀ ❀ ❀

Illinois:
Structural Consensus

School politics in Illinois is in many ways similar to school politics in Missouri. In terms of the type and the nature of state involvement, Illinois and Missouri do not differ markedly from each other. Both states have adopted foundation programs. Both have state-wide school district reorganization plans which were put into effect at the end of World War II, reducing drastically the number of school districts in each. Neither state has an outstanding record in the area of teacher welfare, although Illinois has adopted minimum teachers' salary and tenure laws.

On a fundamental level, the similarities are even more striking. In both states, for example, the goals of professional educators are moderated to fit what the political system will comfortably allow. In neither state do public school issues generate much controversy. Political parties do not divide on education questions, and although there are numerous potentially conflicting elements, differences are reconciled before they erupt openly. In brief, each state has witnessed the evolution of a consensus pattern with respect to the formulation of school policy.

THE ILLINOIS SCHOOL
PROBLEMS COMMISSION:
ORIGIN AND DEVELOPMENT

In Illinois, however, despite the similarities with Missouri, an entirely different organizational scheme and influence pattern produces many of the major decisions. We will describe Illinois school politics primarily through an analysis of the Illinois School Problems Commission, its activity and inactivity, and the interests it serves. Although first established in 1949, merely as a temporary advisory commission for the legislature, the School Problems Commission (SPC) today is actually the arena in which decisions concerning the state's role in education are made. It is uniformly regarded as the state's most powerful agency with regard to school politics. The SPC defines, and thereby limits, the state's role in education. It determines the amount of state financial aid appropriated to each local school district. Its other recommendations affect numerous phases of education policy.

Illinois has arrived at a formula in education policy formation that provides for "progress without significant controversy." The Illinois School Problems Commission is an agency that, for a variety of reasons, has been able to combine the stated goals and ideals of pro-school people with a recognition of the realities of the political system. Although it possesses no *formal* powers other than advisory, virtually all of its recommendations have been incorporated into law. To understand the crucial position this agency occupied in Illinois school politics in 1961, we must examine the situation that prevailed prior to its establishment.

Antedating the creation of the SPC, there was no single agency officially responsible on a continuing basis for the formulation of a state school program. Illinois has never had a state board of education, despite repeated proposals for establishing one; and from 1870 until the late 1940's, the state education system "survived but did not flourish under policies developed by the General Assembly and administered by the State Office of Public Instruction." [1] Dissension and disunity among the education groups blurred their impact and disrupted any plan for a coordinated program which would define and limit the state's role. The State Office of Public Instruction, though responsible for such vital tasks as teacher certification and school accreditation, offered little or no positive leadership and was incapable of assuming a greater role as long as the office remained under the control of a partisan-elected superintendent. In terms of state involvement, Illinois could hardly parade itself as a leader.

During this period, state programs were set up in response to either policies suggested by education interest groups or the recommendations flowing from temporary *ad hoc* commissions established by the legislature to study special problems affecting public schools. It is not difficult to demonstrate the widespread diffusion of responsibilities that made school politics so chaotic and unpredictable in Illinois for over fifty years. Let us examine first the various *ad hoc* commissions created by the legislature to aid in the handling of the public school problems and the role they performed in creating an atmosphere favorable to the acceptance of a continuing or permanent agency.

TEMPORARY STATE COMMISSIONS

Between 1907 and the creation of the first SPC in 1949, the Illinois General Assembly established fifteen special legislative commissions to study the problems of the public school system.[2] (For an over-all summary of the recommendations and adoptions of these commissions, see Appendix

[1] Quoted from an interview with a gubernatorial appointee to the SPC.
[2] A report of one of the first SPC's states that summaries of studies made by temporary school commissions or of education studies made by other state agencies were issued in 1907, 1915, 1921, 1923, 1925, 1931, 1935, 1937, 1939, 1941, 1943, 1945, 1947, 1948, and 1949.

II, pp. 294-99. In most cases these legislative commissions were concerned primarily with immediate problems of financing and organization. Although these commissions proved useful, by the time each had expired the state was confronted with new problems, and each problem appeared more difficult than any of the previous ones. As a result, the legislature had to create an almost continuous chain of temporary state commissions, some of which were successful in having their recommendations adopted, while others proved to be of only nominal significance. (The data presented in Appendix I summarizes the recommendations made by each commission, revealing that only a few met with immediate success.) The report of the School Finance and Tax Commission of 1947, a temporary commission established in 1945 by the state legislature to find an answer to the state's problem of financing the improvements in education, an answer which various groups were demanding, evaluated the work of these agencies as follows:

Although each commission has not always achieved its full immediate goal, they have all contributed to the sum total of guidance which has gradually borne fruit for the benefit of the youth of Illinois and the legislature which bears a direct obligation for the education of youth.[3]

One of the most significant achievements in Illinois public school history—the passage of the foundation program in 1947—was the product of a temporary state commission. Although this program was authorized prior to the establishment of the SPC, it was based largely upon the recommendations of the School Finance and Tax Commission, most of whose members were later appointed to the SPC, and it did not actually take on its present form until it had been drastically revised by the SPC in 1953. According to a member of the SPC research staff, the foundation "is a *program* in the literal sense of the term, not a sum of money as most

[3] *State Support of Public Education in Illinois,* Report of the Illinois School Finance and Tax Commission (March, 1947), p. 22.

people believe; money, of course, is required to put the program into effect." The basic principle underlying such a program is to guarantee a minimum set of standards for each school district in that state, whether rich or poor in assessed valuation: that is, it is designed "to provide a minimum level of educational opportunity for all schools of the state." The program aims to raise all schools which are below this level as quickly as possible.

What are the standards? The following are the major criteria used: a school term of nine months or 180 days; a good building with adequate sanitary facilities; teachers with at least four years of college training; good instruction in fundamental courses; and transportation for pupils residing a long distance from the school.

In 1947, the school districts of Illinois were tested with these criteria in mind, and the results showed that many were operating "substandard" schools. The result of the study showed also that if the state could guarantee $114 for every elementary pupil and $179 for every high school pupil in average daily attendance, they could maintain foundation standards. The total equalization levels guaranteed by the state at that time were only $62 and $90, for high school and elementary pupils respectively, however, with the remainder left for the local districts to raise.

In the years since the establishment of the SPC, the equalization levels and the flat grants (a grant of an equal sum of money to *every* school district) have increased steadily. In 1959, the present level of $252 per pupil was established, along with additional flat grants of $47 per elementary pupil and $32 per high school pupil. Several interviewees felt that $307 should be the next minimum goal.

What generalizations or inferences, if any, can be drawn from the studies conducted by the various temporary commissions created by the General Assembly or by the other state agencies? This question was raised by the Illinois School Finance and Tax Commission. An immediate predecessor of the SPC, this commission summarized the work accomplished by all of these various commissions and agencies in the following manner:

1. Each group recommended the establishment of some type of "nonpolitical" state board of education with an executive officer, the superintendent of public instruction, to guide and direct the Illinois educational system.

2. General agreement existed on the necessity of *larger* administrative and financial local school districts.

3. Virtually all of the study groups favored the use of state aid only as a means of relieving local tax burdens. The majority of studies recommended that less aid be distributed through flat grants and increased equalization aid.

4. Over the years there was increasing sentiment for the adoption of a foundation program.

5. Most studies singled out as the principal cause of local school problems the existing local tax machinery (assessment procedures, tax rates, and assessed valuations).

Although the success of these early commissions was, on the whole, limited, the practice of using them seemed firmly established. The creation of the first School Problems Commission in 1949 to conduct an extensive study of the state's school problems did not depart in any significant way from established procedures. Yet, unlike its predecessors and for reasons that will be discussed subsequently, the SPC became a permanent part of the state decision-making machinery in 1957, and, in fact, informally achieved this status almost from its inception.

Attempts at Collective Action

During the period that the legislature was receiving the reports from temporary commissions, the General Assembly found it necessary to reach concrete decisions on many problems not included within the scope of these commissions. The latter simply could not meet the legislature's need for information, and "as a result," according to one SPC member, "they turned to education groups and individuals concerned with the status of education in the state."

One approach widely subscribed to but not wholeheartedly backed by the subscribers was to unify the various interests into one structural entity which would include all (or nearly all) of the active organizations concerned with education and finance: namely, the Illinois Education Association, the Illinois Agriculture Association, the Parent-Teacher Associations, the League of Women Voters, the Chamber of Commerce, and the Illinois Association of School Boards.[4] Several state superintendents of public instruction called state-wide conferences of representatives of these groups in the hope of developing some form of consensus among the various interests they served.

Those interviewed in the course of the present study did not agree about the role and significance of such conferences. An Illinois Education Association official who had attended many of them described them merely as "a place where the various interests would get together and talk over the problems of education." Others felt that they had helped to define problem areas but they also were quick to admit that little concrete action was ever taken. Attempts to structure a unified education front failed largely because each group held distinct and contrasting views as to what the direction of education policy should be.

It is a not unwarranted conclusion from the interviews that no representative ever felt or demonstrated a high degree of involvement or commitment to any structure designed to promote unity among these interests. However, there was one point of agreement: these nonstatutory meetings laid the broad foundation for the state's principal education interests to accept and to participate in the SPC. From this experience, the interest group representatives

---

[4] Other organizations, including, for example, the Illinois Taxpayers League, the Little Red School House groups, and local school boards, were added to those listed above when specific issues were being discussed.

learned that a united front consisting of *all* organized interests of education was a crucial determinant of policy outcome in the Illinois political system. Eventually, they came to recognize that they themselves must compromise on education policy before they could present their demands effectively to the legislature. If the various active education interests could agree, they concluded, there would be little organized opposition once the measure reached the General Assembly.

The "Go-It-Alone" Policy

Informal alliances were formed only sporadically to achieve educational goals in the legislature. The more common approach was for each organized interest group to go it alone. To get anything accepted, each group found it necessary, according to one representative, "to find a friendly legislator, 'educate' him with the facts, have him introduce your bill, and then see what happened."

The obvious result was a perpetual stream of interests pressing the General Assembly for action. A tremendous number of education bills was introduced in each session of the legislature, largely because each group usually thought it necessary to have every item of its program included. It was typical to have several bills on the same subject introduced by different legislators at approximately the same time. To complicate the scene further, an individual constituent having a complaint concerning education would frequently persuade his local representatives to introduce a bill to correct the situation. Thus, the two permanent standing committees on education in the House and Senate were swamped with bills; neither could handle effectively the constant flood of legislative proposals. With all of the diverse interests represented in the state, "developing a program of school policy which was acceptable to everyone was almost impossible. Every group had its own plan for solving the problems, and if it wasn't accepted completely, that group was not satisfied." [5]

The go-it-alone policy produced at least as many if not more problems than it solved. By the start of World War II, the leaders of the education interests were quite concerned. Nothing was being done and there was not much on the political horizon to indicate that long-range solutions were forthcoming. The war itself gave the legislature a temporary reprieve. Few people expected any real gains in education while the war was in progress. With the end of hostilities, however, interest group leaders began to expect the General Assembly to act with dispatch on the many public school problems that had accumulated over the years.

NEED FOR A NEW AGENCY

Why was it necessary to create a new agency for this purpose? Why couldn't the existing governmental agencies—the General Assembly or the State Office of Public Instruction—provide the necessary leadership in solving education's problems?

We have already alluded to the reasons for the General Assembly's inability to handle education problems. However, the question concerning the role of the State Office remains. Why didn't the General Assembly accept the studies and recommendations of the State Office?

The answer lies in the political nature of the office. The state superintendent was (and is) a political official elected by the voters in a state-wide partisan election. As a result, there was political rivalry between the superintendent and some members of the General Assembly, particularly those of the opposition party. No one felt that the superintendent's discretion should be greatly expanded. Moreover, every superintendent who took office unhappily found himself labeled "weak" by the various education interests, regardless

[5] Quoted from an interview with a representative of the IEA.

of the skills he possessed or devices he used. The attitude of the interests had tended to reinforce the legislature's resistance to expansion.

Secondly, members of the legislature viewed the state superintendent as purely an administrator and therefore incapable of acting as a legislative adviser. A legislative leader summarized the view toward the State Office as follows:

It is an administrative office and couldn't have filled the vacuum; no one was more aware of this than the state superintendent himself. The state superintendent in office at the time of the establishment of the SPC and those superintendents since have been lavish in their praise of the work done by the SPC and are the first to admit that it has fulfilled a function that the State Office could never have done.

"Budgetary" factors were also cited to explain why the legislature refused to extend the authority of the State Office, although it was rather obvious that they were not really significant. A veteran legislator stated that the superintendent "just didn't have the facilities to handle the problems which have since been assigned to the SPC and there was no money that could be appropriated for this purpose." Then he commented wryly: "Of course, we had money but it wasn't going to be used that way."

Finally, the legislators were correct in assuming that there was no support from the main education interests for any expansion of the superintendent's role. It is an article of faith among professional educators that school superintendents, state and local, should be appointed rather than elected. For example, an IEA official described the State Office in the following way:

The State Office is nothing but a partisan administrative department! You just don't get the layman's point of view from the State Office, as you would from a state board or a legislative commission. You need a lay board to mull over the problems, outline policy, and so forth. One man, or one man's office, can't do this; he's too busy administrating to have time to worry about solving problems, and besides the state superintendent is an elected official.

An officer of the State Association of School Boards declared: "The State Office just couldn't handle the job!" And a leader of the Illinois Agricultural Association maintained: "The solving of such complex problems requires a broader viewpoint than that provided by the State Office. *Education has to be taken out of politics.*"

Beyond these considerations, the General Assembly, according to its leaders, felt itself to be the agency most qualified to make the final decisions. As we noted previously, "the state legislature had often boasted that *it* is the state board." [6] Although the members of the General Assembly that were interviewed unanimously agreed that the state's education program prior to the formation of the SPC had become impossible for them and their standing committees to handle and that something had to be done, they were nevertheless determined that control over education should not slip very far from the legislature's grasp.

The conclusion, then, is the obvious one: there was no support for expansion of the State Office's role, either from education interests or from members of the General Assembly. The SPC, a majority of whose members were legislators, was carefully designed to provide expertise and "objectivity" without surrendering any authority to an executive agency.

The Chaos Following World War II

Thus far we have asserted that the state's public school policies were inadequate largely because there was no machinery to which the legislature could turn, and that the state's present system was chaotic. A more detailed examination of this chaotic period should prove useful.

By 1946, the situation concerning the schools of Illinois had become a "real crisis." "Something had to be done."

---

[6] Quoted in an interview with a senatorial appointee to the SPC.

Over 12,000 separate school districts were in operation, many of them of the "little red school house" type. There was a desperate shortage of teachers (over 4,000 temporary emergency certificates had to be issued to mostly unqualified instructors in an attempt to alleviate the situation) and those who were teaching were poorly paid by comparative standards. There was insufficient money to pay for improvements, and the local property taxes were considered too high.[7]

Each proposed solution created additional complications. For example, even if agreements were reached on consolidating districts, who would be responsible for the payment of debts owed by one or more of the merging districts? Who was legally responsible for changing the boundaries of the newly created districts? How much of a voice should the local residents have in school organization? Should the traditional local autonomy of schools be preserved? How were additional qualified teachers to be obtained in time to prevent school standards from dropping further?

Added to all of these problems was one that overshadowed all others: namely, a constantly increasing birth rate which had begun during the war years and continued unabated in the years following the end of World War II. Putting it in more or less mathematical terms, one observer formed the following equation to demonstrate the problem: "Inflation plus many more students plus more unsolved school problems equals too complicated a situation for the existing machinery to handle." In the face of this situation, the pressure for action from the education interests became intense.

Governor Adlai E. Stevenson, immediately after taking office in 1949, and in response to many demands, created by executive order an Advisory Commission on Education.

---

[7] Only 14.6 percent of the funds used to support the public schools of Illinois in 1946 were allocated from state sources.

After a short period of study, this agency issued a series of recommendations designed to guide the governor in developing his education program, although no comprehensive formal report was prepared. High on its list of priorities was the recommendation to establish a *continuing* commission to study full-time the problems of education. The creation of such a commission, so it was argued, would provide the General Assembly with the expert assistance it desperately needed to meet current as well as future dilemmas.

Although the General Assembly was not convinced initially that a *continuing* commission was necessary, the need for some kind of advisory council, even a temporary one, had finally become apparent. True, the pressures of the individual interests and the work of the previous temporary commission had produced some worthwhile legislative results, but the members of the General Assembly had become increasingly aware that the education interests could not agree among themselves on what approach to take. Since the legislative leaders felt unqualified to solve the problems and were now of the opinion that the education groups were drifting too far apart in their points of view, some kind of coordinating agency seemed the most feasible solution.

Late in the session of the Sixty-sixth General Assembly in 1949, the legislators resolved the problem by passing an act which created a commission "to survey and study the problems pertaining to public schools in the state." [8] The act provided that the membership was to consist of the state superintendent of public instruction, the director of finance, three representatives (appointed by the speaker), three senators (appointed by the president pro tempore), and five members appointed by the governor. The members were to serve two years, until July 1, 1951 (at which time the commission was to expire), and were to "receive only actual and neces-

[8] *Illinois School Problems,* Report of the School Problems Commission (March 1951), p. 1.

sary expenses incurred in the performance of their duties." [9]

The commission's delegation of authority was broad; it was authorized to "consider and study all germane factors in an effort to determine the improvements necessary to raise the educational standards of the public school to a desirable level." [1] For SPC Number One, as the first commission was to become known later, $35,000 was appropriated for the biennium in order to employ such technical assistants as it deemed necessary.

The SPC did not become a permanent part of the decision-making process until 1957. Between the expiration of the first SPC and the 1957 act, three additional SPC's were created. In essence, each was similar to the previous one, although a few modifications were made along the way. In 1953, for example, the legislative membership was increased from six members to ten (five from each house). Although the appropriations for SPC Number Two were reduced from $35,000 to $18,000, appropriations for subsequent commissions were steadily increased ($25,000 for SPC Number Three and $40,000 for Number Four).

By an act approved by the state legislature on July 8, 1957, the SPC became a continuing agency. The biennial appropriation was set at $50,000.

THE ILLINOIS SCHOOL PROBLEMS COMMISSION: FUNCTIONS AND PROCEDURES

Anxious to find solutions for the many problems in education it faced and to avoid the constant harassment that would result from failure to meet its obligations to the public schools, the General Assembly delegated broad authority to the SPC. The 1957 act establishing the SPC on a permanent basis provided that:

[9] Ibid., p. 1.
[1] Ibid., p. 1.

The Commission shall study: 1) the progress and problems of school district reorganization and the means of further promotion of an efficient school system; 2) need of further codification and revision of school laws; 3) state, county, and local school administration of the common schools and the interrelationship of such administration; 4) the adequacy and efficiency of present plans of granting State and common school aids of the various types, including the State aid formula and qualifying rates; 5) the methods of acquiring adequate revenue for schools and the definite sources of possible revenue for local school funds and for state school aids; 6) any problems which may arise that may affect the general welfare of the schools.

The Commission shall also counsel and advise the Superintendent of Public Instruction on any school problem that he may bring to them for consideration. The Commission may from time to time make recommendations for consideration of improvement in any public school area.

The Commission shall also make recommendations to the Budgetary Commission prior to February 1, of each odd-numbered year as to the amount of the State school aids required for the succeeding biennium.

The Commission shall consider and study all germane factors in an effort to determine the improvements necessary to raise the education standards of the public schools to a desirable level.

The Commission shall make a detailed report of its findings and conclusions to the General Assembly not later than March, of each odd-numbered year, and shall submit recommendations for such legislation as it deems necessary.[2]

A mere enumeration of the statutory functions obviously does not provide a complete picture of the work performed by the SPC. For example, how does the SPC decide what are the state's most pressing education problems? Does it con-

[2] *Illinois School Problems,* Report of the School Problems Commission Number Six (March 1961), pp. 3-4.

sider all matters that require state action, even those of a purely local application? Is any attempt made to avoid certain issues? After selecting areas upon which to concentrate, how does the commission decide what to recommend? What are the sources of its information? We will attempt to answer these questions in the following pages.

SELECTION OF PROBLEMS

The SPC, operating in the American tradition—if indeed there is a tradition—regards itself as intensely pragmatic. Hence, its responses to public school matters are not fixed *a priori* by a rigid pattern of beliefs about what the school system should be doing. Rather, or so its members stoutly maintain, each policy issue is considered as it arises. This enables the members to tailor the solution to fit the individual situation. Perhaps the only conscious political belief, other than a pragmatic orientation, that seems to affect all commission members in the same way is the belief that more money will help the schools. How much, of course, is another matter, and it is here that the negotiations begin.

Some problems arise more or less automatically, and as they concern mainly the state's public school financial program, they constitute a major part of the SPC's work. Members of the commission describe the following areas as "mandatory and routine": the state aid formula, qualifying rates for state aid, the amount to be provided under the state equalization formula, the amount of flat grants, the sources of possible revenues for local and state school funds, and the anticipation of the appropriation that will be needed to fill the equalization level authorized by the state.

Second, occasionally the General Assembly directs the SPC to take special cognizance of a particular matter. In recent sessions, for example, the SPC has been directed by the legislature, according to one SPC member, "to determine the best methods of obtaining additional revenue, to propose the best methods for reorganization of school districts, and to find ways to improve the methods of transporting pupils." When so directed, the SPC devotes considerable attention to these particular areas.

Third, major problems not pertaining to finance are brought to the collective attention of the SPC through informal communications between commission members and representatives of the state's organized education interests or county and local district superintendents of schools, or among the commission members themselves, some of whom are regarded as outstanding education leaders. Furthermore, the commission retains its own research staff which is constantly investigating and studying a variety of problems. The research reports cover the entire state education field, though most of the emphasis is on finance.

Finally, some problems are brought before the commission through its open hearings, letters from constituents of the legislative members of the commission, conversations with individual members of the General Assembly, newspaper accounts of school problems and needs, and articles in professional education journals.

Almost as significant as what the SPC does and how its responsibilities are defined is what it carefully avoids. The SPC does not consider all matters that involve the public school system; it assiduously avoids some areas. Items, for example, that apply only to a single school district or a few districts within a single geographic area, even though state legislative action is required, generally do not fall within the self-defined jurisdiction of the SPC. Commission members feel that local problems should not come under commission study unless, according to one senatorial member, "an issue is such that it is disruptive to the whole state."

The SPC by general agreement among its members also refuses to tackle problems generally considered to be so controversial that no workable solution is likely. The SPC, of course, does not avoid controversy entirely; conflict is involved in making almost every decision. It does, however, avoid any consideration of issues that it regards as basically irreconcilable. Differences in opinion over the level of state aid, for example, can be settled. But conflicts between parochial and public schools or issues involving racial problems in education do not lend themselves to immediate solutions and involve cleavages so deeply rooted and so broad in scope that the SPC feels that any action it might attempt to take in these areas would be disruptive. Proposals regarding the use of public funds to support transportation of students to parochial schools are normally left to the discretion of the regular education committees of the House and Senate, with the SPC playing no overt or formal role. To a large extent, other agencies of state governments have adopted similar practices, with the obvious result that most conflicts in the state involving racial and religious problems which affect schools go unresolved or are resolved at the local district level.

In addition, the SPC feels that recommendations to the General Assembly concerning some items of teacher welfare (minimum salary laws, tenure laws, retirement provisions) are handled effectively by the various organized interests and that the SPC should not devote much time to their consideration. One interest group representative quoted an SPC leader as having repeatedly stated: "Why should we go into teacher welfare? They seem to be doing right well by themselves."

Finally, the SPC makes no attempt to assume the General Assembly's constitutional responsibility for supervising the administration of the public schools. One commission member explained:

At no time has the SPC gone into the questions of setting up a state board, of getting an appointed state superintendent, or of investigating the work and functions of the county superintendents of schools. We've certainly been requested in hearings and meetings to go into these areas, but we haven't. Our only excuse is that most members of the SPC just didn't believe it necessary.

Thus, from this complex of factors come the problems to which the SPC directs attention. How it does so is described below.

OPEN HEARINGS

Political scientists have long recognized the special significance of certain formal procedures in the functioning of governmental agencies. The formal rules of procedure followed by the SPC provide some insight into the pressures which affect school decisions on the state level and the manner in which the SPC is able to perpetuate its predominant role. One of the most significant formal procedures which the SPC uses is the open hearing.

In July of the odd-numbered years, soon after the new appointments to the commission are announced, the SPC members hold preliminary meetings to determine where and when the commission will hold its public hearings.[3] Between 10 and 12 of these open hearings are usually held at locations scattered throughout Illinois. Several are usually planned for the Chicago area.

SPC hearings, like all of its meetings, are open to the public and are held ostensibly to give commission members an opportunity to hear the recommendations of organizations and individuals actively concerned with education. Members of SPC, however, disagree about the value of the public hearings in the total decision-making process. Interviews with the various SPC members revealed three general evaluations of the open hearings. First, a few members feel that these hearings provide a sounding board for valuable information, information on which decisions may be based.[4] Sec-

[3] In most cases the SPC chairman determines the location and time of the open hearings in advance, with the entire membership voicing its approval or disapproval during its preliminary meetings.

[4] Among those who found the hearings informative and worthwhile, one said: "I would say that these hearings are of great significance, for it is here that we are able to gain an understanding of the situations existing in the state so that possible solutions to all trouble spots can be contemplated." This evaluation was shared by a senatorial member of the SPC.

ondly, some feel that they are a nuisance and are of only minor significance; but none who took this view was in favor of abolishing the hearings since they believe that "the democratic system requires them." [5] A majority of the members hold a third view, that the hearings provide some useful information but that their main purpose is to give representatives of the organized interests, local school district administrators, or anyone interested in education an opportunity not only to feel that they are a part of the decision-making process but also an opportunity "to just blow off steam." This view is based on the theory that if interested groups and individuals feel that they are playing a role in the making of decisions, they will provide the necessary base of support when the SPC presents its recommendations to the General Assembly and to the governor.

Informed observers of the political scene are very much aware of the fact that appearances before committee hearings have significant compensatory value.[6] The safety valve

---

He viewed the open hearings as being "very significant! The needs of the local districts (whether they be in the area of curriculum changes, of consolidation of districts, of financing, or whatever) are brought to our attention by the people who have had experience in those areas." One of the members of the House of Representatives pointed out that it is from these hearings "that the SPC collects the information by which it determines which areas of education will be dealt with during the next two-year period . . . Those appearing before these hearings represent school administrators, agricultural groups, chambers of commerce, PTA's, teachers' groups, the Illinois Taxpayers Association [an organization described by a senatorial commission member as an organization which "has kept an open eye on us but has been most cooperative"], and oftentimes people interested in special phases of education: handicapped children, visual aids, and so forth. Of course, the opinions of these people would be significant in the making of our decisions."

[5] One member commented: "Most of the time we just have to sit there listening to real crackpots!" Another legislator stated, "We let them come in and tell us their problems, which generally concern every possible phase of education; one hour's testimony may range from construction of new buildings to the education of gifted children. Many of these speakers frankly bore us stiff since we've heard the same material presented so many times. We feel, however, that each is at least entitled to a hearing."

[6] For a discussion of the significance of open hearings, see, for example, David B. Truman, *The Governmental Process* (New York: Alfred A.

function of adjusting group conflicts and relieving disturb-ances has frequently been noted as an important role which open hearings play. The testimony presented at the hearings is of little value compared to the fact that a public hearing is held. An education interest group representative, an out-raged citizen, or the spokesman for any interest may be mol-lified, even if no concrete results are produced. As such, the public hearing is viewed as one of the "democratic rules of the game." It conforms to the procedural expectations of the community and facilitates acceptance of the legislative decision, since it has been arrived at "in the right way," with "everyone" having a chance to be heard.

A Senate appointee to the SPC discussed the open hear-ings in the following manner:

There are of course perennial problems which are brought up at hearings year after year. Some I'm afraid won't ever be solved; others are regarded as merely "problems in the mind," not really problems at all. Sometimes we do get new problems brought up in hearings, and occasionally we even get a few new ideas. *How-ever, the real significance in holding these hearings is to give the school people a chance to feel close to the legislation eventually recommended.*

One of the interest group representatives holding mem-bership on the SPC stated that while the hearings are not actually very important in the making of policy, "they are *psychologically* very important in that they make school ad-ministrators and interest group representatives feel that they have a significant part in the process by which decisions are made. Only once in a while do we get a good idea from one of the people appearing at one of our hearings." Another SPC member maintained:

Of course, we receive some important information from these hearings, but their real value is that they give the people inter-

Knopf; 1951), pp. 372-377; and Murray Edelman, "Symbols and Political Quiescence," *American Political Science Review,* LIV, No. 3 (September, 1960), pp. 695-704.

ested in education a chance to get their problems off their chests and to make them feel a part of the whole process. Oftentimes, we are able to solve their "problems" on the spot just by giving them advice based on the wealth of information we've accumulated from the years of experience and study we've had.

Whatever significance the members of the SPC attach to the open hearings, all feel that they are a necessary part of the procedure. Every SPC has begun its biennium with a series of hearings held in the various sections of the state.

USE OF SUBCOMMITTEES

Once the major problems are determined and the hearings planned, subcommittees (composed not only of SPC members but of educators, non-SPC legislators, interest group representatives, administrators, and interested citizens as well) are appointed to study each item in detail and to propose recommendations to the entire commission. The listing of subjects for which SPC subcommittees have been appointed gives some insight into the type of major problems with which the commission has been concerned in recent years. Subcommittees were created to study pupil transportation, special education, revenue, the duties and functions of the county superintendent of schools, school district organization, summer schools, a number of technical matters pertaining to the length of the school day and year and with the so-called federally impacted school districts, recodification of the school law, and problems involved with special charter districts.[7]

The subcommittees hold open hearings in various sections

[7] A significant feature of these subcommittees is the extensive use made of outside experts. For example, the subcommittee set up to study revenue included, in addition to three legislative members of the SPC, six legislators, an official of the Department of Revenue, the Chicago superintendent of schools, two real estate brokers, an insurance company executive, a banker, and a representative of the Illinois Agriculture Association. Other subcommittees have frequently included faculty members and administrators of the state teachers colleges and universities.

of the state (in addition to those held by the entire commission), make statistical surveys, and prepare and collect
research materials. Each subcommittee presents its recommendations to the full SPC membership which then votes to
accept, reject, or amend the subcommittee report. The SPC
is not bound by any subcommittee action. One SPC member
observed: "Of course, we give the subcommittee reports serious thought, but we don't have to accept them."

FINAL ACTION ON RECOMMENDATIONS

How does the SPC formulate its final recommendations?
An SPC member gave perhaps the best answer to this question:

Our SPC meets and discusses the problems placed on our agenda.
We discuss each of the various proposals suggested for solving
the problems; some are considered important enough for special
study by subcommittees. Following our discussion of each, we
vote, with a majority deciding a recommendation; however, we
are not bound to support it if we still oppose it.

Though most decisions follow this general pattern, a more
specific analysis is helpful.

Many problems are handled by the entire commission,
with no special subcommittee appointed.[8] In such cases the
personal judgments and evaluations of members with longstanding reputations in public education form the basis for
SPC recommendations. On matters pertaining to finance, the
commission's research director and his staff do most of the
research and study. The accuracy of the staff's financial reports is seldom, if ever, questioned. Following the studies of
the various problems by either special subcommittees or by
the entire SPC membership, the final recommendations to

---

[8] The usual procedure is for the SPC to delegate only two or three special problems a session to subcommittees. The remaining recommendations
are based either on the knowledge of the individual members or on reports
submitted by the research staff.

the General Assembly are decided. Most recommendations are agreed to unanimously, although roll call votes are taken.[9]

Reports of the SPC are published in March of each odd-numbered year. The 1961 recommendations were grouped into sections concerned with finance (sixteen recommendations including keeping the equalization formula at the $252 figure established in 1959, appropriating $50,000 to the superintendent of public instruction to continue a pilot study on a program for gifted children, and appropriating $15,250,000 to reimburse school districts for transporting pupils to and from school); local district organization (nine recommendations which included passing a county school district survey act, the creation of a State Reorganization Committee, and the setting by law of mandatory standards for reorganizations); state, county, and local school administration (thirty-one recommendations which included increasing the minimum academic training required for provisional certificates, permitting township school treasurers only in counties having at least one million population, and recodifying the School Code); special education (four recommendations); and a short section on the School Building Commission (seven recommendations).

ACCEPTANCE OF RECOMMENDATIONS

Formal presentation of its recommendations does not conclude the SPC work. On the contrary, for the legislative members in particular, the work has only barely begun. SPC members are keenly aware that a crucial aspect of their role is to do everything possible to see that the recommendations are accepted.

[9] A few recommendations (one, for example, permitting all unit districts, excluding Chicago, to levy $1.25 for education purposes without a referendum and to levy $0.25 for building purposes without a referendum) have been made after causing an open division among the Commission members. Several of these conflicts were so intense that the biennial report of the SPC made mention of individual dissents to various recommendations.

The first job encountered after the report of the recommendations has been made concerns the *drafting* of the legislation necessary to implement the SPC recommendations. This function is performed soon after the final recommendations are made, under the direction of the chairman and *with all of the major interests taking part*. The purpose of broad coverage of education groups is to prevent any comparable bills from being drafted independently. At this point each group indicates what items it feels deserve the highest priority in the legislative session. Also at this juncture, the SPC decides which group will be responsible for which bill.

The next step is for the SPC to determine what other bills must be drafted in order to have all of their recommendations ready to present to the General Assembly. As one member says, "When necessary, the SPC does actually draft the bills."

After the bills have been prepared, the formal task of introducing them into the General Assembly obviously falls to the legislative members of the commission. The usual procedure is that each measure is jointly introduced by the legislative members of each house, with the chairman handling most of the details. Occasionally one commission member will introduce an education measure individually, although even then he will make it clear that the bill has SPC support. In a few instances—but only a few—the SPC legislative members, while not personally introducing commission-supported legislation, have found it expedient to have other legislators introduce it.

Although we deal with the relations between the SPC and the legislature in detail below, we must here point out that the legislative members of the commission deem it their personal responsibility to see that all SPC bills are passed, except of course in those few cases where several members of the commission are opposed to the recommendations agreed to by a majority of the SPC. The nonlegislative members of the SPC also contribute by answering any questions a legislator may raise, talking to legislators about the merits of the recommendations, and appearing as witnesses before any committee that considers an SPC measure.

Finally, commission members do everything possible "to insure the governor's support of its recommendations since all of their efforts would be futile without the backing of the state's chief executive." [1]

SPC: COMPOSITION AND INTEGRATION

Virtually all of the policy recommendations of the SPC are *underpinned by the support of its members.* No deep-seated controversies rage within the agency. Outward appearences, therefore, might suggest that it deals more with matters of detail than with policy questions, but this is not so. Thus, in order to understand Illinois' brand of school politics, it is necessary to determine the basis for consensus; that is, how the problems are ironed out and how the anxieties of those most immediately concerned with public school policy are eliminated. Two factors seem significant. First, the internal composition of the SPC has been carefully calculated to produce a high degree of "integration." Second, the SPC has developed working relationships with the other governmental agencies that have final authority in determining education policy and with the interests most vitally concerned with policy results. Each of these aspects requires exploration.

COMPOSITION

The salient feature of the composition and organization of the SPC is that it includes most of the major interests that have a direct and tangible stake in the outcome of the public school decisions. It is structured to provide these interests with a formal and official voice in its deliberations. The Illi-

[1] Quoted in an interview with a legislative member of the SPC.

nois constitution, though rigid with regard to the separation of powers principle, is flexible enough to allow for the creation of a special commission to deal exclusively with one major policy area that includes in its membership legislators, gubernatorial appointees, an elected state official, and representatives of organized interest groups (see Appendix III).

Selection of Members. By law, the size of the commission is fixed at seventeen members, each of whom serves a term of two years. The legislative membership is fixed at ten, the governor appoints five, and two members (the state superintendent of public instruction and the state director of finance) are ex-officio. Immediately after the appointments are announced, the members elect a chairman, vice-chairman, and secretary. In addition, a research director and staff are appointed early in the SPC's biennium.

No description of the formal organization of such an agency will provide a complete picture of its internal workings. For example, what criteria are employed in the selection of members? Who makes the legislative appointments to the SPC? Does it have the characteristics of a group? Is it cohesive? Is any aspect of partisanship ever involved?

Legislative Membership. The act creating the SPC specifies one formal rule governing legislative appointments: it requires an equal number of senators and representatives. (Originally, three members were appointed from each house but this was increased to five in 1953.) Beyond this ground rule, the main criterion in the selection of legislative members is to insure representation on the commission of all conflicting, or potentially conflicting, elements within the General Assembly. Members from both parties are selected. The majority party in each house appoints three members, while the minority selects the remainder.[2] Officially, these ap-

---

[2] One senatorial leader pointed out that one Commission included four Republican senators and only one Democrat, "but this was very unusual and the three-two breakdown is normal."

pointments are made by the speaker of the house and the Senate Committee on Committees. In reality, the party representatives on the SPC name the new members.

More specifically, in the House the SPC chairman suggests to the speaker and the minority leader individuals whom he believes would serve effectively and efficiently on the commission. These recommendations are followed almost without exception. Likewise, in the Senate, the Committee on Committees and the majority and minority leaders usually look to their respective party members on the SPC for suggestions on appointments to the commission.[3]

The representation of the various geographical or area interests of the state are of considerable significance in the assignment process. Although the legislative leaders may not define these interests very precisely, they are acknowledged, and they do enter into the calculations. For example, the division between the Chicago and downstate Illinois representatives, a division which permeates virtually all phases of the legislative process, must be reconciled. Democrats from Cook County expect to have—and indeed insist that they have—at least one member from each house on the commission. To illustrate, the Senate's Democratic membership on the commission has always included a Cook County representative and a downstate representative, the latter usually from central or southern Illinois. Representatives of the heavily Republican areas of central Illinois have maintained a majority of that party's SPC representation.[4]

[3] It might be interesting to point out, for example, that the appointments to the SPC Number Six agreed upon by the Democratic leaders of the Senate were not acceptable to all of the members involved. One of the commission appointments was given to a downstate senator who was actively engaged in a local campaign for judge. Believing the SPC to involve what one senator described as "too much work and too little to be gained politically," he exchanged commission assignments with another downstate Democrat. Although this was accomplished unofficially, it was ultimately ratified by the appointing powers.

[4] It is evident from the comment of one SPC senator that legislators see themselves as representatives of geographical areas: "I am certain that I will be reappointed to the SPC although I could serve on almost any of

Previous experience in education matters also weighs heavily in any assignment. Almost invariably, new appointees have had previous experience on either the House or Senate Education Committees. Reputations of concern for and knowledge about public education are established there. It is "almost automatic," according to one legislative leader, that ranking or senior members of these committees will be designated to fill any SPC vacancies.[5] Interviews indicated that nearly all of them had extensive backgrounds in areas concerned with the public schools.[6]

Careful attention is given to the personalities of applicants. Members of the commission tend to recommend for membership only those whom they feel will not upset the delicate unity the SPC has been able to achieve. Legislators who are thought to be seeking to manipulate the political process for their own personal advantage or who fail to gain the respect of their colleagues have little chance of being selected. Although it is somewhat difficult to document this point, those primarily responsible for making the selections indicated that to be eligible for SPC work, a member must be moderate and willing to compromise. Membership on the SPC is restricted to only those legislators who are

the many other commissions. However, I am probably the most available downstate Democrat who could serve on the SPC and will be reappointed as such."

[5] Included in the SPC Number Six membership were four legislators, each of whom either had been or was currently chairman of an education committee of the legislature.

[6] One House member of the commission had been actively engaged in public school activities for "over thirty years," with experience as a teacher in a rural school, a high school teacher and principal, a county superintendent of schools, and a local district superintendent; he had also served as president of the County Superintendents' Association and president of the Southeast Division of the State Teachers' Association, in addition to being a twenty-year member of the IEA and twice a delegate to the NEA convention. Another legislative member, while an attorney, had often worked on court cases concerned with schools, often representing school districts in cases involved with reorganization. One member had majored in education while in college and had taught for about five years, besides serving on the House Education Committee for his entire legislative career. Other members showed similar backgrounds.

sensitive to the predominant "moods" of the General Assembly. Whether all assignments live up to expectations is of course debatable, but as a ranking member of the commission put it: "The leadership is usually *very* careful about whom they appoint to the SPC; this is not always true of the memberships of commissions of this type."

Not all members of the General Assembly regard SPC service as especially desirable. Several suggested that the senior members of the commission monopolize the limelight, thereby preventing a newcomer from becoming expert in this area. A few have even requested transfers on the grounds that there is little operative political warrant for remaining.

The SPC members who for various reasons have achieved the status of public education experts vigorously insist upon their right to retain membership. Interviews with the leading legislators on the commission indicated that all expected and desired to be reappointed.[7] Seniority, however, does not guarantee tenure on the commission.

Nonlegislative Membership. A majority of gubernatorial appointees since 1949 have been representatives of organized interests concerned—directly or indirectly—with education. The SPC has always included in its membership the research director of the Illinois Education Association, the secretary of legislation of the Illinois Agriculture Association, a representative of the State Association of School Boards, and a member, often the president, of the Chicago Board of Education. The fifth gubernatorial appointee has varied from commission to commission, although this position has on two occasions gone to representatives of the Illinois Chamber of Commerce.

These individuals have brought the SPC a wealth of per-

---

[7] One veteran legislative member who did not seek reëlection to the General Assembly was subsequently appointed to the SPC, this time by the governor.

sonal experience in and knowledge of the problems faced by the public schools. One senatorial member credited the "excellent appointees made by the governor" as the most significant reason behind the success of the SPC. Lester R. Grimm, John K. Cox, and Harold W. Norman (see Appendix III), each of whom has served as a member of every SPC since its creation, are recognized by the commission members and by most of the legislators as being among the state's most informed leaders in the area of education. Grimm became research director of the IEA in 1924 and has been "studying school problems ever since," after having held positions as teacher, principal, and local superintendent of schools.

Norman, a Chicago attorney, became active in education matters during the 1930's, when he helped to organize a school district in his home area. He was subsequently elected to the school board and eventually became its president, in which capacity he "really served as principal and superintendent as well." As a result of this activity, he "became vitally interested in all phases of education and well acquainted with the problems it faced." Soon after, he became active in the State Association of School Boards and from that time on engaged in "almost all of the informal conferences called concerning state problems of education." ("I even drafted a good deal of the proposed legislation.") He was appointed to the School Finance and Tax Commission (along with Grimm) and was chairman of Governor Stevenson's Advisory Commission on Education; he has been a member of every state commission on education in the years prior to the establishment of the SPC. Cox, as Secretary of Legislation of the IAA, had taken a leading role in the school reorganization controversy, an area of great interest to the IAA membership. This association has been instrumental in obtaining rural acceptance of the consolidation of districts. During the period of 1944-50, Cox pointed out, "I attended several hundred meetings on reorganization and since then have had a great interest in the problems of education."

One gubernatorial appointment is traditionally reserved for a representative of the Chicago Board of Education since, according to one member, "so many of the state's school problems are centered in that area." As one legislative leader pointed out: "There's always a representative of the Chicago public schools on the commission; the membership of a state agency just wouldn't be complete without him."

The conditions surrounding the selection of the fifth gubernatorial appointee are somewhat vague. The appointee is usually a new one. Some members maintained that the reason for this is that it is the only political appointment open to the governor.[8] The fifth appointee to the SPC Number Seven (appointed in 1961) was Edwin Haag, who had served four years as a legislative member of the commission before his retirement from the legislature. The person filling this appointment on SPC's Number Five and Number Six was John R. Kinley, a Rockford attorney, whose special interest was school law and who had often represented local school boards in litigation.

Although the statute establishing the commission gives him broad discretion, the governor is limited in his appointing power by custom and common sense considerations that require that the aforementioned organizations and interests select their own representatives. Such appointments are not rewards for political work: that is, the power to appoint is too restricted to be used as a political weapon.[9] Therefore,

[8] One appointee holding this position predicted successfully that he would not be reappointed to the commission because of the election of a new governor. He was subsequently replaced by a member of the governor's party.

[9] One gubernatorial appointee stated: "I've been appointed to seven state education commissions by both Republicans and Democrats, and at no time have I ever been asked about party connections by either the governor or the legislature . . . I don't even know the party affiliation of the four other appointees of the governor, and it really makes no difference."

the appointees to this commission do not incur the same obligations to the governor that many appointees to other state agencies do. In actual practice, the governor has only two appointees for which he alone is directly responsible: the director of finance, an *ex officio* member; and the one appointee not dictated by organized interests.

State Superintendent of Public Instruction. The remaining commission member, the superintendent of public instruction, serves in an *ex officio* capacity. It is his office, of course, that has the most direct and continuous contact with the local school districts, and it is only logical, if only because of the information at his disposal, that he should be included.

Role of the Chairman. The chairmanship of the SPC has been held since 1951 by Representative Charles W. Clabaugh (Republican of Champaign). Interviews with the commission members indicated that this post is crucial in the formulation of school policy. There was also agreement among all concerned that had it not been for the personal prestige and hard work of the chairman, they would have found it much more difficult to capitalize on the structural advantages of combined legislative and interest group membership.

LEADERSHIP ROLES

The formal and informal leadership positions on the SPC tend to coincide. The chairman, while not dominating the commission, does lead and direct it. In addition, he sets the limits in which the specialities of the individual members can be employed. Some members whose training or knowledge in certain areas are extensive, are generally referred to when problems in such areas arise. It should prove useful, therefore, to study the roles performed by the various commission leaders.

In several ways, the SPC chairman is the most important member of the commission. His jobs are varied and numerous. First of all, he presides over all SPC meetings and open hearings. As such, it is his responsibility to call each meeting, to arrange for the presence of those wishing to testify, to notify the commission members of the meeting, to appoint subcommittees, and to assist in the setting of the agenda.[1] In addition to these duties, the commission's research staff is directed under his personal supervision. He normally devotes at least one day a week "to the administrative work necessary to keep the SPC operating." Acting in this capacity he handles all correspondence to and from the commission office. More significantly, it is his personal responsibility to make sure that all SPC recommendations are drafted into bills, to designate the individuals to introduce them, and to handle the details of mobilizing support for their adoption. One member described the chairman as being "the commission's executive officer," in which capacity he "coördinates all of its activities."

Probably, the chairman's most significant function, however, is "just being chairman." He is the one member of the commission who devotes many hours each week to the work of the SPC. Few people in Illinois understand the state's school problems as well as the chairman. According to one legislator, "Anybody who would devote as much time to studying the problems of education as the SPC chairman has to devote would automatically be in a strong position whenever such matters are discussed." Another described him as "the best informed man on the Commission." It is obvious that in the General Assembly (and in the communities of the state) he would be looked to as the chief repre-

[1] The agenda is actually the result of collective action. The research staff (under the direction of the research director) collects the vast amount of pertinent data into a workable form. On the basis of this data, the chairman, usually assisted by the research director, the commission recording secretary, and any other SPC members whose advice the chairman seeks, sets the agenda. It is described, however, as being "very informal," and in actual practice anything can (and is) discussed at any time a member wishes to bring it up.

sentative of the SPC. When he is recognized during debate on an education issue in the House of Representatives, he speaks with authority, his "facts are never challenged, and his opinions are challenged only rarely."

In the case of the present chairman, long tenure has enhanced his status and increased his influence. Although not a member of the first SPC, he has been a member and chairman of every commission since that time. His continuous service as chairman even during times when the opposing party was in numerical control of the SPC is due as much to the respect of the other commission members as it is to the nonpartisan atmosphere surrounding the commission activity.[2]

Role of Informal Leaders. The members of the SPC were in general agreement that while the ideas, opinions, and comments of each member were to be respected, several commission members had achieved special status by becoming specialists in particular areas of education policy. Commission members considered certain of themselves as "informal leaders." One member put it this way:

Informal leaders? Of course we give added consideration to the comments of certain people. Lester Grimm is an expert in the field of education; he has great respect; anything he has to say on school matters is of significance to the SPC. Harold Norman is an astute attorney specializing in school law; on any legal question we listen to him attentively.

[2] One Democratic senator stated: "We all have a great deal of wholesome respect for Representative Clabaugh; he is the most informed man on the commission." A Republican senator agreed: "Clabaugh was chosen chairman because he is the best man in the field. He is acquainted with every phase of education. He isn't autocratic and runs a good commission." An interest group representative added: "Representative Clabaugh combines his influence as chairman with his many years of experience into a strong leadership position; he is well-qualified and experienced." This idea was also stated by another education man: "Clabaugh has been an excellent chairman; his knowledge of schools and his willingness to organize and spend hours and hours on SPC business make him very effective. He is very capable and does a fine job in a difficult position."

Another added:

Each member of the commission is probably looked to for advice in some specific area. I look to Grimm, for example, in matters pertaining to teachers, to Davis in taxation matters, to Kinley in special charter district questions, to Dale in matters of rural schools, and so on.

The informal role of the two Chicago members merits special attention. Our analysis of the internal politics of the SPC revealed that on most matters of state-wide application the Chicago representatives were *not* the innovators, rather they were the ones who would raise the question: "Look boys, how will this affect Chicago?" Although we cannot document this as an incontestable fact, the Chicago representation was there primarily to make sure that the state's largest school district was not damaged by any state-wide actions and that its special status in state law was preserved. The relationship of Chicago school men and the basis of their bargaining power (resources) will be examined later on in this chapter.

The role of the research director also merits special mention. Section Six of the act creating the SPC authorizes it to "employ and fix the compensation of such employees and technical assistants versed in the aims and problems of public education as it deems necessary to effectuate the purposes of this act." [3] Since 1951, Dr. Orville Alexander, Chairman of the Department of Government at Southern Illinois University (Carbondale), has held the position of staff director. [4]

The research director's role, as defined by other members,

[3] *Illinois School Problems,* Report of the School Problems Commission Number Six, March, 1961, p. 4.
[4] The research director for the SPC Number One was Dr. Richard G. Browne who was then Head of the Social Science Department of Illinois State Normal University and who had previously been research director for the Illinois Legislative Council and the School Finance and Tax Commission.

is largely a "technical or statistical" one.[5] But it seems to embody more than this might imply, and in fact SPC members tend to contradict their own overall assessments of his influence. As one might expect, a significant part of the director's work involves the area of school finance; it is his job, for example, to project the school costs for the forthcoming biennium. Most members indicated, however, that the director usually acts at the request of the commission and does not himself really initiate any proposals.[6]

In essence, the director of research is considered by the other members as an advisor to whom they can look for assistance in *any matter under discussion*. It is here that his influence is felt the most. Several members who said that his overall role was nominal added that his informal opinions were extremely helpful in deciding some of the more difficult problems faced by the SPC.[7] It was also pointed out that a significant part of the director's influence lay in controlling to a large extent the time at which the various issues are brought up in the commission. Although the chairman prepares the agenda, nothing is considered until the staff has completed the research on it. As one legislative member summed up the research director's position:

The director of research has an impossible job! He is personally responsible for studying *all* the problems. He must give assistance

[5] One SPC leader stated: "We tell him we want something done and what material we need, and he proceeds to get it for us.

[6] One member pointed out: "The research director is deferred to on technical problems; on financial matters, expenditures, etc., we accept his views. He has no role, however, in policy matters; his work is pretty well centered in digging out facts for us." Another member suggested that his role "could best be summarized by saying that the SPC guides the direction his research takes, but once he completes it, the commission accepts his results with few questions. He actually does little without general instructions of the SPC, however."

[7] One member pointed out that "the research director's informal role may be more significant than his formal powers. He often gives his 'educated' opinions at our meetings and is often quite influential in the decisions reached by the SPC." Another commented: "He may come in with suggestions which are usually of considerable value to us in the reaching of decisions."

to all subcommittees requesting his help. He must do independent study and must anticipate the problems even before they actually arise. He must write committee reports and really has innumerable responsibilities. However, with all this, neither research director appointed has ever been domineering; both have been objective in presenting the facts on both sides of every issue debated.[8]

THE INTEGRATION OF COMMISSION MEMBERS

Once assigned to the SPC, a member knows that he has joined a going concern, an established group with its own set of norms.[9] From then on, a major factor in any decision he may reach in this commission is the influence on him of this institutionalized group. But the SPC is more than just a group with its own norms; *it is a highly integrated group.* We use the term *integration* in the same sense that Richard Fenno does, that is, "the degree to which there is a working together or a meshing together or mutual support among its [a committee's] roles and subgroups" and "the degree to which a committee is able to minimize conflict among its roles and its subgroup, by heading off or resolving the conflicts that arise."[1]

The characteristics that explain or affect group integration are the length of time an individual belongs to a group, the expectations the group imposes upon its members, the evaluation or image the members of a group have of it, their degree of satisfaction that the group is performing an important task, and the attitudes and respect the members have for each other. We shall examine the SPC in terms of each of these variables.

First, the membership of the SPC has remained gener-

[8] Quoted in an interview with a legislative member of the SPC.

[9] For a study of group norms of committees, see Ralph K. Huitt, "The Congressional Committee: A Case Study," *American Political Science Review*, XLVIII (June, 1954), pp. 340-365.

[1] Richard F. Fenno, Jr., "The House Appropriations Committee as a Political System: The Problem of Integration," *American Political Science Review*, LVI (June, 1962), p. 310.

ally stable in the years since its creation. Three of the gubernatorial members have served on it since its inception. The chairman and vice-chairman, both legislators, are members of long commission tenure. The turnover in legislative membership is never complete and seldom drastic at any one time, thus indicating a continuous group life (see Appendix III).

Legislative members serve an average of four and one-half years. Of the 10 legislative members on SPC Number Seven, 1 had served on the commission since 1951 (SPC Number Two); 2, since their appointments to SPC Number Three; 7, from SPC Number Four to the present; and 8 had also served on SPC Number Six. This means that Veteran Commission members, by articulating and reinforcing group norms, can easily transmit them to new members. "The opportunity exists . . . for the development of a stable leadership group, a set of traditional norms for the regulation of internal . . . behavior, and informal techniques of personal accommodation. Time is provided in which new members can learn and internalize (SPC) norms . . ."[2] Thus the SPC "does not suffer from the potentially disruptive consequences of rapid changeovers in its leadership group, nor of sudden impositions of new sets of norms governing internal committee behavior."[3]

Second, every member of the SPC is expected to be interested in public education and to strive for its improvement. He is supposed to devote a considerable amount of his time and effort, both within the commission and within the legislature, toward this end. The General Assembly provides practically no surveillance of the commission's work, and the SPC operates under the assumption that in the field of education policy formation, it has preëminence.

This common interest in education problems helps to pro-

---

[2] Fenno, Jr., p. 315. We are using Fenno's terms because they seem especially appropriate.
[3] *Ibid.*

mote integration. The members deal with the same subject matter year after year—and frequently more than once a year. "Substantive and procedural repetition," Fenno has pointed out, "promotes familiarity with key problems and provides ample opportunity to test and confirm the most satisfactory methods of dealing with them." [4] The absolute necessity to finance education makes it urgent that the commission find such methods. Moreover, the selection process serves as a deterrent to fragmentation. As we have noted, only those individuals who are predisposed to be coöperative and moderate in their approach and who have a strong commitment to education—either by virtue of their past performance or their group membership—are selected. One SPC legislator pointed out: "By dealing with the problems over and over, we become rather well educated to the problems of public schools. We then in turn have to 'educate' the others: the legislators, the governor, even the communities. This is our responsibility." [5]

Thus, the consensus of the commission is based on the conception that it has one paramount task. That task is to solve the major problems of the state's public schools in a businesslike fashion while guarding against unreasonable drains on the state treasury. The members express their satisfaction in the knowledge that the commission is performing an important role, which in turn means that membership on the SPC insures one of having a major voice in public school policy. Interviews with the commission members revealed the extent to which they feel the state's education decision-making machinery depends upon their work. "The SPC can almost say 'yes' or 'no' to any bill concerning education," was the way one member put it. Another com-

[4] *Ibid.*, p. 312.
[5] Another senator stated: "The SPC develops a know-how of education problems that the average legislator just doesn't have. . . . The SPC members, by being able to have the education experts come to them and explain the situation to them, have in a sense become 'education experts' themselves. This has greatly contributed to the success of this commission."

mission member described the pattern of consensus as follows:

It is a working commission—we take a businesslike approach in
attempting to solve the needs of schools which the state should
solve. We are able to recognize the local needs and problems; we
then try to recommend legislation within the framework of these
needs. We are conservative in our recommendations; people by
nature object to change and as a result we don't try to force undue change upon the General Assembly.

The members speak of the agency as a "hard-working
commission." All agreed that the SPC "involves a tremendous amount of hard work, much of it rather tedious and
perhaps dull." The commission members meet frequently,
the sessions are long, a great deal of traveling is necessary,
and each member, to keep current, must do considerable
individual research. This respect for the commission itself,
as well as for the position of each individual on it, results
in a strengthening of the SPC position.[6]

Moreover, the importance the SPC members attach to the
notion that the SPC is a "hard-working commission" and
that hard work is part of the group's "recognizable and
distinctive political style" may suggest a uniformity in the
political process. Fenno, for example, found that the attrac-
tiveness of the United States House of Representatives'
Appropriations Committee is heightened by "the committee's self-image that [it is] 'the hardest working committee
in Congress.'"[7] SPC members, similar to House Appropriations Committee members, believe that "willingness to work"
is a "badge of identification that is to be proudly worn."[8]
SPC members feel that the long hours that they put in ac-

[6] A former member of the SPC research staff stated: "All of the members are actually close friends, all devoted to the cause of education. Although they may not always agree in policy discussions, at least they all
understand and respect the other fellow's opinion. Not very many other
state commissions can say that about their memberships." For a discussion
of the significance of such respect, see Fenno, Jr., pp. 310-324.
[7] Fenno, Jr., p. 314.
[8] *Ibid.*

tually serve to increase both group morale and identification, and again as Fenno found in his study, "prolonged daily work together encourages sentiments of mutual regard, sympathy, and solidarity. This *esprit* is, in turn, functional for integration." [9]

Data on this point reveal that SPC members are satisfied with the actions of this commission as a whole. A quantitative measure of dissatisfaction is group departure, and it has already been indicated that most members are not interested in relinquishing their memberships. Of greater significance, however, is the high regard the members themselves openly express for the commission. "It is a source of pride to be part of it," one member said. All agreed that "the SPC has been one of the most successful agencies operating in the state." One member explained:

The SPC has done everything it was designed to do. The public in general is enthusiastic about it. The state superintendent has been lavish in his praise of it. Educators in general have been too. I regard my service on it as one of the major accomplishments of my political career.

Integration, of course, helps to prevent stalemate. All express willingness to abide by majority rule. Members never attack each other publicly and rarely criticize SPC procedures. "If a member doesn't agree, he simply says so and that ends that. We then move on to something else," reported one member.[1]

Thus far, we have dealt largely with the attitudes and images that the commission members have as a group. But

---

[9] *Ibid.*

[1] For other studies on factors involved in committee integration, see Nicholas A. Masters, "House Committee Assignments," *American Political Science Review*, LV (June 1961), pp. 345-357; Ralph K. Huitt, "The Congressional Committee: A Case Study," *American Political Science Review*, XLVIII (June 1954), pp. 340-365; James A. Robinson, "Decision-Making in the House Rules Committee," *Administrative Science Quarterly*, III (June 1958); and Seymour Scher, "Congressional Committee Members as Independent Agency Overseers," *American Political Science Review*, LIV (December 1960), pp. 911-920; among others.

why has the SPC been able to achieve integration and how has it been able to maintain it? What keeps the SPC from flying to pieces? Since the essence of politics is conflict or competition for scarce resources and the processes by which these conflicts are resolved, an examination of SPC's efforts to minimize or resolve conflict will give us further insight into Illinois school politics.

Part of the answer seems to lie in the SPC's previously discussed internal composition and procedures: that is, the selection of members of the "right temperament," deliberate avoidance of highly controversial questions, and permission to all groups to participate in its deliberations. But other factors are involved. A major taboo in SPC work is to raise any issue or to manipulate any situation that will divide or bring about serious conflict among commission members. Partisanship, for example, has no place in any of the commission's deliberations, regardless of the intensity of feelings or rivalries among the members in other policy areas. Willingness to compromise, respect for the ideas of other members, and deference to the informal leaders who are specialists in a particular area, are *expected* of SPC members. Let us examine some of these factors more closely.

Agreement on Priorities. In interviews, commission members repeatedly stressed that the SPC was neither designed to solve nor was capable of solving all the state's education problems. The membership (even those representing organized interests) agreed that consensus *on fiscal policy* was more imperative than pressing for advancement in other areas.[2] One interest group leader, for example, stated that the SPC record in areas such as local school administration and teacher welfare was not outstanding. "However," he

[2] One member stated: "The real controversial questions—those dealing with religion, race, federal aid, etc.—are just never brought up in the commission." Another mentioned in regard to these same issues: "Questions in all of these areas have been brought up from time to time, but by default we just haven't acted on them. They are too controversial, and would divide us."

continued, "when you consider the many advancements that have been made in the state aid program, this is not too expensive a price to pay." Another interest group leader told how his group annually proposes a series of recommendations to the commission but actively seeks the passage only of those receiving SPC support. "To do otherwise would be breaking down the consensus which the SPC has worked so hard to achieve," he added. Another pointed out: "Sometimes we ask the SPC for too much; we realize that we might have to take a half loaf instead of a whole, but I think it's obvious that a half loaf is better than none at all."

Recognized Need for Internal Cohesion. All SPC members insofar as the public schools are concerned interpret the political world that affects them with striking and somewhat surprising similarity. All believe, for example, that internal cohesion is vital to their effectiveness and that maintaining it is worth almost any price, even the total sacrifice of some long-term goals. These are the lessons of power that all have learned. One member observed: "Almost all SPC decisions are made as a result of a consensus of the various members; very rarely is there a division of opinion that necessitates an actual vote. If this unity were ever to break down, we would be in serious trouble." Disagreements, of course, are never completely eliminated. But the SPC has found ways to ventilate them before they disturb the cohesion of the entire group. The device commonly used is to appoint a subcommittee and give it ample time to reconcile all the conflicting elements. In this regard, one member stated: "If for some reason a problem should arise, we will usually put it in the hands of a subcommittee to fight it out. The fighting is done there. When the final report is given to the SPC, it is normally received with little controversy. Our meetings are cordial, informative, and conducted with little hostility."

The overt attempt to avoid controversy whenever possible may have resulted in the Illinois public schools occasionally not getting all that they might have if policies had been formulated in the partisan, conflict-oriented, legislative channels. Education interests, however, have come to realize that the "avoidance of conflict" policy *insures* them passage of what *is* recommended by the SPC, whereas "there would be no assurance of anything being passed without it."

Nonpartisanship. For the most part, Democrats and Replicans are not at this point in Illinois in conflict over matters of education. If partisanship were generated from any source, it would probably come from the governor, as indeed it did in 1959; this, however, was the exception and not the rule. Party identification, as well as a party program, was of virtually no importance to the members of the SPC so far as its *work* was concerned.[3]

Partisan considerations in recent years, however, have had some effect on the internal organization of the SPC. In 1962, for example, in the election of the commission chairman, a tie vote resulted in a contest between Democratic Senator Edward C. Eberspacher and Republican Representative Charles W. Clabaugh, with the Democratic members supporting Eberspacher and the Republicans and organized interest representatives favoring Clabaugh. It was rumored that the split was caused by Speaker Paul Powell (Democrat, Vienna) who felt that Clabaugh was pushing too hard for a reorganization of a school districts bill that, if adopted, would adversely affect his district. He used his powers as speaker to force a party-line vote. Clabaugh, sensing that the interjection of partisanship in any form could deeply divide the commission, withdrew his candidacy and was immediately elected vice-chairman.

Until that time, no partisan matters of any great signifi-

[3] When asked about the role played by political parties in the decision-making process of education, one senator replied: "Political parties are just not important in matters of education. Members don't usually follow any party-line thinking. If a person knows a lot about education, I listen to him, and I usually follow his suggestions, whether he's a Republican or a Democrat. Partisan politics just isn't interjected into education situations."

cance were introduced. In fact, several members pointed to the elections of a Republican chairman, vice-chairman, and secretary at a time when numerically the Democrats were in control of the commission as examples of the nonpartisan policy followed by the SPC and of the desire of the whole membership to subordinate party affiliation to education policy considerations.

In election campaigns too, there seems to be little connection between public school issues and party activities. While a review of previous state party platforms indicates that a portion of each was usually devoted to education proposals, the positions taken by the two parties rarely differed and the planks were broad in scope and general in terminology. Except perhaps for federal aid, there is no ideological division between the parties on public school policy in Illinois. The campaigns that followed the writing of these platforms, moreover, almost never included debates over proposed education policies. One member explained: "We feel that party platforms don't say much about education. They're awfully general—both parties have been rather conservative in this area and public school matters do not become campaign material."

Members of both parties on the Commission tend to condemn or censure any member who has the audacity to make education a partisan consideration. We were told: "Only one member of the commission ever tried to turn the SPC into a political agency and even members of his own party [on the commission] realized this and strongly disapproved."

The absence of partisan battles over education issues within the SPC is normally carried over to the floor of the General Assembly. As one commission member describes it:

In a typical legislative session, school bills are not party bills . . . Only several times in the last twenty years or so do I remember open partisan fights over issues directly concerned with education. Governor Stevenson was very liberal in his views on public education and went so far that he produced one party fight. Although he had very progressive plans and the appropriations for schools in his budget were very liberal, there just wasn't enough money to cover everything. His own party leaders told him that all he wanted couldn't be done within the monetary limitations. They informed him that they were obligated to cut some of these to a level that the state could afford. Stevenson protested loudly, but his budget was cut, leaving him without his great improvements. That was one instance where a party as a bloc went against the governor—and it happened to be his own party. . . . However, I haven't known of either party, *as a party*, ever standing in the way of any public education issue. School bills are generally not considered along political party lines.

Records of final votes on education bills in each house add weight in support of the contention that such issues are not decided along party lines. In sum, the SPC has been the least affected by partisan considerations of all the advisory commissions on the state level, despite the fact that it is not totally immune. Some potentially controversial issues, only remotely or indirectly concerned with education, have been purposely "transformed" into "education bills" in attempts to secure their passage by capitalizing on this nonpartisan framework. The presence of conflicting viewpoints on public school problems is obvious, for the existence of such conflicts was a contributing cause in the establishment of the SPC. But in essence these differences were not then and are not now partisan.

Combining Educational Expertise with Political Experience. Integration of the SPC rests on a *recognition* by all the members that its work is the result of consultation, compromise, and agreement by the representatives of the state's education interests and by the leading "education" members of the legislature. They feel education theory is tempered by practical politics. According to one commission member: "When some of us educators get involved in education theory and start recommending accordingly, the legislative members will remind us 'that won't pass,' and we then alter our recommendations into a form that will pass." [4]

The crucial fact is that certain SPC members are *recognized* and *acknowledged* by the others as fulfilling specialized roles in the education decision-making process. The informal leadership roles mentioned above are not subtle, as they often are in organizations or committees. Interest group representatives, for example, recognize the legislative members on the commission as the best judges of what education bills will pass the General Assembly. SPC legislators, in turn, recognize the representatives of the interest groups on the commission as the best judges of what the state should be doing.

Thus all members are expected to observe and acknowledge the particular expertise of their colleagues, and in this sense, role specialization has become a vital commission norm. The SPC as it operates today virtually requires each member to play the role as a specialist in some substantive area or in the legislative process generally. His contacts, energy, and time are expected to be devoted primarily to his own peculiar specialized function. SPC acceptance of specialization has been an important integrative force in all phases of its decision-making deliberations.

In sum, our analysis of the Illinois School Problems Commission strongly suggests that its high degree of integration has important consequences for the public school policy-making process. Integration of the commission is one big factor, along with several others, that has produced a long

---

[4] This process was described by one legislator in this manner: "You can't use the bulldozer approach in getting changes passed in the legislature. You must first recognize the problem, proceed slowly to confer with educators, find out how it can best be solved, but always keeping in mind that the solution will have to be practical enough so that it will pass the General Assembly. This way you arrive at recommendations that are acceptable to everyone." Another legislative leader pointed out: "We screen our recommendations in the SPC with the ideas: Can this be enacted if recommended, and, if so, will it do the job it is intended to do? This gives us a more practical approach to solving the problems." For this reason, according to one interest group leader, those problems "on which legislative pressure is greatest—school finance, taxation, state aid, and so on—are those which are first discussed and acted upon by the SPC."

string of legislative victories. In the section that follows, we will attempt to test the effect of the commission's integration on its relationships with other governmental agencies.

The commission's integration has also had a demonstrable influence on the access and strategies of the various interests that operate on the state level. The organized groups concerned with public school policy—IEA, ISASB, PTA, etc. —channel virtually all their major policy demands through this agency and adjust or modify their priorities in accordance with its decisions. *Even in areas where the SPC does not act, its informal support is openly solicited.* Moreover, the ways the commission achieves integration affects its policy proposals. Matters pertaining to finance and reorganizational school districts are given the highest priority; teachers' welfare is given only secondary considerations or is left to others to handle; and some matters are as a matter of policy not touched upon at all. High integration has also meant that party interests have little or no influence and play no role, subtle or overt, in public school decisions.

Finally, a substantial part of education decision-making process is highly stable and predictable as a result of the commission's integration. "Everyone knows just about what the commission can and cannot do," one legislator commented. Thus, as Fenno found in his study of the House Appropriations Committee, integration is "a stabilizing force." "Nobody," an interest group leader said, "is going to upset the applecart when he knows that the SPC can always get something done."

SPC RELATIONS WITH OTHER GOVERNMENTAL AGENCIES

The vitality of the SPC springs from the nature of its membership. The presence of influential legislators, the state's chief school and budget officers, and interest group leaders on the commission is its greatest leverage in gaining the

General Assembly's approval of its recommendations. Because there is no state board of education—or any other agency that can speak authoritatively in education matters —the SPC provides important links among the General Assembly, the governor, and the state office of public instruction, as well as the major education interests.

Yet the SPC's effectiveness depends on something more than its internal cohesion. It is, as one member said, "only an advisory body," and if the governor or certain elements within the legislature opposed it, it would soon cease to exist or would play only a nominal role. The question then is how the SPC maintains the relationships with other agencies of state government, as well as private groups.

THE SPC AND THE GENERAL ASSEMBLY

"The most important thing to remember is that in education matters the legislature is all-powerful," one senator declared as he described the role performed by the law-making body in formulating public school policy. The General Assembly of Illinois has never delegated any of its formal authority over education decision-making to any other agency. Thus, in the performance of its functions, the SPC operates in a context different from that of the state board of education in Missouri. SPC members say that since the state legislature of Illinois reviews all of the commission's recommendations, "the General Assembly, in effect, is the state board, and thus in principle, though perhaps not in fact, its preëminence is preserved." Even though all major public school decisions in Illinois either originate in, or flow through, the SPC, the fact that the formal authority rests with the General Assembly is not ignored by SPC members. They are indeed extremely cautious about what type of relationship they maintain with the parent body.[5]

---

[5] It should be noted at this point that the House and Senate Education Committees play only a modest role in the formation of policy. Since the ranking members of both committees maintain influential positions on the

Legislators frequently disagree, not only about what they think should be done to alleviate a particular situation but also about the underlying facts. But the SPC's proposals and facts go virtually unchallenged. Records of sessions of the Illinois General Assembly reveal that the legislature and the governor promptly accept *all major* SPC recommendations. There are few, if any, floor debates; neither of the regular standing education committees in the House or Senate holds very extensive hearings or ties up SPC proposals in committee; and at the time of a final vote, few if any questions are raised. The percentage of SPC recommendations accepted by the legislature is fantastically high when compared with the record of any other state commission.[6]

Outward appearances would suggest that SPC recommendations pass with very little effort. There are no external pressures to combat; there are no hostile committees to overcome; and not even such old and reliable political obstacles as inertia and ineptness seem to rear their heads. There seems to be no argument that SPC backing of a measure insures its passage. But why has the commission been able to command such widespread respect and acceptance from the members of the General Assembly? It is a commonplace that outward appearances are frequently deceptive. So it is with the SPC; for in reality, the respect and acceptance of the SPC rests on an elaborate foundation of practices, procedures, services, and policies.

Inclusion of Legislative Members. One of the SPC's principal aids in achieving its goals is its inclusion of re-

---

SPC, there is generally little controversy within these committees on any policy recommended by the SPC.

[6] One might point out that some SPC recommendations are disapproved by means other than being voted down in the legislature. The commission members have on occasion withdrawn their support of a proposal previously recommended by the SPC when circumstances arose affecting its passage. The commission has also been known to "try out" a recommendation to see how it is received by the members of the legislature and by the various organized education interests. If the proposal is received unenthusiastically, SPC support will probably be withdrawn.

spected legislators among its members. Of the ten legislative members, five are ranking members of the education committees of both houses, and all have acquired a reputation for being informed and concerned about education policy. This obviously is a matter of more than passing importance to those interested in achieving results. It means that the SPC's recommendations have received some bipartisan support *prior* to their consideration by the General Assembly. Of equal significance, ten legislators are prepared to lead the fight for final passage. Meetings are held in the offices, on the floor, and in hotel rooms where SPC policy is carefully explained to any legislator who may have doubts. In brief, the commission includes members who have an intimate working knowledge of "legislative give and take" and who know "what goes on inside." Their views are given the additional weight that is accorded by legislators only to those who are themselves on the inside and who play the political game for similar stakes.

One Democratic senator claimed that the SPC had achieved such a record for success because:

we, as legislators and as members of the SPC, are able to recognize the local needs and problems; we then try to recommend legislation within the framework of these needs . . . We legislators know what the General Assembly will accept. From this know-how, we guide the SPC into recommending proposals which *are passable.*

A Republican senator strongly seconded this interpretation of the General Assembly's respect for the commission. He said:

The SPC is a *legislative* commission whose purpose is to inform the legislative members of the problems of the schools existing in the state. Our chief strength lies in the fact that when we come in with recommendations, we have five members in each house who have fairly specific knowledge of the background, the need for, and the situation surrounding each recommendation. . . . The fact that the SPC membership includes ten members who are actively engaged in the practice of politics gives us a more *practical* approach to solving the problems. We screen our recommendations with the question: can this be enacted and, if so, will it do the job it is intended to do? If the State Office recommended bills, they would come before the General Assembly with no one on the floor cognizant of the background or able to speak with any authority as to the need for the bills. The SPC, however, has people on both sides of the aisle in both houses who know from months of study both the needs for and the reasons behind each of its recommendations.

Everyone interviewed agreed that without legislative members, education bills could conceivably produce bitter partisan controversies once they reached the floor of the legislature or perhaps even in committee. The research director of the SPC explained:

The two parties' leaders [in the legislature] agree on a program while it is being discussed at the SPC level. Since several of these legislative leaders are members of the SPC, agreement is worked out before the recommendation is even announced by the Commission; obviously, little difficulty is found by the time the program reaches the state legislature. The SPC does not recommend any program until it has "lived with it for two or three years" and knows it will pass and will work.[7]

[7] An example of how decisions reached before the proposals are officially announced oftentimes determine whether or not they are accepted was the passage of the 1959 sales tax increase, whose funds were to be used for the state's foundation program. The commission believed that an increase in the sales tax was the only tax increase possible without increasing the already overburdened local property owners. "Property taxes were as high as they can go" was how one member described the situation. However, it was feared that this tax increase might have difficulty in being passed by the legislature, since representatives of the so-called "richer" districts might be inclined to vote against any increase in taxes on the grounds that their local districts, while having to pay a high percentage of the increased taxes, would in fact not benefit at all from the amounts collected. The SPC recommended, therefore, in addition to an increase in the equalization level paid by the state to the poorly financed districts, an increase in the amounts of *flat grants* paid by the state to *every district* in the state, regardless of its financial capabilities. Since all local districts would benefit from the new increase, this resulted in the acceptance of this proposal by most legislators. One observer thought this was "an excellent example of

Thus, far removed from some of the more dramatic spectacles of the General Assembly, the SPC legislative members formulate recommendations in which few of their non-member legislative colleagues express any real interest, although all acknowledge their importance. The point is that all members of the General Assembly are prepared to accept SPC recommendations because they know the legislative members of the commission have insured that every decision is "readied" for final action. They know that step by step, the commission members have worked out the delicate compromises necessary for political consensus, thereby significantly reducing the chances that a non-commission legislator will be hurt by a vote on an issue which he does not understand.

A United Education Front. The General Assembly's confidence in the SPC is also based on the knowledge that the latter has the solid backing of the state's principal education interests. By the time the General Assembly is ready to act, all of the principal groups have made their positions clear and are prepared to press for favorable action. The importance of such unity among the education interests to the SPC in its relationships with the General Assembly cannot be underestimated. It means that the General Assembly will not itself be the target for all types of demands, many of them conflicting and many of them unworthy of detailed consideration. It also means that the legislators are politically safe in the education field; they are not forced to take sides, favoring one group over another, or to compete with other legislators to win the favor of a particular group. Finally, the individual legislator is relieved of the responsibility of introducing legislation with which he may not agree, of fighting for causes that he knows have little chance of success, or of generally using his political currency on issues that have few, if any, political payoffs.

how the SPC, through its practical knowledge of the political picture, can obviously increase the chances of its recommendations being accepted."

Interviews with the nonlegislative members of the SPC disclosed that they, like their legislative colleagues on the commission, take an active part in the legislative battle for passage of the SPC recommendations. When asked about his role in securing the passage of these recommendations, one interest group representative who serves on the SPC said:

It consists mainly of explaining the bills and answering the questions of legislators. I get many questions every week asking the pros and cons of each bill. My lobbying is just answering questions—for committees, for individuals and at meetings . . . Many interest groups, in addition to those represented on the SPC, will pressure the SPC members for certain programs and will also help us secure passage of our programs once they are presented to the legislature.

An "Objective" Approach to Education. The influence which SPC legislators and interest group representatives wield in passing commission recommendations only partially accounts for the SPC's unusual position in Illinois state politics. There is one other variable, the myth of objectivity and nonpartisanship that surrounds the SPC. Members of the General Assembly say that they have learned from experience to trust the advice given to them by SPC members. All legislators interviewed believed the SPC was sincere in its efforts to separate school problems from purely political considerations and to make recommendations without seeking political advantage. They said that they look to the SPC as an agency expertly equipped to deal with problems generally considered to be too hot for the inexperienced to handle.

One senator, when asked to compare SPC suggestions with those offered by other state agencies, immediately replied:

The work done by the SPC could not be accomplished by any other state agency. The State Office is a *political* unit and therefore could not be trusted by both sides of the General Assembly. The legislature recognizes the SPC as *nonpolitical* and just wouldn't be as enthusiastic about recommendations made by the State Office.

In this "nonpolitical" role, the SPC has been able to concern itself with problems previously considered politically impossible to solve. It serves as a buffer, eliminating or reducing the conflict and pressure on public school matters, particularly those concerned with finance, to a minimal level. The SPC *settles* public school questions and frees legislators to devote their energies elsewhere. Moreover, the SPC is one of the few agencies in the history of Illinois politics whose functions have not been constantly hindered or complicated by problems that arise from the persistent division in Illinois between the Chicago and the downstate interests.[8] One leading senator summarized the situation in the following way:

The Chicago-downstate division, which is involved in practically every phase of Illinois politics, would probably extend even to the public schools if it weren't for the SPC. With the *objective* role played by the SPC, the school problems area is one where the problems can be solved with all of the disputing factions generally being satisfied.

Another senator shared this opinion:

I think it's obvious why such a commission could better handle the great variance of problems that exist in Illinois between Chicago and the downstate areas than an agency like the State Office.

[8] On the surface it might appear that the bitter Chicago versus downstate controversy in the 1961 session over state aid for transportation of Chicago students to school was an exception to this rule. This issue, however, had not been considered by the SPC, and the proposed bill was neither endorsed nor opposed by SPC members acting in that capacity. In fact, several members of the SPC claimed that the issue was not a school problem at all, but rather one of state subsidization, "a direct appropriation from the general revenue of the State of Illinois to the Chicago Transit Authority," as one member of the SPC put it. It is generally agreed that when the SPC is not involved or refuses to take a position on issues affecting public schools, consensus breaks down. Only this agency has been able over time to eliminate and reduce conflict over school legislation to the satisfaction of both sides, Chicago and downstate, of the most pervasive conflict in Illinois politics.

The SPC, by including members of all sections, all parties, all interests, and all factions, obviously could arrive at a better solution for the *whole* state than could one political office.

Trusted Advisers to the Legislators. This broad sketch of SPC-General Assembly relations conceals the many daily little services and favors the SPC, especially its legislative members, provides for the members of the General Assembly. A closer inspection of these relationships shows why the SPC enjoys such a high level of confidence. For example, in situations where the SPC has not concerned itself with legislation introduced by other legislators, or where the decision of the SPC, after discussing the matter, is not to offer any recommendation, the members of the SPC perform a rather specialized role. They become the *trusted confidants* of their legislative colleagues to whom the latter look for advice or leadership in matters pertaining to the public schools.

Out of conviction, habit, and convenience, an overwhelming majority of legislators who plan to introduce education bills or who are considering bills not sponsored by the commission will take the following steps: they will ask whether the commission's legislative members have considered the matter and, if so, what their decision was. Is a recommendation concerning this matter forthcoming from the SPC in the near future? If the matter was not discussed there, why not? What were the pros and cons? Why was no action taken? If a decision was reached, was it unanimous?

If the SPC has not acted, legislators then ask members' advice. What do you personally think of the bill that has been proposed? Would it get SPC approval if it were considered? Does it conflict with our existing programs? Is it really a local bill? Would this affect my district and in what way? Are you personally going to support it or oppose it actively?

In such circumstances and in the absence of SPC official policy, the legislative members of the SPC become the educational experts whose advice is likely to influence a large portion of the General Assembly. Although the SPC members obviously do not exercise complete control over all public school matters, when they agree as to whether a bill should pass or fail, their opinions virtually always prevail. In brief, the chances of any education bill passing in the absence of official SPC action depend almost entirely on whether the SPC legislative members approve or not.

Data from the interviews reveal how crucial this informal role of SPC legislative members is regarded. One senatorial member of the SPC put it this way:

The members of the General Assembly look to the SPC for leadership in education matters. An individual legislator wanting to introduce a bill without SPC approval would first take it to one of the legislative leaders on the SPC for his opinion. If one of these disapproves, the bill would have little chance of being passed.

Another SPC senator stated:

I seldom see a bill on school problems brought up in the Senate where the sponsor hasn't first come in to see if the SPC is doing anything about it, too. If we haven't done anything and aren't doing anything, he will probably go ahead and introduce it. After studying it, I may favor it, or I may oppose it.

Another member agreed:

There is an unfortunate and growing tendency on the part of the legislative members to do *nothing* in the realm of education until they have checked it with the SPC or with its individual members.

And a fourth senator was rather blunt in his analysis:

Very rarely do legislators bring up bills concerning education on their own. They always come to us first. If they don't, I would say that their bills have little chance of passing.

Perhaps even more crucial, given the propensity of politicians to want to remain in office, is the SPC's function as the buffer between elected representatives and their constituencies in matters of public school policy. In this regard, the SPC's role is analogous to the Missouri State Teachers Association's. Because of the active and widespread interest in schools, a phenomenon generally not characteristic of other state government functions, legislators are often subjected to an almost continuous barrage of requests to "do something about the school situation." Realizing the practical problems of trying to get an education bill passed in the General Assembly without SPC support, and also realizing that many of the demands made by the constituents are oversimplified or distorted, individual legislators rely on the SPC for aid and assistance in answering their constituents. SPC members may also suggest the type of legislation other legislators should introduce to alleviate particular problems. On numerous occasions, SPC members draft the bills, prepare letters to constituents informing them of what the experts say about the situation, and use their influence to help their colleagues pass bills designed to remedy local problems.[9]

Of equal importance is the assistance the SPC provides to the individual legislator by the fact of its existence. Constituents demanding legislative action on certain school problems are directed to the SPC; the immediate pressure is thereby removed. Legislators have found it to be a mechanism, a process, or a procedure that allows them to respond to their constituents in simple, easily understood terms. Legislators can simply say, "The SPC has studied those matters carefully; the people on it are experts."

Several SPC members mentioned this as one of its most vital functions. A House leader said:

Often certain legislators who have a particular problem of education will come to us for advice; I will then give them any position that the SPC has settled upon. Also we help these legislators draw up their bills on particular problems so they won't affect our al-

[9] One legislative leader of the SPC disclosed that much of his time is spent in drafting specific replies concerning public school problems for legislators to send to their constituents.

ready established overall policy. As such, the legislators look to us as a buffer between themselves and their constituents: when they receive pressures from local interests to introduce controversial, unpopular, questionable, or unwise legislation, they can tell their constituents that they are ill-equipped to handle it and send them to our commission. We can answer any question that any member might bring up concerning a problem his local district is having; although the SPC might not officially take a stand, we can help the legislator solve his problem.

This opinion was shared by an interest group leader who pointed out some of the SPC experiences:

Oftentimes constituents and interest group representatives come to their legislators asking that a particular education policy be passed. Perhaps this is a controversial issue, perhaps the legislator himself is opposed to it, or perhaps he doesn't really understand the situation. In all these cases the legislator's way out is to advise the demanding groups to take the matter to the SPC since its members are the ones who know something about it.

Few state legislators could make the claim of the little wooden ornament that used to sit on President Harry Truman's desk with its inscription, "The buck stops here." Legislators are as well known for avoiding decisions as they are for making them. So when there is a problem in education or when irate citizens complain that too little is being done, the SPC becomes a convenient scapegoat. Illinois legislators have not hesitated to say, "If not enough is being done, it's not my fault; the School Problems Commission should take care of it." Although they refer to the SPC in this manner only rarely, legislators freely admit the security of knowing that the SPC can take the blame for them.

In sum, the SPC in its relations with the General Assembly serves as a constant source of information, a conclusive answering-service for constituents, and an occasional scapegoat. Since the SPC is recognized as the principal agency in the formation of school policy, individual members of the legislature can remove any pressures from themselves by transferring requests to the SPC and informing their constituents that "little can be gained without SPC support anyway; that's where you'll have to exert your pressure."

Reducing Controversy on Public School Issues. Legislators know that although failure to enact satisfactory school legislation can hurt them politically, there is little to be gained by advocating changes in the school policy. "After all," one legislator said emphatically, "isn't everyone for the public schools? Who's against them? Everyone wants to be a friend of the schools."

Stated somewhat differently, the atmosphere surrounding education practically eliminates the public school issues from the *normal* flow of legislative business. There is little political currency (such as patronage appointments) for the ordinary legislator in being a "public school advocate." As a result, a common attitude found in the General Assembly is that members "just don't want to be involved with education." Another legislative leader commented wryly, "If the SPC wants to handle education, let it do it. It takes the heat off us and what can one get out of it anyway?"

In fact, in the eyes of most legislators, there are few reasons against permitting the SPC to continue handling the major school problems. Since it is doubtful that anyone would gain and more likely that everyone would lose in any prolonged conflict over public school policy, the SPC performs a vital service for the General Assembly by reducing the probabilities of political fights over education.

Moreover, long habituation to SPC decisions produces a strong disposition to accept the agency's views on pending school matters. The bits and pieces of information collected for this study make this argument more than merely plausible. Although speaking in a much broader context than we do here, V. O. Key makes the point: "The experience of agreement . . . may enlarge the capacity to do so."[1]

---

[1] V. O. Key, Jr., *Public Opinion and American Democracy* (New York: Alfred A. Knopf; 1961), p. 48.

The SPC and the Governor

In Illinois the governor plays a predominant role in virtually all important public decisions.[2] Two recent students of Illinois politics point out:

The governor of Illinois, whether or not his party controls the legislature, has more opportunity to influence legislative action than any other outside source. The governor is the only nonmember of the legislature with a continuous and direct access to the General Assembly, access starting with a biennial message that the constitution directs him to submit to the legislature at the convening of each session, with regularly scheduled meetings with legislative leaders of both houses. The governor is required to and does submit an executive budget containing a statement of expected revenues and expenditures for the biennium. Thereby, he has a further control over the state purse to supplement his item veto power over money bills. Finally, he is head of the political power that controls the bulk of the patronage, and he can be personal dispenser of patronage if he so chooses.[3]

Since all of these gubernatorial powers can affect public school policy, the SPC proceeds cautiously with each incumbent, regardless of his party affiliation.

Influence of State Chief Executive. The governor's influence on the SPC has been apparent from the time it was established. Five members of the first SPC were gubernatorial appointees. In addition, the director of finance, who serves as an *ex officio* member of the commission, is a gubernatorial appointee. For the first several commissions (until 1953 when the legislative membership was increased to ten), the six appointees of the governor were equal in number to the representatives of the General Assembly.

[2] The Illinois governor, in contrast to his counterpart in Missouri, serves a four-year term and may seek reëlection an unlimited number of times. In the years since the creation of the SPC, the governorship has been held by one Republican (Stratton, 1953-1961) and two Democrats (Stevenson, 1949-1953, and the present Governor Kerner, 1961-   ).

[3] Gilbert Y. Steiner and Samuel K. Gove, *Legislative Politics in Illinois* (Urbana: University of Illinois Press; 1960), p. 33.

Gubernatorial appointees provide the governor with direct access to internal negotiations and developments. "The governor's appointing power is really his most significant function relating to our work," is the way one Senate member viewed the relationship. Another believed that the agency's close working relationship with the governor is attributable to the "outstanding appointments" which the governors have made to this commission.[4]

The governor's power to influence SPC deliberations extends far beyond any gains he might have made from his appointive power. With his support, the SPC is a key agency; without such support, it probably would have little impact. Why? What gives the governor such life and death power? First, his veto power is virtually absolute. Steiner and Gove have stressed this:

The veto power is of critical importance in Illinois legislative policy-making because of the finality of gubernatorial disapproval. Even an attempt to override a veto is a rarity; only three vetoes have been overridden since the adoption of the constitution of 1870 . . . The relatively equal party division in the Illinois House of Representatives, a result of the cumulative voting system, makes it virtually impossible to obtain sufficient votes in the House to override the governor's veto on those rare occasions when the legislature is in session to receive a veto message . . . The Illinois constitution requires the affirmative votes of two-thirds of the members elected to each house to override a veto.[5]

The General Assembly usually completes most of its work during the final weeks of the session; a veto by the governor is therefore final because normally the legislature has adjourned by the time it takes place.

SPC members are more fearful of the governor's veto power than of General Assembly disapproval. As one of the gubernatorial appointees expressed it:

---

[4] Also, according to this member, "the outstanding qualities of these appointees has helped this agency to produce the truly needed solutions to education's problems. This fact has made the SPC a very successful agency."

[5] Steiner and Gove, *op. cit.,* pp. 33-34.

Usually the SPC recommendations meet with great success in the legislature . . . Generally, however, the SPC does not fear defeat of its recommendations by the state legislature as much as it fears the veto of the governor. This fear is based on two facts. One, the SPC has a built-in lobby in the legislature—the legislative members of the Commission; no such situation exists with the governor. Two, past performances show that a governor's veto of SPC recommendations comes more frequently than a defeat in the legislature.

This same member later added: "We must always consider the governor's opinions since his real significance comes in that he can, and on occasion does, veto recommendations after they've been passed by the legislature."

Moreover, an Illinois governor, like the governor in Missouri, controls the state's purse strings. The governor and the director of finance (a gubernatorial appointee and an *ex officio* member of the SPC) prepare the state's budget and recommend the tax program that is necessary to finance it. Public school expenditures constitute approximately 20 percent of the total state budget. Since the legislature seldom departs drastically from the governor's fiscal program, it would be virtually meaningless for the SPC not to negotiate on this level. Such negotiations are normally conducted through the director of finance who attends the SPC meetings and plays the role of the governor's personal representative. This does not mean, of course, that other members do not contact the governor about school matters. They frequently do. But it is the responsibility of the director, along with the commission chairman, to keep both the SPC and the governor fully informed as to the other's views and current policies.

More specifically, the usual procedure in financial affairs is for the commission to make a preliminary estimate of the revenue needed for the state's public schools during the forthcoming biennium. This temporary report is then presented by the director of finance and other SPC leaders to the governor, who in turn discusses it with his financial advisers. The governor then informs the commission of the state's total financial picture and how the estimated school expenditures fit in with the entire budget situation. The commission must often, of course, revise its original estimates in view of the total budget. Otherwise, as was the case with the 1959 sales tax increase, methods are found by which the preliminary estimates of the commission can be accepted. Here, as in other areas, the SPC and governor attempt to eliminate any possible areas of disagreement before the commission makes a recommendation to the General Assembly.

The necessity for a close relationship between the governor and the SPC is best illustrated by describing what happens when communication between them breaks down. The 1959 legislative battle to increase the equalization level is an excellent example of one of the few times that this has happened since the SPC was established. When the SPC and the governor failed to agree on a public school recommendation concerned with finance, the result was controversy and chaos. In this instance, indecision on the part of the state superintendent introduced a further complication. In fact, the controversy reached such a peak that the SPC was almost wrecked as an effective agency.

The facts were these. The March 1959 report of the SPC recommended an increase in the equalization level "from $200 to not less than $245 per pupil in average daily attendance." According to the commission members, the decision was agreed upon in the SPC by a bipartisan vote, although a few Democratic members had been in favor of raising the figure to $262. Before the report was published, the state superintendent, apparently in the hopes of gaining a political advantage before the governor could make the same recommendation, publicly declared that Illinois could afford a figure of $248 per pupil. The Republican governor, influenced by the passage of a sales tax increase and by the statement of the Democratic superintendent, announced he would support a $250 equalization level. The majority of SPC members, hoping to achieve the highest level possible without stirring up a controversy within the legislature, stuck with the $245 figure, although "we would have been happy to take the $250 figure," commented one member. But by the time the SPC issued its formal recommendations, the political battle had already begun, and "the controversy which the SPC had hoped to avoid was well on its way."

Legislative leaders of both political parties immediately entered the battle. The Republican leadership supported the governor's position. On the other side, the Democrats on the SPC, enthusiastically supported by their party's leaders, decided to push for the $262 figure that had been killed previously in SPC deliberations. A stalemate ensued almost immediately. The House of Representatives, with a Democratic majority claiming "the children of Illinois deserve it," passed a bill providing for the $262 figure in almost a straight party-line vote. The Senate, controlled by a Republican majority, acted differently. Senate Republican leaders claimed that "the state just didn't have the money to support that high a level of state aid," and passed instead an act calling for $250 per pupil. At this point, the governor left the country for a trip with a group of governors to parts of Europe and Asia.

On the night before the legislature adjourned, a conference committee composed almost entirely of SPC members finally reached a compromise calling for a figure of $252 per pupil. Republicans claimed that the compromise was "a face-saving device" for the Democrats which actually gave them no real political advantage. "The $262 figure would have surely been vetoed, and the level would have reverted to $200. The $252 figure was as far as the state could go within the limitations of its funds." [6] A Democratic leader explained: "We realized our $262 figure was really out of

[6] Quoted in an interview with a Republican leader of the Senate.

line and were shooting for $255. By getting the Republicans to raise their figure to $252, we felt we had accomplished a great deal." Thus, as is so often the case in politics, both sides claimed victory.

But in fact the consensus that had existed in the determining of education policy had been upset, first by a refusal of the governor to go along with the SPC on a financial recommendation, and second by the resultant interjection of partisan conflict into the making of school policy. Partisan division developed almost immediately and the SPC and its work was shoved out of the picture until the final hours when a conference committee was appointed that included SPC members. After the action was over, all agreed that the SPC could not survive many more onslaughts such as this; but perhaps of even greater importance, the leaders of both parties indicated that they had learned a real lesson. They expressed the opinion that there was little political advantage in getting involved in education issues and that it made much more sense to allow the SPC "to take care of such problems."

An additional power of the governor should be mentioned here: namely, his control over approximately 20,000 state positions. The patronage at his disposal gives him a bargaining position which one legislator described as making it possible for him "to gain the support of any legislator who might have earlier differed with his position."

Another legislator went even further: "Ordinarily, any governor who so desires can dominate the legislature. . . . Anytime the governor wants something, he can get it. The governor controls 20,000 jobs; anytime he needs a vote bad enough, he can go to a legislator of either party and offer three, four, or however many is necessary in exchange for his vote." The disposition of patronage is especially important to the downstate legislators who consider it imperative to their electoral success. "We *have* to have it to win," pointed out one legislator.

Insuring Gubernatorial Support. To insure gubernatorial support, the SPC has adopted the self-image of the governor's research staff on public school problems. The information that the SPC compiles or collects is as a matter of procedure fed directly to the governor and his staff. It would be most difficult for the governor to duplicate or replace this service on his own, and the State Office and the major interests are both so directly concerned that their objectivity might be questioned. The years of educational experience represented on the SPC, along with the knowledge the members have of political practicalities, have since its inception provided all of the governors with a research staff upon whose recommendations they can safely rely. "The governor shares the General Assembly's respect for the SPC," a commission member commented. "The almost total absence of conflict between the governor and the SPC indicates the degree to which the SPC has gained acceptance by the state's chief executive, no matter who holds this position."

From the governor's vantage point, the SPC is strengthened by the strong *bipartisan* support it receives for all of its proposals. Moreover, it is politically inadvisable for a governor to disapprove measures that have received nearly unanimous support in the General Assembly.

It is also significant that the governor appoints six members of the commission. Although the majority of these appointments are not rewards for political work and are in fact dictated to a large extent by the major organized education interests, it remains true that these members owe their appointment to the governor. Obviously, it would also be politically inadvisable for a governor to oppose with any frequency the recommendations made by a commission at least partially composed of his own appointees.

Another reason underlying gubernatorial backing for SPC findings is that its actions are invariably endorsed and supported by the major education interests. The governor, like the legislators, is a political official; he is as anxious not to acquire new enemies as he is to hold old allies. "No governor would want to alienate the public school people; constant bickerings with the SPC would inevitably have this result," commented one education representive. Yet he is by no means their tool. "The two [the governor and the SPC] have learned to live and work together; nobody gets hurt this way."

The SPC apparently fully understands and appreciates the governor's strong institutional position in the state and therefore makes special efforts to accommodate its policies to his. The SPC advises the governor as to what the problems of education are, which can be solved, how best they can be solved, what is politically possible, and how the governor can use his influence to the best possible advantage to assure passage of these recommendations. The governor, meanwhile, as the state's most powerful political official, relays his opinions, ideas, and recommendations to the SPC, where they are carefully considered—particularly in the area of finance. In essence, this is the relationship between the two: the governor depends on the SPC and the SPC will not act, in fact cannot act, without the governor's support. The two "live well together," and each respects the other's role. Mutual cooperation between the chief executive and the SPC, strengthened by mutual respect, has guaranteed general agreement between the two. It thus fits them into the general pattern of achieving maximum consensus from all parties to the decisions.[7]

[7] With almost tedious regularity, each interviewee talked of the reliance of the governor and the SPC on each other. "Usually the chairman and/or some of the other leaders of the commission talk over each of the recommendations with the governor," one SPC member said. "This is especially true in the case of all recommendations concerned with money matters; it is imperative to see how far the finances of the state will permit us to do what we want to do. We always did this with Governor Stratton just before we held our final meeting, so if it was necessary to change our plans to stay within his limit, we could do it." A senatorial member gave this opinion: "The governor relies on us. We serve as his education advisors. Of course I should imagine that this would depend somewhat upon the

THE STATE SUPERINTENDENT AND
OFFICE OF PUBLIC INSTRUCTION

Among students of public administration and professional education the office that is criticized most frequently and perhaps is least understood is that of the chief state school officer. The areas of his operations with which the majority of school people are most familiar include such functions as school accreditation, teacher certification, building inspection, and related supervisory functions. His role in the policy-making process is another matter, however. It is in this regard that there seems to be little understanding. In Missouri, we found the chief state school officer's role to be nominal or at least indirect and not highly visible. In Illinois, the chief state school officer plays a different role, a role based on the peculiarities of his own state. It should prove useful to explore briefly the substantial content of this role as it has developed in this state.

The state superintendent is elected in a state-wide partisan election and heads an office staffed largely with patronage appointees.[8] The close and direct involvement of the state superintendent (and of the State Office) with partisan politics has significantly restricted his role in public school matters.

In the chaos which existed in the area of education prior to the creation of the SPC, the superintendent, as the elected leader of the state's educational system, was frequently suggested as the man to provide the leadership necessary to bring together the various education groups into a unified force. In fact, several individuals elected to

---

individual governor but this has been true in the case of all recommendations concerned in any way with money matters."

[8] Professional educators now hold most of the top administrative positions, but this is a relatively recent phenomenon. All clerical appointees must be cleared by the state committee of the party of which the state superintendent is a member and are regarded as patronage appointees.

this position attempted to carry out this role.[9] None of their efforts filled the leadership vacuum. The inability of the state superintendents to provide leadership, of course, left the way open for the establishment of the SPC. Today, the superintendent's political role is determined almost entirely by his relationships with this commission.

When the SPC was established, the state superintendent was included as an *ex officio* member; he has been included ever since. Precisely what is his role? How significant is it? What relations exist between the state superintendent and the other members of the SPC?

The inclusion of the state superintendent as a member of the SPC has given the State Office of Public Instruction a more respectable façade than ever before but probably has not changed its basic character. Although the state superintendent's role is largely that of an adviser to the commission, his position as chief of the state's education administrative office makes him a valuable and necessary participant in the decision-making process. Coöperation between the State Office and the SPC appears to be an important goal of both agencies and one that has been largely achieved.[1]

[9] One state superintendent, for example, called state-wide conferences at which the leading educational administrators were represented to discuss the problems of the public schools and to seek proposals for their solution.

[1] One SPC member described the relationship in the following manner: "The SPC influences the thinking of the state superintendent and *vice versa*. Off hand, I can remember no instance where the SPC recommended anything to which the superintendent was openly opposed; however, I would not go so far as to say that the SPC accepts *everything* which the superintendent proposes." A legislative member described the superintendent's role similarly: "As a member of the SPC, he has a pretty influential role. For example, the state superintendent has one advisor who deals with nothing else but transportation of students; when an issue concerning transportation arises, of course we listen to his advice; who could be better qualified to advise us on something like that? I would say that only on very rare occasions would the SPC recommend something to which the superintendent was openly against."

A legislative veteran pointed out that a portion of each SPC meeting is devoted to hearing proposals of the state superintendent. "We usually give special consideration to these since we realize the work that has gone into them. We very seldom turn down anything he's supporting. We also make

The state superintendent offers perhaps more proposals to the SPC than any other member. A significant number of these are of a more or less routine nature, which would suggest that the superintendent has little power of his own to influence legislative decisions. Most of his proposals are approved by the SPC, and of those that are rejected, many are brought before the SPC later. In 1961, for example, while the SPC accepted almost without question the majority of the proposals the superintendent advanced, it refused to consider his one major suggestion, namely, to establish a commission to study vocational and technical education. The superintendent has indicated that he intends to bring the matter before the SPC again in 1962 or 1963. In an atmosphere of apparent mutual respect, the superintendent makes available to the commission all facilities of his administrative office to assist SPC members.

In assessing his own role in the SPC, the present superintendent, George Wilkins, Democrat, admits that he is greatly handicapped by the "political nature" of his office and by the fact that he is thought to head a patronage-oriented, partisan-controlled administrative department. He points out that even his close political associates, the people who helped to elect him, look to the SPC rather than to the superintendent's office for guidance in education matters. This is especially true if the office is held by a downstate Democrat. As a member of a state-wide party, the Democratic candidate for state superintendent is often the "place on the ticket" offered to the downstate interests by the Chicago-controlled state machine. According to one education interest group leader, educators regard the superintendent as a "successful politician" rather than an educative statesman. "Education and overt politics just don't mix!"

The representatives of education interests who are SPC members view the state superintendency as a job for "some

use of the research staff of the State Office. I would say the relations between our commission and his office are very harmonious."

politically ambitious party worker who, once elected, would be in a position to strengthen his role in the state political arena." Because of his control over large numbers of jobs, he is able to bargain with his legislative colleagues if he wishes to enhance his office (and, therefore, his own role) by gaining larger appropriations, larger staffs, and more significant duties. Such attempts are often hindered, however, by two factors: namely, the personality of the individual holding the position and the belief that actually the office of state superintendent is not and should not be a strong party office. The view that the State Office should be kept out of partisan politics is shared by every interest group concerned with education. Obviously, legislators are aware of this. Increasing the appropriations, staff members, and responsibility of an office which the most concerned interests already distrust would result in political discomfort for every legislator who supported such measures.

Membership on the SPC tends to blur somewhat the superintendent's image as a partisan official and in this way helps him to be more influential. Actually it gives him an opportunity for a larger role in the decision-making processes of education than he might have if he were forced to go it alone. The commission provides him with a protective shield which permits him greater flexibility. Many of the suggestions which have been adopted and supported by the SPC and eventually accepted without controversy by the legislature and governor would probably have met with great difficulty (had they ever been proposed) if introduced in the General Assembly merely as "a recommendation of the state superintendent."

On the other hand, SPC membership means that most of his recommendations eventually reach the legislature via the SPC. The result is the obvious one: the credit goes to the SPC—not to the superintendent. This gives him little ammunition for the next election. The lack of this type of political currency, therefore, makes it necessary for him to strengthen his political connections with his most available weapon, patronage, which, in turn, reinforces his negative image as a political official. As the representative of one education interest group said: "An elected superintendent will always be caught in a vicious circle and there is very little that we can do about it."

In sum, the harmony and coöperation that exist between the SPC and the state superintendent result largely from the superintendent's recognition that the SPC is the key decision-making agency in education and that his office will become largely a "paper affair" if he chooses to ignore the SPC or attempt to by-pass it.

THE SPC AND THE ORGANIZED EDUCATION GROUPS

Illinois, unlike Missouri, has no *one* group that speaks for all the school interests, although the Illinois Education Association clearly plays the major role in the articulation of new proposals. The IEA consists of more than 63,000 members and is divided into twenty-one regional divisions and scores of local sections. Its principal governing agents are a representative assembly held annually, a board of directors elected by the assembly, and three governing committees elected by the divisions.[2] The Association has a full-time staff in the state capitol, a large part of which devotes full-time to pending legislative matters. The IEA's principal legislative agent is a twenty-one member legislative committee elected by the twenty-one regional divisions. This group, each year, formulates the legislative program, submits it to its own representative assembly for approval or amendments, and then proceeds before each session of the legislature to work out the details of its position and to devise the strategy it will employ.

Once the program of the IEA is determined, it is pre-

[2] An association of local superintendents does exist but is considered as a part of the IEA. There is no distinction between teachers and administrators in the membership.

sented to the SPC, both in open hearings and in a written report given to each member. From that time on, the chairman of the legislative committee is in frequent contact with individual members of the SPC. However, IEA's major contact with SPC has always been and remains the IEA's own representative on the commission, Lester Grimm. As a result, the SPC has stayed largely within the framework of the IEA program, and the IEA has adjusted its program to meet conditions set by the SPC. An official of the IEA remarked that he could "think of no time that we have been in direct conflict with the SPC. The SPC has pretty well attempted to meet our demands, and we have attempted to meet the conditions laid down by the SPC. There is great mutual respect because of our constant research and because the SPC has been objective and nonpartisan."

The IEA of course does not confine all of its legislative activities to its support of the SPC, for the commission does not deal *formally* with the whole gamut of education policy-making. For example, the IEA has close working relationships with the state's Pension Laws Commission which handles many matters pertaining to teacher retirement. To carry out these functions, the IEA has found it necessary to extend its contacts beyond SPC legislative members and thus occasionally provides specific services to individual legislators concerned with school needs. The IEA's staff has written speeches for legislators, and though not very often, like the MSTA in Missouri, serves as a research staff for the House and Senate education committees, as well as for the individual legislators.

In terms of the resources of influence, the IEA, according to one official, feels that its greatest asset "is its facts and figures rather than its large membership. Our program is so carefully thought out that when we present it, it is difficult to oppose. We have the full faith and confidence of the legislature and the governor as to the authenticity of our facts."

The IEA, though equipped to do so, does not rely extensively on grass-roots pressure because, as an IEA official put it, "ordinarily, we do not find it necessary. Usually, it's a matter of contacting legislators; it's merely routine." For those occasions when grass-roots pressure is thought to be necessary, the Association has created a system of contacts with influential local members who, in turn, will contact their state representatives. Another strategy of the IEA's is to present petitions to the governor indicating public support for a measure it favors.[3] But in final analysis, the IEA's avenue to state policy is the SPC, where it is formally represented; it provides the structure for the articulation of demands and negotiation of agreement.

A second group concerned directly with school policies is the Illinois Federation of Teachers. This group is composed of approximately 13,000 members, of which over 7,000 are in the Chicago area. The group's principal concern is with matters pertaining to teacher welfare, and it has not been identified with the SPC in the way other major interests have. Legislative leaders and officials of the SPC do not regard the IFT as a powerful interest. It is a relatively small group in comparison with the IEA; it has no central office and only limited research facilities. Moreover, because of its affiliation with labor and because the bulk of its membership is centered in the Chicago area, the IFT is viewed with suspicion by downstate legislators of both parties.

The IFT has not had a close relationship with the IEA, which is similar to what we found in Missouri.[4] The two

[3] In 1959 the IEA, in coöperation with the Congress of Parents and Teachers, the Illinois Association of School Boards, and other organized interests, conducted a four-month public relations program which resulted in the collection of over 1,000,000 signatures which were presented to Governor Stratten in support of a one-half cent increase in the sales tax. As a result of these petitions, the governor supported the tax increase and the legislature subsequently accepted it.

[4] In the following chapter we will discuss in connection with Michigan interests some of the reasons why this relationship is strained. The political impotence of the teachers unions in Illinois and Missouri makes such a discussion less relevant in Chapters 2 and 3.

groups neither cooperate with each other very often nor agree on the facts. On at least one occasion in 1961, the IEA felt it necessary to circulate among its members and friends comments on a legislative report of the IFT which its secretary, Paul E. Woods, had prepared. The IEA's covering letter stated: "This report [the legislative report of the IFT] contains so many errors, substantial and otherwise, that it is deemed necessary to supply you with a 'comment' or 'comments' on each item. In this way misunderstandings and consequent erroneous actions may be avoided." [5] The IEA officials feel that the "teachers union" is concerned only with expanding its membership, whereas IFT officials feel that the state's other education interests have not shown sufficient concern for teacher welfare.

The State Association of School Boards plays a more active and direct role in Illinois than does its counterpart in Missouri. It is widely acknowledged that this group is one of the most effective and powerful forces in public education. Founded in 1913, the Association presently represents over 70 percent of the school boards which govern over 95 percent of the state's pupils. The Association states as its objectives the study of education problems and the furnishing of the General Assembly and other public officers with information pertaining to education proposals. It maintains a full-time staff in the state capitol for these purposes.

The IASB does not regard itself as an innovator in the education field. It does not ordinarily formulate specific proposals, nor does it conduct elaborate research designed to bring about major changes in school policy.[6] As one of the

[5] Wayne Stoneking, Research Associate, Illinois Education Association, in mimeographed letter circulated by the IEA, dated October 28, 1961.

[6] The executive director of the IASB described his position and that of his association in the decision-making process in the following manner:

At that time the SPC was first created, I, as Executive Director of the state's association of local school boards, was invited to attend as an advisor all meetings and hearings of this Commission; I have been so invited ever since . . . When our association has a proposal or suggested program we would like to see enacted, we of course do *not* officials explained: "We rely primarily on the IEA, State Office, and the SPC to formulate policies. Our role is largely a supportive one." [7] In essence, however, the IASB's political role, much the same as the IEA's, is carried on through its representation on the SPC.

The state's largest education interest, the Illinois Congress of Parents and Teachers, plays only a nominal role in most policy decisions. The role of this organization, which claims approximately 700,000 members organized into 144 councils and 2,476 local PTA groups, has been largely determined by its relationships with the IEA. The group is in close contact with IEA officials and usually, although not invariably, will support attempts to bring grass-roots pressure on the legislature and governor. The PTA also enthusiastically supports the SPC, and its representatives indicate that they have complete confidence in this agency's capacity to meet the state's school problems.

Thus far relatively little mention has been made of the influence relationship between the Chicago public school system and the state's policy-making processes, procedures, and machinery, although we did point out a little bit about the nature of Chicago's representation on the SPC. A brief account of this relationship seems warranted at this time.

The role of the state's largest school system, which is itself

---

draft the bill and present it to the legislature ourselves. We communicate with the SPC on all things we think need attention; we present to them our facts and any other advice we think necessary. Only if the SPC approves of it does a proposal of ours end up on the floor of the legislature . . . Before the SPC, we had to go directly to the General Assembly with our plans, try to convince each legislator of their merits, and hope we could get the needed votes. Now, we convince the SPC members our ideas are sound . . . We never, and would never, by-pass the SPC by going directly to the General Assembly . . . That's the way to lose friends and influence. If I disagree with something the SPC is considering, I go directly to one of its leaders and talk to him about it. If they still can't see my side of it, the matter rests. I don't believe in trying to knife them in the back.

[7] This Association was represented, however, at meetings conducted throughout 1962 of a committee studying the problems and proposals of legislation on teacher certification.

a separate identifiable interest, is in many respects comparable to the role of St. Louis and Kansas City school systems in Missouri, recognizing that there are some important deviations in detail. The Chicago school system, like those in St. Louis and Kansas, has over the years been delegated considerable local autonomy and is presently the subject of considerable separate or special provisions, particularly in such areas as structural arrangements, taxing power, pupil transportation, etc. These separate delegations of authority and special provisions are protected and negotiated by a bloc of Cook County legislators, mostly Democrats, who are controlled by the Cook County Democratic machine. It is this dependence on Chicago legislators that partially accounts for the Cook County Democrats' influence on Chicago school decisions. More precisely, the Cook County delegation becomes the bargaining agent and negotiates with downstate delegations on matters affecting Chicago's schools. Although we did not explore this relationship in detail as we did in Missouri, it seems safe to say that the influence of the Chicago school system is substantial (though not a fixed quantity) whenever the Cook County delegation does its bidding.

On matters of *state-wide application,* many of which vitally affect Chicago, the Chicago school men seldom directly intervene or initiate proposals. Rather, the essence of that relationship seems to be that Chicago school men keep their "finger" on state-wide issues by having a Chicago legislator (who, of course, is backed by the Cook County delegation) and one of their own school board members on the SPC. Unfortunately, our data allow only these few brief general statements about this relationship, which involves numerous subtleties and nuances. But if we were forced to define the relationship as succinctly as possible, we would say that Chicago school men have concluded a treaty with the state government, and that the principal provision of the treaty is that in return for special legislation and the protection of its special interests, the Chicago public school system will stay clear of or support only upon request school measures affecting the remainder of, or the entire, state.

In sum, the major education interests in Illinois, with the exception of the IFT, have enthusiastically endorsed and supported the SPC. In the interviews, SPC members were fully aware of the importance of maintaining the active and enthusiastic support of the organized interests primarily concerned with the development of public school policy. "We attempt to use every avenue possible to insure that our work is consistent with what the various groups want and need. We seek their advice, and we keep them informed of what is going on at all times so that when recommendations are made, we can count on them. That is why there is never any organized opposition to anything recommended by the SPC." [8] Thus, the SPC has provided an arena in which the various and sometimes conflicting aims of organized groups can be compromised or decided upon, where a common program can be formed.[9]

It becomes evident from this analysis that the politics of public school decision-making finds expression through an agency unlike that described in the conventional discussions of the instruments of state government. The specialized role and function of the SPC in Illinois illustrates the proposition that states as separate entities develop structures that reflect local cleavages, customs, and traditions, and that these very structures may shape the content of public policy.

[8] Quoted from an interview with an SPC official.

[9] The groups discussed above do not, of course, constitute all of the organizations concerned with state policies. The discussion has been restricted to those interests that are continuously and actively concerned with major state policies affecting the public schools. The Illinois Agricultural Association, for example, though represented on the SPC by one of its officials, no longer plays as active a role in state politics as it did prior to the organization of local school districts.

CHAPTER IV

⚜ ⚜ ⚜ ⚜

Michigan:
The Lack of Consensus

Explaining how major public school issues are decided—or not decided—in Michigan is much more difficult than it is for either Illinois or Missouri. In the latter two states, formulas have been developed to achieve consensus. The MSTA in Missouri, representing virtually all of the claimants, adjusts its demands each year to what the other participants in the decisions will accept, and consequently most of its recommendations are adopted. Similarly, in Illinois the School Problems Commission, combining the stated goals of the professional educators with a recognition of political realities is able to formulate proposals acceptable to all elements within the legislature, as well as the governor. Although it is true that a whole series of elaborate negotiations, clearances, and strategies are necessary to achieve consensus on education recommendations in these two states, each of them presents a much simpler picture than Michigan, where there is no group that has come to represent the "best thinking possible to solve the state's education problems."

In Michigan there is no continuous or regular pattern of decision-making, or at least none that is easily visible. The final outcome of recommendations cannot be safely predicted as it can much of the time in Illinois and Missouri. That is, there is no established process in Michigan to eliminate or modify the factors that cause conflict over education issues. Does this mean, then, that Michigan has a "better" or "worse" record than Illinois or Missouri? Does it mean that there is never a consensus in Michigan, or that there will invariably be conflict and unpredictability in the Michigan scheme of things? The absence of a clear, visible pattern of decision-making in Michigan does not necessarily imply that the results achieved are less impressive than those in other states or that it is impossible to bring about wide acceptance of a policy proposal or series of proposals. But each year a new pattern emerges with the outcome in doubt until final decisions are reached.

The factors that make Michigan contrast so sharply with the two other states are easily identified but not easily explained. First, the education groups that make demands on the legislature are no longer unified. Second, the failure to adopt a state-wide school district reorganization plan immediately after World War II has resulted in a situation where the wealthy and poorer districts display a considerable self-consciousness over their conflicting interests, and these divisions are reflected and articulated within the legislature when school district reorganization or state aid is the issue. Third, there is a longstanding cleavage between two ideologically oriented parties. Since one party controls the governor's office and the other controls the state legislature (particularly the Senate), and since they disagree widely over the extent and method of financing state services, their division has caused education "to divide along political lines." Finally, it should be mentioned that there is a division between the proponents of public schools and the protectors of the parochial and private schools. This division seems to be based more on economic than religious grounds, but in any event it is largely latent at present.

·   ·   ·

In this chapter we will first identify the various groups that make claims on the state concerning education and analyze the potential resources of influence of each. Secondly, we will discuss the political context in which the education interests must operate and their relationships with the governor and the state legislature. Thirdly, we will examine two issues, one involving state aid and the other involving reorganization of school districts, to determine how the aforementioned factors—lack of unity among education interests, wealthy *vs.* poor districts, and partisanship—have been more disruptive in this state than they have been in either Illinois or Missouri. The major question this chapter attempts to answer is why a clear decision-making pattern was not operative in Michigan.

EDUCATION INTEREST GROUPS

"I was elected to the Senate Education Committee to keep those bastards in education in line." This remark, made by a ranking member of the Senate Education Committee of the 1961 Michigan Legislature, indicates more than just his personal feelings toward public school interests; it captures the essence of the reaction of many legislators to the demands made by public school interests in Michigan.

During the past decade the groups advocating major changes in public school policy in this state have faced a legislature that was sometimes hostile, sometimes indifferent, and only occasionally sympathetic to their demands. In the face of rather formidable obstacles, the public school interests have sought, through various means, to create an alliance capable of obtaining the legislation they want. The nature of the alliance that has evolved and the potential and actual influence of each group is the focus of the study of state politics and the public schools in Michigan.

Michigan has no dominant spokesman for the public

schools. It has no governmental agency analogous to the School Problems Commission in Illinois and no group which has influence comparable to that experienced by the Missouri State Teachers Association. Nor does Michigan have a state board to back policy proposals or decisions with prestigious lay support. Rather, in Michigan, demands for changes in public school policy are voiced by an array of groups that are seldom in complete agreement but which sometimes join together to push for favorable action on a particular issue. Frequently, their approach and their views as to what issues should be given highest priority differ sharply.

There have been efforts to unite the education interests behind one common authoritative spokesman. The superintendent of public instruction, seeking a broad base for the development and support of his education program, attempts to unify the various groups through an Educational Council, composed of representatives from each public school interest. The council, which meets weekly throughout the year to consider major education issues, has, for reasons which will be discussed later, enjoyed only limited success. To a large extent the various participant groups still follow their own individual programs, regardless of the decisions reached within the council.

There are two types of groups that make active demands for public school legislation in Michigan. (We did not make this distinction in Illinois and Missouri because it appeared less relevant to a meaningful discussion of school politics in those states.) In the first category are the groups whose members have *a direct tangible stake* in the legislative decisions on education questions and which *make specific demands* upon the various decision-makers. In this category the major groups are the Michigan Education Association (MEA), the Michigan Association of School Administrators (MASA), the Michigan Association of County School Administrators (MACSA), the Michigan Federation of Teachers (MFT), and the Michigan Association of School Boards (MASB).

We call the second type of group a supportive group. A supportive group has *a major interest* in education policy, but either its members are normally not directly employed by public schools or the organization does not consider itself a spokesman for the professionals. Groups of this type make fewer specific demands upon the decision-makers and do not usually initiate policy proposals, although they may exert considerable influence on the decisions reached. The significant group that falls in this category is the Michigan Congress of Parents and Teachers Associations (PTA).

THE MICHIGAN EDUCATION ASSOCIATION

Of the major professional education groups with a direct interest in public school legislation, one of the most influential is the Michigan Education Association. At one time, we were told, this group virtually monopolized the policy articulation process, and operated in a manner not dissimilar to the MSTA in Missouri. But the rise of separate and competitive interests within the education establishment has significantly curbed its influence. Yet with its 58,000 members comprising 85 to 90 percent of all public school professionals in Michigan, the MEA comes closest to representing all phases of the public schools. It operates under the assumption that the political process holds the key to the ends it seeks. Its major resource is its possession of information about school issues and its ability to supply this information to decision-makers. Only rarely does the MEA rely upon the mobilization of its membership to affect political decisions. It conducts substantial research and transmits its findings to the legislature through distribution of its weekly, biweekly, and monthly publications. Its representatives testify before legislative committees and meet privately with legislators and representatives of the governor's office. The association's legislative representative, Dick Adams, is always available to supply information to inquiring legislators. The MEA also provides legislators with such services as research reports, briefing papers on education questions, and technical assistance in drafting bills.

An example of the type of service MEA supplies to the legislature is the information the association provided in 1961 on the proposed increase in state financial assistance to local school districts. The MEA had requested an eight percent improvement factor in the amount of state aid over the previous year. To support this request, MEA provided the legislators with figures indicating the condition of classrooms, income of teachers, increase in student population, financial condition of local districts—all information derived from their research which showed the need for the eight percent increase in state aid.

Legislators' comments in interviews showed that they frequently rely upon the MEA for information and that invariably they have found its data accurate and useful. Several legislators further indicated that they conceive of MEA as an informational service rather than as an education interest group. One said, "We don't think of Dick Adams [the MEA legislative representative] as a lobbyist; rather we think of him as a person who gives us good, reliable information on education questions." It would be misleading, however, to suggest that all legislative leaders view the MEA simply as a service-oriented group. In fact, a few felt that this group was the most prominent and visible lobby in the state. But this is not the general view. It minimizes the importance of information to the politician, who is in "continuous need of current information because he is at the mercy of the changes as they occur." The effect of information—or the lack of it—extends to a legislator's status with both his colleagues and his constituents. Information is significant to a legislator in two respects: it helps him, first, to arrive at what he considers the proper decision, and, second, to gauge the political consequences of alternative decisions.[1]

Although the majority of legislators interviewed were favorably disposed toward the MEA, two members were of a decidedly different opinion. The chairman of the Senate Education Committee, who regards himself as a conservative Republican, stated:

I don't look to any interest group in the state for information. I look instead to educators I know in various areas of the state. The MEA is the most powerful lobby in the state; most of the fellows [his legislature colleagues] rely on them but I don't. I don't because the MEA is partisan; I know it is not openly partisan *but* it is for spending more when we haven't got it and that is a partisan issue.

The chairman added that although he felt that most of the representatives of the MEA were Republican or "sympathetic to the Republican cause," most of the educators were not. "Republican Senators know that most of the educators in education groups are Democrats and of course this affects their decisions." Our impressionistic evidence does not, however, support the Senator's conclusions. In fact, we are inclined to suspect that most public school people are Republicans. What is significant for our purposes is that this was his perception of reality.

A Democratic legislator from Wayne County who is a ranking member of the House Education Committee felt that the MEA was "too aggressive" and that it was too biased to trust. He contended that it made very little difference whether educators were Republicans or Democrats, "that in fact they did not favor either party." He maintained

[1] Forced to make choices of consequence and to minimize serious disturbances in his established relationships, the legislator is constantly in need of relevant information. Access is likely to be available to groups somewhat in proportion to their ability to meet this need. David B. Truman, *The Governmental Process* (New York: Alfred A. Knopf; 1951), chapters XI and XII.

that the major problem in Michigan was to find a "meaningful criterion to measure school needs."

The MEA is self-conscious about its image. Its representatives say that the organization prefers to be regarded as an information service rather than as a political lobby. Political bargaining must be done outside the purview of the rank and file membership. The leadership considers expertise its most important single source of strength and likes to think of the association as furnishing significant information to the political leaders of the state at all times. The association leadership feels, for example, that the work of a full-time research person borrowed from the faculty of Michigan State University influenced education legislation during the 1960 legislative session. But organization representatives are aware that their services are regarded with suspicion. In their view, the Senate is more "hostile" or "unfavorably disposed" than the House, and they attribute this hostility largely to what the chairman of the Senate Education Committee suggested, namely, their "partisan image."

The MEA does not, of course, rely exclusively upon specific services to legislators in order to influence policy decisions. It makes a concerted effort to create a favorable climate of opinion in support of the public schools among both legislators and the general public. For example, all legislators, regardless of party, area, and voting records, receive a personal letter from the president of the MEA congratulating them for work they did on behalf of public education. Moreover, regional representatives of the association make personal contact with the legislators in their home constituencies. At the state capitol in Lansing, the MEA does a moderate amount of entertaining. It usually holds a joint dinner for the House and Senate Education Committee members each year, where it gives a thorough explanation of the important education issues confronting the state.

In the face of a legislative crisis, the MEA has attempted to activate its membership, to make them aware of the issues, and to stimulate them to contact their representatives. In some instances, the MEA has informed incumbent legislators that they would probably lose the support of many MEA members by unfavorable votes on key issues. On the whole, however, the MEA does not make any effort to gain legislative backing for its programs by threatening legislators with reprisals at the polls. In the interviews, legislators said that this is an important resource that the MEA has at its disposal, but all stated that MEA exerted little or no perceptible influence in this manner. In assessing the organization's influence potential, an MEA representative said:

We are successful as long as we remain nonpartisan. This has been difficult to do lately with the governor and legislature in a fight over how much money to spend. We want to spend more on schools and that makes us seem partisan. Our problem, then, is to prove that schools need the money, and information, not theories of government, is the only nonpolitical approach to this problem that will keep us from being drawn into a partisan battle.

The Michigan Association of School Administrators

If information is the major resource of the MEA, an influential membership is the most important resource of the Michigan Association of School Administrators (MASA). This group of 700 school administrators, representing 96 percent of the superintendents, assistant superintendents, and county superintendents in the state, is frequently cited by members of the House and Senate Education Committees as "potentially the most influential" education group in Michigan, although the organization has never fully realized its potential. All members of the House and Senate Education Committees contend that the strength of the MASA lies not in what services it provides for them, but rather in the *nature of its membership*. School superintendents, they point out, are respected members of their communities and are regarded as local authorities on education. Since they enjoy leadership positions in virtually every community in the state, local district superintendents generally find access to state legislators easier than do classroom teachers.

The MASA is a federated unit of the Michigan Education Association; the MEA is the parent organization, with MASA as a specialized subordinate organization within the MEA. As the MASA has grown in membership, however, it has tended to pull away from the MEA. The result is that the MEA is more teacher-oriented, while the MASA is concerned mainly with the needs and views of administrators. A basic reason for this development is that the MEA has been forced to compete more vigorously in this state with the teachers union movement. Such competition requires more active concern with teachers' welfare. This, in turn, tends to alienate school superintendents and school boards who are facing budgetary pressures. This separation, to the degree it is perceived by the legislators, has tended to place the MASA in a stronger bargaining position for the schools as a whole, whereas the MEA has become increasingly identified as the teacher-welfare bargaining agent. MASA officials tend to view the MEA in this manner. MEA, on the other hand, prefers to view the organizational relationship as it is formally established and considers the MASA as a subordinate, specialized agency.

Because the MASA leadership realizes that legislators see its strength in terms of its capacity or potential capacity to bring grass-roots pressure to bear upon them, MASA feels that the most potent weapon in its arsenal is its ability to persuade the local superintendents to support a piece of legislation by contacting their local senators and representatives at home. From the organization's vantage point, this type of action yields more impressive results than any services or entertainment it can provide for legislators while in Lansing. As a result, the MASA leadership encourages each local superintendent periodically to discuss the problems of

education with his legislators at home and to offer suggestions for solutions.

The MASA maintains contact with its local members
through its ten regional chairmen. Action plans initiated by
the State Legislative Committee of the association are transmitted to the local membership through the regional chairman. The committee uses this mechanism when it wants
local superintendents to act.

The effort of MASA officials following the 1961 legislative
session illustrates the importance MASA places on the influence of its local membership. That summer, "leadership
teams" were dispersed throughout the state for the purpose
of organizing local superintendents into "minuteman" units,
to be on call when the MASA leaders in Lansing send down
an action plan on a piece of legislation. The minutemen are
to keep in continuous contact with their individual legislators, and when the association's Lansing office sends out
an impulse, the minutemen are supposed to transmit it immediately to their legislators. MASA officials hope that ultimately these minutemen will meet periodically with their
legislators as a forum and will keep the pressure up throughout the year. According to the executive secretary, however,
MASA's greatest problem at the moment—and perhaps the
greatest problem of all the public school groups—is "getting
our own boys interested."

While the MASA leadership assiduously tries to cultivate
more political activism on the part of its membership, it
expends great effort to ensure that contacts with legislators
appear locally initiated. For example, when the MASA
joined the other major education groups in a crash effort to
get an increase in state financial aid during the 1961 session
of the legislature, the executive secretary, in a flyer to the
local superintendents, urged them "to get a carload of people to come to Lansing [to] take your representative out for
dinner and make the plea to give something for public edu-

cation." The local superintendents were instructed as follows: *"Don't tell the legislators you are coming at my suggestion or Max Cochran's* [the Department of Public Instruction's legislative representative]. *Indicate you are concerned about financial aid for your own school."*

Not all efforts of the MASA, of course, are directed through its local membership. Association officers have active personal contacts in Lansing. These contacts are maintained, to a large extent, for the purpose of keeping up to date on legislative activity. In addition, however, the leadership discusses the MASA position with the legislators, urging their support, as well as maintaining rapport with the other public school interest groups. Although MASA does not maintain elaborate research facilities, it does provide the legislators with substantive information, when requested, on pending legislation.

Even though the personal influence and contacts of its membership are the strongest assets of the MASA, this group is hesitant, save in its recent minuteman effort, to make full-scale use of these resources through more active political participation. The association states that it does not want its members characterized as politicians, but rather as educational statesmen. Several legislators cite the association's reluctance to use its full political potential as its major weakness. But MASA officials point out that full and continuous displays of strength might, in the long run, prove self-defeating. MASA officials contend that they cannot run to the membership every time they face a difficult or closely contested issue. The question they must constantly face, they say, is "Will the members respond?" And even if they do respond, "wouldn't the extensive use of power serve only to activate and consolidate opposing forces?"

The principal difference between this group and its counterparts in Illinois and Missouri is its insistence upon an independent status within the professional education establishment.

THE MICHIGAN ASSOCIATION OF
COUNTY SCHOOL ADMINISTRATORS

The Michigan Association of County School Administrators (MACSA) shares substantial common ground with MASA: both are affiliated with the MEA, and their memberships overlap. The county superintendent group, however, is on more tenuous ground than MASA or, probably, any other public school group in Michigan. The county school district in Michigan, as in other states, is now fighting for survival. With the expansion in the size and resources of local school districts, the county school district—whose function has traditionally been to assist marginal school districts—has experienced a diminution of responsibility in recent decades. The county school district today performs little more than a few housekeeping functions, such as taking the annual school census and collecting delinquent school taxes owed to school districts within the county. Its major substantive function—to furnish supervisory and consultative services to the local school district when requested—has dwindled in significance as the local districts have grown and developed their own supervisory and consultative staffs.

In recent years, the legislature has given county districts some new responsibilities. For example, they now are authorized to conduct cooperative programs among school districts within the county, area studies to analyze the educational conditions and needs within the county, and special education programs to bring training to children who are deaf, blind, crippled, defective in speech, mentally handicapped, or housebound. But these new functions have failed to enhance the status or insure the longevity of the county school district.

The strength of the Association of County School Administrators reflects the present condition of the county school district. The association, founded in 1924, realizes that it, too, is at the crossroads; it knows it must rebuild or perish.

MACSA has never exerted much influence at the state level; its activities have always been more county-directed. In recent years, however, because of the requirement of state action for reorganization of county districts, it has become a more active force at the state level. This contrasts sharply with what we found in Illinois and Missouri where comparable organizations had little or no concern with most state-wide policies. It has the endorsement of the other key education groups, but not their strong support. The association's access to the legislature is limited because each county district has a limited amount of patronage at its disposal. As one legislator put it, "This group has no bargaining power since county superintendents have no jobs that legislators could use to get support." In addition, even MACSA leaders contend that many of its own members have never been sure whether their primary allegiance should go to the County Administrators Association or to other professional education groups. In recent years, county school administrators have become increasingly involved in the MASA and the MEA. And recently the association longevity received another blow when the administrators from large counties split with the small county people to form their own group. Although MACSA still has over eighty percent of the county school administrators as members, these defections have hurt.

Realizing the portents of doom, the MACSA leadership has vigorously sought the passage of an intermediate school district bill to inject new life into the county school district. This bill, which we will examine presently, provides, among other things, for the consolidation of county school districts.

There have been difficulties in getting unanimous support for the bill from within the organization, however. County superintendents who fear losing their jobs in such a consolidation have voiced their opposition to legislative leaders. This internal dissension, coupled with the weak bargaining position of the group as a whole, has rendered the MACSA's efforts on behalf of this bill ineffectual.

The leaders of the MACSA have staked its entire survival on the proposal for reorganizing the county school districts. Without it, they claim, the association will continue to decline in strength. The real dilemma facing the MACSA leaders is that the major source of the group's weakness—a low level of cohesion—is aggravated by the bill on which the organization is staking its survival.

THE MICHIGAN FEDERATION OF TEACHERS

The fourth major education organization in the category of groups whose members have a direct interest in the outcome of decisions that affect public schools in Michigan is the Michigan Federation of Teachers (MFT). The "teachers' union" has approximately six thousand members and is affiliated with the American Federation of Teachers. The federation, its leaders assert, is proud to be identified with the labor movement and casts for itself the role of bargaining agent for the classroom teachers in their relations with the school administration. In terms of policy, it considers superintendents to be employers and thus on the other side. "The superintendents represent the administration, we represent the teachers." Federation leaders believe that many superintendents have failed to meet their responsibilities to the teacher. Although its leaders say the organization has many goals identical with those of the MEA, they firmly believe that only an organization composed of classroom teachers exclusively can properly represent the teachers.

MFT's close identification with labor has contradictory effects. On the one hand, it helps secure support for the MFT program from legislators sympathetic to organized labor, primarily Detroit and Wayne County Democratic legislators. This is its major source of strength. On the other hand, in a state where the division between the Democrats and

Republicans is ideological and is predicated on a corresponding split between urban labor interests and rural agricultural interests, the MFT relationship with urban-labor Democrats alienates outstate Republicans. Interviews with several key Republican legislators indicated that they found this group and its demands offensive. As one ranking House Republican put it, "I am highly offended by the federation's practice of calling teachers 'scabs.'"

MFT demands are occasionally inconsistent with and contrary to the position of other public school interests, in particular the interests of the superintendents and school board members. As an organization it poses a direct threat to the MEA since it competes for the membership of the classroom teachers. In fact, the National Education Association, MEA's parent group, views the teachers union movement as a major threat and has encouraged all of its state affiliates to take an active stand against its operations. The reader will recall that the same antagonism was present in Illinois and Missouri. As a consequence, the MFT does tend to alienate these interests, the result being the obvious one: sincere attempts at a closer alliance with these groups are often futile. Even with these basic differences, however, surprisingly good rapport exists between the MFT and other education groups. Again, partisanship is part of the explanation.[2] The Democratic commitment to labor—including the MFT—gives the federation some bargaining power with the other public school groups in terms of the perceived number of negative votes the MFT could potentially marshal in order to derail pet projects of the other groups. Moreover, the other education groups realize they are dealing with an organization which has considerable support and sympathy among Democrats, many of whom are dependent on or in sympathy with organized labor generally. Working rela-

---

[2] In the case of the MFT, partisanship seems accepted as a group tactic, and thus denotes a high degree of cohesion and serves to lessen the threat of cleavages along party lines within the group.

tionships have thus become more imperative, particularly when the Democrats control the governorship.

MICHIGAN ASSOCIATION OF SCHOOL BOARDS

The Michigan Association of School Boards (MASB) is the most rapidly growing organization among Michigan public school interests. Although it is the newest group on the Michigan scene, it should not be construed as only a minor influence. Indeed, it is quite possible that this group might, in the near future, become the most influential of all the education groups in the state. At the present time, it has access to the legislators and other public school groups view it as their strongest competitor for the legislature's attention.

A particularly notable feature about the School Board Association is its recent growth in membership. From a roster of 300 school boards in 1957, the association had mushroomed to 809 member boards by 1961, representing districts that include 94 percent of the public school children of Michigan and 90 percent of the public school systems offering classes from kindergarten through twelfth grade. In 1961, approximately 5,000 members were included in the School Boards Association.

It is difficult to identify the precise reasons for this rise in membership, but representatives of the organization and informed onlookers have some explanations. As it became clear that the state government would assume an increased share of educational policy decisions, the local school boards organized into a state-wide group to function more effectively at the state level—organizing, in effect, for the tasks at hand. They considered themselves to be the governing units for the local schools, and if part of the governing authority was to shift to Lansing, they saw their task as one of reorganizing in order to gain access at the new points of decision. The School Board Association's first major step into the state arena was to sponsor the 1957 legislation which provided for a guaranteed continuing appropriation for state financial assistance to local school districts. Political observers in Lansing indicate that the School Board Association first emerged as a strong force at that time.

Encouraged both by effective reorganizing and by success in its first legislative venture, the organization began to operate vigorously. It could then compete with other interests for the scarce fiscal resources at the state level for public schools. Some educators list as a contributing cause for the association's rapid growth and increased activity the aggressive developmental policy of the National School Board Association.

The Michigan Association of School Boards makes policy proposals only rarely. It has no research facilities to support such activity. Rather it acts as a watchdog over public school legislation that is introduced and offers its support or opposition as appropriate.

The organization sees itself as the only major education interest group that is not on the public payroll and so has no immediate and direct interest in the outcome of public schools legislation. It sees itself as disinterested and public-spirited, with only the best interests of the schools in mind. The leadership of the Association is quite emphatic on this point.

An underlying antagonism between the School Board group and the professional educators stems from the former's self-image. Viewing themselves as the only duly elected authorities for the local schools, they feel that they can best represent *both* the schools and the taxpayers; they feel that they and not the professional educators (whom they regard as their employees) should represent the schools at the state capitol. This concept of employer-employee relationship is illustrated in a statement of one of the Association leaders. In explaining why the experiment of organizing the School Board Association as a branch of MEA failed in 1947-48, he said: "It was just like General

Motors operating as a branch of the United Auto Workers."
And a School Board Association official observing the Education Council, a body including all key education groups,
said, "I find it most disturbing that School Board officials
are sitting down with all divisions of their employees."

Meanwhile the professional educators express *their* antagonism against elected governing boards. One leader in
the Association of School Administrators states quite bluntly:
"We are not going to let these *lay people* come down here
and run things."

The differences of opinion between the School Board
Association and the professional education groups flare into
the open from time to time. In the showdown fight on public school appropriations in the 1961 legislature, all of the
professional education groups moved to a compromise three
percent improvement factor in state financial assistance to
local schools, while the School Board Association stubbornly
held out for its request for five percent.

Virtually all of the professional education groups whose
representatives were interviewed indicated that they saw
the School Board Association as something of an "antago-
nistic force" in the education family. At the same time, the
School Board Association leaders warned their members of
a "prospective MEA-MASA coalition," and urged their people to "head off this coalition." The significant variable in
this regard in Michigan is the absence of any *effective alliance* in which differences can be absorbed or reconciled.
Unlike its counterparts in Illinois and Missouri, no long-
term and stable relationships have crystallized in Michigan.

The strength of the School Board Association springs
largely from the elected status of its members. This makes
an impression on both Democratic and Republican members of the Senate and House Education Committees. They
reason that, in the first place, the school board officers are
elected because they have strength at home; they must, in

general, be esteemed members of their communities. They can translate this into influence at the state level because they do get votes at home. As elected school officials, their voice on public school matters is generally respected in local communities. Because of this, a legislator is reluctant to arouse their opposition.

If the political activism of its members is one important factor in the group's strength, another is the position of its membership in the social structure. School board members are usually property owners in their communities and often have a sizable financial stake there. As a result, they often reflect a conservative view, leaning toward preservation of the *status quo*. They usually come from and represent a selected layer of influential and relatively satisfied people in the community. In this sense, they are joined by many legislators of the same kind who share the same perspectives and enjoy the same status. In general, the school board people speak the language of the legislators. On the other hand, several legislators went so far as to say that the professional educators are usually loquacious and somewhat suspect. The fact that school board people are not on the public payroll is also a large factor in their favor. Legislators tend to view their requests as representing less self-interest and more common concern for the community as a whole.

Since its strength is largely a result of the home town prestige and position of its members, the School Board Association directs most of its activity to the individual community. The Association places great emphasis on having the local school board officials maintain constant contact with their legislators at home. When action is desired, the association leaders contact local school board people to put the pressure on. The association has not yet perfected this device but it has been improving it. It recently held a series of meetings throughout the state to activate its local memberships and will possibly demonstrate more success in mobilizing local strength in the near future.

THE DETROIT PUBLIC SCHOOL SYSTEM

Michigan's major metropolitan school district, Detroit, also constitutes a separate interest that intervenes at various points in the state's political actions. Like Chicago, St. Louis, and Kansas City, it has as its major resource of influence a bloc of urban legislators which, when unified, is able to bargain and negotiate with outstate legislators for the special legislation Detroit's schools need and desire. The Detroit public school system, again like the metropolitan systems in our other two states, has not played a highly active or visible role in deciding education matters of state-wide application, being content to leave such deliberations to other interests. However, we must report that at the time of this research and apparently because of the failure of the state's other major education interest to achieve results, Detroit in conjunction with some adjacent school districts in Wayne County has begun to "step up" its activities at the state level. "We have begun to recognize," a high official of the Detroit school system stated, "that we can no longer operate effectively by leaving state-wide decisions exclusively to outstaters. The concerns of schools in this area where most of the state's people live are vital and they demand state attention. We will simply have to take more firm action than in the past." A decision on strategy is one thing, implementation of course is another matter. The same official did not hesitate to point out that the seemingly inherent urban-rural cleavage had been effectively overcome under the old formula of area delegation bargains. "The urban-rural conflict could rear its head if Detroit pushes too hard," he said. Conceding the thinness of our data, we can report that this new strategy of active involvement, if it is carried out, will make Michigan stand in sharp contrast to school decision-making patterns in Missouri and Illinois.

MICHIGAN CONGRESS OF PARENTS AND TEACHERS

Moving now to the second category—supportive groups which have a major and continuous concern about education but whose members are not so directly affected by the outcome of education decisions—we find one major group in Michigan politics, the Michigan Congress of Parents and Teachers, commonly referred to as the PTA. Although its membership includes professionals it is nevertheless an essentially lay group and so regards itself. Although the PTA's 390,000 members make it the largest education organization in the state, the minimal level of political activism and political commitment of the membership, coupled with the purely local outlook of many of the members, reduces the group's political significance. Few, if any, politicians see the PTA as a major voting bloc. (They certainly do not conceive it anywhere near comparable in power to the United Auto Workers, which has only approximately 254,000 members in Michigan.)

In a certain manner, however, the tactics of PTA leadership render the size of its membership a source of some strength. It is a prestige group of high status, organized to promote closer coöperation between the teachers, the public schools, and the parents. In that sense, it concerns itself with a broad range of education issues, giving the nominal support of 390,000 prestigious citizens to specific programs which have been formulated by other education groups. The PTA is not in any sense a rubber stamp group, but operates with the expectation that it will be used for the benefit of the public schools—or, more precisely, in support of those proposals that win its favor. The leaders visualize the group as largely a supportive group. Consequently, PTA membership is not stimulated to militant action, but the Association relies instead on face to face contact between the PTA leadership and the legislators in Lansing.

The PTA does not have a large degree of cohesion, and

since "the degree of unity sets limits on permissible partisanship," it is not surprising that the PTA is perhaps the
most hesitant of all the education groups in Michigan to be
identified with any partisan political activity. As one PTA
leader put it: "There is absolutely no partisanship in the
PTA; we do not even want politicians to speak at our meetings." In sum, the Michigan PTA is a useful friend, but not
a very bothersome enemy.

Another category of groups which touch upon education—
including both supportive and nonsupportive groups whose
major concern is with issues other than education—will not
be described in this section. Suffice it to say that these
groups—organized labor, chambers of commerce, taxpayers
associations, etc.—can create a broad favorable climate for
education programs and they can also create a substantial
residue of opposition to many proposals. Their support or
opposition is sporadic, rising and declining as the issue at
hand affects or does not affect their interests. Such support
or opposition, especially when generated to protect perceived interests, can obviously be one of the deciding factors in some instances, as will be seen later on in this chapter. However, detailed analysis of these groups, no matter
how attractive the prospects it offers, is not essential to an
understanding of the public school interest group structure
in Michigan. Their existence and sporadic participation can
be accepted as facts of political life in the public school
policies of the state.

THE SUPERINTENDENT OF PUBLIC INSTRUCTION

No investigation of the education interest in Michigan is
complete without discussing the legislative and political
role of the superintendent of public instruction and the
State Department of Public Instruction. With a popularly
elected superintendent of public instruction, who sees his
role and that of the Department as integral parts of the education policy-making process, the machinery of the Depart-

ment is constantly thrust into the decision-making arena.

The Department becomes engaged in policy-making in three ways: through the superintendent personally; through the Department's legislative representative; and through the Department's own internal administrative machinery which systematically prepares policy positions.

The most overt—and the most controversial—involvement is that of the superintendent, who, since 1957, has been an elected Democrat, Lynn Bartlett. He has closely adhered to the education planks of the Democratic platform, and is perceived as presenting to the legislature partisan proposals for the solution of education problems. The Michigan legislature, on the other hand, has consistently had a Republican majority in each house. In this political environment (where there not only is a divided government, but where the parties are more ideologically oriented than in most American states), the pursuit of Democratic programs along strictly party lines spells continuous defeat. Therefore the superintendent has faced the dilemma of having to maintain a partisan stance toward public school issues in order to retain the strong support of his party and thus remain in office, while at the same time he must support a bipartisan program in the legislature in the hope of legislative victory.

The nature of the office of superintendent of public instruction compounds the difficulty. To gain acceptance and respect within the public school system, he must be regarded as an educational statesman, not a politician. This informal requirement has given the superintendent very little political leverage for the promotion of his own programs even when they bear the Democratic label. Unlike the governor, for instance, who is in a stronger political position, it is difficult for the superintendent to transfer his ballot box popularity into voter support for his programs in the legislature.

To offset this position of relative political impotence, the superintendent has attempted to fuse the education groups into a unified voice, the Educational Council, in order to present a "consensus program" to the legislature. This group is composed of representatives of the MEA, MFT, MASA, and the MASB. The council has had only a limited success. Agreements reached in the Council are not binding and on numerous occasions they have been ignored by member groups. Moreover, the MEA desires to create its own council and has tended to resent the leadership efforts of the superintendent. As a result, the superintendent has found his bipartisan education support unreliable and his program often defeated in the legislature along party lines.

The superintendent has been unable to erase his partisan image in the eyes of numerous legislators. Virtually all of the education committee members interviewed said they identified the superintendent and his programs as partisan. As a Republican member of the House Education Committee put it, "He [the Superintendent] couldn't get away from his partisanship if he wanted to; the nature of the office wouldn't allow it." He added that "the partisanship is inherent, and he [the superintendent] doesn't try to hide it." Another House Republican mentioned the superintendent's partisanship with disfavor: "The superintendent is little more than a party politician rather than an 'educator.' He has cheapened his position by engaging in lobbying activities." Democrats in the legislature look upon the superintendent's legislative efforts with more favor than do the Republicans, of course. Said one House Democrat: "The superintendent rates high among the Democrats in the legislature, and he also has some support from the Republicans. The two together could add up to a winning ticket. He wouldn't even have this strength if the office wasn't an elected partisan post."

Despite Republican antipathy to the superintendent's lobbying activity, all legislators, including Republicans, indicated that they sought out the superintendent's office for information on education issues and, perhaps with some qualifications, generally trusted the information they received.

The legislative acceptance of Department of Public Instruction information and counsel may be more attributable to the efforts of the Department's legislative representative than to the superintendent's. While the superintendent must carry the party banner, his legislative representative, Max Cochran, who is highly respected by many legislators, quietly goes about the legislature in nonpartisan garb (although it is well-known that he is a Republican), informing and advising the legislators.

The legislative representative is, in fact, a key to the Department of Public Instruction's influence. His job is to keep on top of all legislative proposals. As a result, he keeps the Department personnel, the various education groups, and, at times, the legislators themselves informed on the various public school proposals before the legislature. He prepares an analysis of each education bill.

In his role as lobbyist and legislative trouble-shooter for the Department, he maintains close contacts with the legislators. In general, the legislators interviewed indicated respect for his advice and counsel. A ranking Republican senator indicated his confidence in this way: "I have more confidence in Cochran, the Department's legislative representative, than in any other member of the Department of Public Instruction." A Republican leader in the House indicated that "Max Cochran wields substantial influence in the legislature." A freshman Republican senator indicated that he got no information from the Department of Public Instruction "except through Max Cochran." He added, "I am inclined to lean heavily on Cochran in the future because I have confidence in his information." Also, all Democrats interviewed said they found Cochran to be very reliable and helpful.

The legislative representative also functions as a catalyst in the operation of the Department's internal legislative policy-making machinery. This activity is centered in the Department's Legislative Committee. This committee, composed of a representative from each of the six divisions of the Department of Public Instruction, meets weekly during the legislative session to consider public school proposals before the legislature. The committee is a clearing house for proposals already submitted rather than a policy initiating body. Proposals presented to the Legislative Committee are referred back to each division before a committee decision is made. This allows the professional administrators to pass judgment on the proposals from their administrative point of view. Decisions reached by the committee serve as a way of keeping the superintendent informed as to how Department personnel feel and of keeping them, in turn, up to date on pending legislation. The Legislative Committee's final decisions are transmitted not to the legislature, but to the superintendent.

Department of Public Instruction personnel have some additional activities that bear on public school policymaking. These include testimony by Department personnel before legislative committees, preparation of research papers, and the drafting of legislation.

Perhaps the key to understanding the role of education interests in this state is a recognition of the following two points. (1) To a much greater degree than in our other two states, the various groups act independently. In the remainder of this chapter, we will attempt to show that at this point in time Michigan has no stable education power structure in the sense that Illinois and Missouri have. Our data suggest that until fairly recently, 1959 to be exact, a power structure consisting mainly of the MEA and its contacts in the state as a whole and certain key officials in the legislature, did indeed exist, a structure capable of keeping education issues from becoming controversial. At the time of our study, however, only the remnants of that structure remained and new groups, powerful in their own right, had begun to exercise influence and move in different directions. (2) The emergence of conflicting elements beyond merely the teachers union *within* the education lobby, coupled with broader political conflicts in the state's total political system, some of which are between the two major parties, creates a problem for the majority of the education interest groups. That problem is that this type of political atmosphere does not fully lend itself to the basic strategies of neutrality, objectivity, nonpartisanship, and low conflict appearance that most of these groups have adopted. By examining the role of these interests in the larger political context and in two specific situations, we hope to illustrate these points.

THE MICHIGAN POLITICAL SYSTEM AND THE EDUCATION LOBBY

For over a decade, the public school interests just described have operated in a political context significantly different from those in Illinois and Missouri. Although the overall objective of the professional educators in Michigan has been to minimize conflict over their demands, they have been comparatively unsuccessful. While in Illinois and Missouri, state participation in school matters has been greatly expanded, particularly in the area of finance, almost the opposite is true in Michigan. For example, state aid in support of the public schools has declined from over 50 percent of total operating costs in 1950 to less than 43 percent in 1961. Not only have the public school interests been unable to reverse this trend, they also have been unable to persuade the legislature to take any major steps in other policy areas. They could not obtain the necessary support in the legislature to adopt a foundation program; instead they have had to be satisfied with a continuing appropriation act which embodies only some of the features of the more desirable foundation program. There have been no giant strides in teacher welfare (except perhaps in teacher retirement), or local and county school district reorganization, and the state legislature has steadfastly refused, despite repeated requests, to approve of state participation in several federal programs authorized under the National Defense Education Act.

As we have noted previously, public school issues are not normally hotly contested in either Missouri or Illinois, and the public school interests have been largely successful in their efforts to achieve fairly wide consensus. Why is Michigan different? There are no simple answers, but the interviews do provide a perspective.

In the first place, in terms of expenditures for services, Michigan is not a conservative state if judged by Illinois or Missouri, or for that matter, national standards. The state government in Michigan plays a much more prominent role in the total economy of that state than do the state governments in either Illinois or Missouri. Public schools have been much more generously supported in Michigan than in either Illinois or Missouri. During the 1950's, however, general concern with public schools appears to have leveled off, at least partly because of an early impressive record of financial support. Table 1, while establishing the high dollar investment in public education in Michigan, also indicates that the state's role in educational finance has become less impressive when compared with that of Illinois and Missouri. The figures are given below. The question is why.

"With service levels and expenditures relatively high," one Republican legislator commented, "demands for more money run into stiffer resistance." "It is no secret to the Republicans," a Democratic member of the Education Committee said, "that Michigan is spending a lot more money for schools than are many of the neighboring states." Representatives of the various organized interests all agreed that

TABLE 1

PUBLIC SCHOOL REVENUE RECEIPTS

(In Thousands).*

	Illinois		*Michigan*		*Missouri*	
	ALL SOURCES	STATE SOURCES	ALL SOURCES	STATE SOURCES	ALL SOURCES	STATE SOURCES
1951-52	490,797	62,938	319,404	177,206	135,866	48,197
1955-56	437,945	105,251	528,281	256,257	200,045	72,917
1957-58	622,644	127,419	636,768	278,780	242,646	79,879

* U.S. Office of Education, *Biennial Survey of Education in the United States, Statistics of State School Systems:* Organization, Staff, Pupils, and Finances, 1951-52, Table 18; 1955-56, Table 24; 1957-58, Table 25.

because the state did spend considerable funds for education at all levels as well as for other services, their "demands were much more difficult to support and justify."

Several interviewees referred to various statistics to buttress their argument. For example, in per capita total state expenditures for all purposes in 1960, Michigan ranked eighteenth, spending $171.46 as compared with Missouri's $120.31 (forty-sixth) and Illinois' $120.12 (forty-seventh). In terms of per capita *state* expenditures for *all* public education, Michigan ranked eleventh, spending $66.38 as compared with Missouri's forty-second position ($32.93) and Illinois' forty-fourth position ($30.04) in 1960. Although Illinois spends more per pupil in average daily attendance than Michigan—$502.00 as compared to $440.13 in Michigan—significantly less money comes from *state* sources. (Missouri spends less than either state, the figure being $386.17 per pupil in ADA.) That is, the degree of state participation in financing public elementary and secondary schools is higher in Michigan than in either of the two other states. In 1961-62, Michigan contributed 42.2 per cent of all revenue for public schools as compared with 35.7 per cent in Missouri and 22.8 per cent in Illinois. In dollar amounts per pupil in average daily attendance, Michigan contributed $224 in 1961-62, Missouri contributed $159, and Illinois $129. In brief, then, Illinois and Missouri rely more extensively on local resources; whereas in Michigan, state resources have been tapped more often and to greater extent, despite the decline in recent years. (See Appendix I.)

Moreover, Michigan's commitments and obligations in the field of higher education are vastly more extensive than in either of the other two states. Michigan's total expenditures on education in 1960 were approximately $520,000,000. This compares with only $302,873,000 in Illinois and $142,247,000 in Missouri. Obviously, drains on the state treasury of this magnitude make the task of any education proponent, regardless of the level on which the support is sought, an exceedingly difficult one. We were told time and again by legislators that the state was "over-committed," "the funds are simply not available." Furthermore, as far as long-range planning is concerned, the educational establishment in Michigan is in disarray, which has led to some competition between the proponents of the public schools and the representatives of the institutions of higher learning (which often compete among themselves) over the state's scarce fiscal resources. Perhaps the most significant finding was not that competition exists, but that when expenditures reach these levels, most legislators are not inclined to make any distinction between money needed for public schools and money needed for higher education. Rather, we were told by one informant they think simply in terms of "how much money will the *educators* want this year."

A second major variable affecting school politics in Michigan is the pervasive conflict between the two major parties and the interests that support them. The exact nature and historical development of this conflict need not concern us here, except to demonstrate the manner in which public school policy and the public school interests have been affected. John P. White states:

What seems to have happened in Michigan since 1928 is that a great national electoral realignment rejuvenated the previously moribund Democratic party. For a time in the late thirties and early forties, the well-fortified political position of the long dominant Republicans, coupled with the political inexperience and ineptitude of many Michigan Democrats, seemed strong enough to survive the assaults of the New Deal era. But since 1948, the Democrats have been able to produce a leadership group and a party organization strong enough to gain and hold control of the state government. . . .[3]

The emergence of the Democratic party as a dominant force in state politics has been accompanied by a realignment of the major parties. The forces that have gained control of each have succeeded in making the parties more responsible in the classic sense of the term: that is, each party is programmatic or committed to certain specific policies. Thus, in Michigan, the parties present alternatives, clear-cut alternatives, and their disparate views are reflected in the day to day operations of government.

FISCAL CONFLICTS

The party cleavages in Michigan relate, first of all, to political ideology and then to implementation. Much of the conflict in Michigan centers on questions of fiscal policy; more specifically, parties divide over how much money should be spent for public services generally and what type of taxes are equitable and raise enough money to finance existing or expanding programs. At various stages, these conflicts have reached crisis proportion and have become the subject of considerable national public discussion and debate. The primary protagonists—the "automobile manufacturers and rural interests versus organized labor—each identified with a political party, have not entered the political arena for the traditional prizes, but are more inter-

[3] *Michigan Votes: Election Statistics, 1928-1956* (Ann Arbor: Institute of Public Administration, University of Michigan; 1958), p. 118.

ested in controlling the total social and economic policy of the state government." [4]

One side is led by the Democratic party, strongly endorsed and supported by the United Automobile Workers Union, having as its principal spokesmen two of the state's past governors, G. Mennen Williams (1949-1961) and John B. Swainson (1961-62). The solid Democratic vote for state offices during the past decade, even during the Eisenhower years, is generally credited to the drawing power of one man. "If any coat-tails were important, they were those of G. Mennen Williams." [5]

On the other side stands the Republican party, in control of both houses of the state legislature during the entire period of the two Democratic governors' incumbency and prominently identified on a state-wide basis with the conservative economic interests, including General Motors, Chrysler, and the Ford Motor Company as well as agricultural and small business interests.

During the course of these years, the public school interests have operated in a political context where the economic posture of the two parties varied more perhaps than in any other state. Republicans accused the Democrats of being "fiscally irresponsible," "dominated by labor," "anti-free enterprise," and "socialistic." Democrats attacked Republicans with equal vigor and dispatch at the slightest provocation. Democrats viewed the Republicans as being "dominated by business interests," "friends of the rich and enemies of the poor," "anti-progress and pro-stagnation," "right wing and authoritarian" and "rural and backward in outlook."

Throughout the state, debates between party adversaries flared up whether it was election time or not. The debates covered a wide range of issues; the principal ones were, however, the representativeness or apportionment of the

[4] Stephen B. and Vera H. Sarasohn: *Political Party Patterns in Michigan* (Detroit: Wayne State University Press; 1957), p. 69.
[5] John P. White: *op. cit.*, p. 111.

state legislature, the nature of the state's fiscal policies and
concern that present policies had caused industrial enterprises to move outside the state, and "welfarism." Did this
mean that the state was hopelessly deadlocked and that
nothing could be done? On some issues, yes. At other times
and on other questions, no.

The one major issue that persistently plagued both sides
and that was never resolved during the Williams years nor
during Swainson's 1961-62 term in office was the question of
a state income tax as a means to finance expanding state
services. There was wide agreement that additional revenues were needed and that a revision of the tax structure
was in order, but the type of the tax and who was to be affected by it was the subject of the deep cleavage. To the
Democrats closely aligned with labor, a sales tax or any
other form of taxation which they considered "regressive"
or adversely affecting lower income groups was out of the
question. Similarly, the Republicans' base of support—big
business, high income groups, conservative rural farmers—
was during these same years vigorously opposed both on
economic and constitutional grounds to any corporate or
personal income tax. The present constitution provides for a
"uniform rule of taxation" which some Republicans argue
prohibits the enactment of a graduated income tax.

Agreement on the need for additional revenue if state
services were to be maintained at present levels or raised,
and disagreement on the source of the additional revenue
complicated the public school interests' position in Michigan.
Unlike the MSTA in Missouri, or for that matter the education groups in Illinois, the organized interests, while requesting additional state aid, could not endorse tax measures
proposed by the governor without incurring direct opposition
from Republican legislators. On the other hand, to oppose
the governor's tax measures might mean the loss of the
Democratic support they had in the House as well as that
of the governor. It would also place school interests in

the untenable position of opposing the only long-range proposals that had been presented at a time when everyone agreed that increased revenues were imperative. ("We Republicans did not offer any long-range alternatives because it was the governor's responsibility to propose a sensible tax program," said a Republican spokesman. "All the Democrats did was to promise more and more and present tax proposals everyone was against, including the Democratic legislators privately.")

Neutrality on the tax question was the only alternative open to the education groups, but this too was an almost impossible position, since they had already admitted that new taxes would be necessary to increase appropriations. "The only alternative we had," a representative of MEA said, "was to present our case and try to gain bipartisan support by appealing to all sides to examine school needs critically." "In this atmosphere, the organized public school interests' chances for success," said one educator, "hinge on the extent of the conflict at the moment our proposals are submitted and on our ability to separate public school issues from other policy questions."

In sum, the fact that so many people have taken sides or believe that the conflict is irreconcilable creates the psychology that reinforces the conflict. Unfortunately for the public school interests, they have found no device in the Michigan political system for coherent education decision-making comparable to the School Problems Commission in Illinois, and no group similar to the MSTA in Missouri was able to fill the gap. Therefore, timing is of greater significance in Michigan, and if measures are introduced at a time when conflicts over fiscal policies are at their peak, *any* influence attempts may appear chaotic, unwise, and predetermined to fail.

One effect of all this has been that each organization, particularly the MEA and the State Association of School Boards, depends heavily on its state-wide campaigns to gain wide public support for school needs. This strategy contrasts sharply with the one followed by Illinois groups, which are represented on the School Problems Commission. It also contrasts, though perhaps less so, with the strategy of the MSTA in Missouri, where state-wide campaigns to generate citizen interest are used only for major and fundamental changes in the direction of public school policy, such as the foundation program in 1955.

Another effect has been that the interest groups in Michigan do not have the same symbolic advantage as do the groups in Missouri and Illinois. Although there is no anti-school lobby operating in the state capital and no one opposes the schools *per se*, resistance to school demands is more open. "We are doing enough for the educators," a Republican member of the Senate Education Committee said, "and until tax questions are settled there is no more money to give them."

Finally, in the political context, representatives of education groups point out that one of their main difficulties has been to gain political mileage from their acknowledged expertise. "We are regarded as experts on school needs all right, and have no trouble on that score, but nobody consults us on revenue-raising matters; and if we got involved in that fight, we would be ruined." The pervasiveness of conflict has further complicated attempts to maintain unity among the various organized education interests. An MEA representative summarized the situation thus:

The state superintendent and the Michigan Federation of Teachers are with the Democrats. The Association of School Boards is for more state aid, but its membership and leaders are generally thought to be conservative and against an income tax. And to complicate matters further many groups, including the PTA, have their own view as to how much we can get or what the Senate will accept. We don't disagree on needs, we disagree on how much we *should* ask the legislature for. Certainly all of this dis-

organization among the education groups limits our chances for
success.[6]

CONFLICT BETWEEN "HAVE AND HAVE NOT"
SCHOOL DISTRICTS

Although the split between the governor and the state
legislature over fiscal policy tends to overshadow and receive more publicity than other controversies, a division
within the state legislature itself—not based on party lines
—has demonstrably affected public school policy perhaps to
an even greater extent. This division is between the legislative representatives of areas which contain wealthy school
districts and the legislative representatives of areas which
contain poor districts. The cleavage is aggravated in Michigan because the state has never adopted a state-wide
school district reorganization plan, the reasons for which
will be discussed subsequently. State representatives from
areas such as Grosse Point, Pontiac, and Bloomfield Hills are
inclined to oppose changes in the state aid formula that would
provide more state money to poorer districts on the basis of
need. Conversely, representatives of the areas containing poor
districts, with the general support of most education groups,
favor a state aid formula weighted more heavily on the side
of such equalization. These representatives feel that they
have the full support of their local school officials in maintaining their position. Obviously, such a situation tends to
weaken the bargaining power of state-wide organizations
claiming to represent all of the claimants.

The chairman of the House Education Committee says:
"This division is the most serious problem we face. The partisan fight gets all of the attention and right now it is of more
far-reaching consequence, but that has in the past and will
again die down and dwindle in significance."

[6] The breakdown of unity among the members of the school lobby will
be discussed subsequently in connection with issues before the 1961 session
of the state legislature.

A Democratic member of the same committee commented:

The biggest split is between the high and low valuation districts; this split is justifiable since the higher the valuation the less aid. The rift is greater in the Republican ranks than in the Democratic ranks. Our distressed aid formula takes care of the metropolitan districts, but many of the rural districts represented by Republicans don't benefit from this. If we had reorganization and eliminated a lot of these low valuation districts the picture would change, but there is so much opposition from the little red school houses and the Farm Bureau that this is not feasible on a state-wide basis; not to mention the tax problem it would raise because of the constitution.

All of those interviewed agreed that the differences between the wealthy and poor districts over the state aid formula would be reconciled only if and when: 1) the majority of poorer districts were eliminated through state-wide action or a series of local annexations and consolidations which would result, according to an MEA representative, in all new districts having "a more sound and sensible financial base"; and 2) there were a basic change in the constitutional provisions dealing with county and city tax limits, which regulate or affect school district tax rates.

Why has a state-wide school district reorganization plan never been adopted in Michigan? Representatives of the various organized interests agree as to the reasons. As one explained it:

After World War II, the state had plenty of money and in comparison with other states we were doing more. Over fifty percent of school revenue came from the state. Add to this the fact that at that time the local school district situation was not as bad as it was, say, in Illinois or Ohio. By comparison, we had fewer districts than most. Thus, there just wasn't the emergency that there was in other states.

A representative of MEA added: "The local districts were in good shape after the war and wanted local control pre-

served. There seemed to be plenty of money, so we didn't
push very hard to change things then; but the simple fact is
we did not remain in favorable comparative situations for
very long and now reorganization has become a hot political
football."

Although both legislators and representatives of organized interests agree that a state-wide plan might have been
approved immediately following World War II, they also
agree that each succeeding year made it more difficult to get
one passed. In the first place, following the war a number of
groups, particularly the Michigan Farm Bureau and the
Friends of Michigan Schools (Little Red School House
group), opposed vigorously any proposals to change local
school districts by action initiated at the state level. "These
groups were very vocal and swamped us with mail," a legislator asserted. "In fact, the biggest and loudest hearing
ever held in the State Capitol was when the opponents of
reorganization came down to tell us about it."

Despite this opposition, representatives of all of the major
school interests felt they would have been successful had it
not been for constitutional provisions differentiating the
limits of city and county taxes. The efforts of the Michigan
Municipal League, an organization representing municipal
officials, were perhaps of most significance in the defeating
any reorganization scheme. The basis of this opposition was
that inclusion of outside city-limits school districts would
subject city schools to the 15 mill county tax limit, thus lowering the quality of existing city schools, which can tax on a
higher level. The state Supreme Court held that inclusion of
school districts located in the county would require the entire district to tax within the 15 mill limitation. Representatives of the education groups admitted that reorganization
was practically impossible with such an interpretation. Their
next tactic was to advocate a change in the state constitution, and the constitutional convention was considering a
proposal to this effect.

Although the organized education interests in Michigan have been too weak and divided to overcome many of the forces in the Michigan political system, they are strong enough to block any proposal they consider detrimental to the public schools. In the absence of a clear test, it is, of course, impossible to say exactly what would happen, but no one disputes this view. Legislators agree that they would never initiate or attempt to push through a program without the active support of at least some of the major groups.

THE POLICY-MAKING STRUCTURE

For certain analytic purposes, one may look at Michigan's House and Senate as entities. However, the picture is not complete until the executive branch and its troubled relationship with the legislature, past and present, are considered. That large portion of state politics in Michigan which involves ideology, policy priorities, and personality has centered to a striking extent around the state's current (1961-62) and preceding Democratic governors. Because of the repercussions for education affairs, we shall focus briefly on the institutional roles of the governor and the legislature in the policy-making process.

THE GOVERNOR

The constitution in force in 1962 plus certain statutory provisions require the election of seven other top administrative officials who, with the governor, make up the State Administrative Board. These offices are those of lieutenant governor, secretary of state, state treasurer, auditor general, attorney general, superintendent of public instruction, and highway commissioner. Advocates of the strong governor system find the current situation theoretically, if not always in fact, intolerable. If all state officers are members of the same party, as they have been in recent years, a strong governor may direct them as a team; however, when party

membership is not identical, the governor finds his administrative powers limited to an even greater degree than already
exists in the nature of the arrangement. (Governor Williams
attempted to by-pass this problem in the early fifties by use
of an unofficial "Little Cabinet.") Also, each of these officials
has, like the governor, a state-wide constituency, which supplies the potential for party factionalism.

The governor in Michigan is elected for a two-year term;
he may succeed himself indefinitely. One of the items on the
constitutional convention agenda, which will be discussed
below, was to increase the governor's term to four years. As
the situation stood, a governor spent half of his two-year
term at less than full efficiency, since he must occupy months
with familiarizing himself with the administrative process
and campaigning for reëlection. It was one of Governor
Swainson's strengths that he offered to the voter extensive
prior experience both in the state Senate and in the lieutenant governorship.

Another constitutional area in which the gubernatorial
powers are curbed in Michigan is that of appointment and
removal of public officials. The Michigan constitution does
not specify a method of creating new executive offices and
filling them, although the governor may appoint persons to
fill vacancies; therefore, an important aspect of the great
modern-day proliferation of the state administrative services
still rests in the hands of the legislature. By statute some department and agency heads were made appointive by the
governor; but the Senate had held on to extensive consen-
tual powers in this matter.

The formal delegation of gubernatorial powers in Michigan would appear to put the governor in a weak position.
However, the political culture of the state provides some
balance. The governor, as leader of a fiercely partisan, ideologically oriented political party, has many resources at
hand. Perhaps his clearest advantage is the wide-spread attention and consideration that his proposals, fiscal and oth-

erwise, receive throughout the state. The governor is always in a position to dramatize an issue or appeal to the public interest. G. Mennen Williams, during his six terms as Michigan governor, relied heavily on this approach rather than on any of his constitutional powers. As a result, Williams vetoed a much smaller number of bills during his tenure in office than is the average in most states.

One commentator on the small number of vetoes explains: "This phenomenon would appear to emphasize less the existence of coördinated action between the political branches than unusual awareness on the part of the majority party in opposition to the Governor of the latter's tolerance limits."[7]

One of the clearest distinctions between Williams' political style and that of his successor, John B. Swainson, was Swainson's extensive use of the veto. It did not become a factor in the educational picture, however, because the legislature has not passed any major educational legislation since the Continuous Appropriations Act in 1959.

But even though the elements of power a governor has cannot be ignored, he is not in a strong bargaining position with the state legislature. Unlike the Missouri and Illinois governors, the governor in Michigan does not dominate the revenue picture. Legislative leaders are not committed to push or to give high priority to any of his recommendations. Moreover, there is no presumption—as there is in Illinois and Missouri—that the governor's allocation of resources will be accepted. Perhaps the situation would be different in Michigan if recent governors had been more low-pressure and had not attempted to exercise broad programmatic leadership. As the situation stands, however, the institutional limitations—no patronage, the two-year term—make it possible for the legislature to thwart the governor almost at will, even while he remains politically popular and gets reëlected.

Education leaders claim that Michigan needs executive

[7] Peter J. Turano: "Governor Williams' Use of the Executive Veto, 1949-1956," *University of Detroit Law Journal* (October, 1956), p. 13.

leadership with more teeth in it. As the representative of one education interest put it:

The recent governors of Michigan have been on our side and they have both been strong personalities, though Williams was the stronger. But they don't have much power over the legislature. Our governors have to spend too much time running for reëlection.

According to another educational leader:

The weakness of the governors in this state is well-known to anyone who has ever observed the legislature in this state. Recent governors have, on the whole, supported most of our proposals, but, without trying to minimize the importance of this support, I can tell you it was less than half the battle. A governor with a strong personality and strong public image still can't do much in this state even when he attempts vigorous leadership.

As we will see in the following case studies, Swainson's term in office, in relation to the legislature, can be characterized as a political impasse.

THE LEGISLATURE

In contrast to the situation in Missouri and, to a lesser extent, Illinois, the Michigan political context can be called a high-pressure system, high enough to be periodically explosive. We have already discussed the orientations of political parties and interest groups in Michigan. Now we turn in more detail to the Michigan legislature as it existed in 1961.

As is frequently the case in America, under-representation of urban areas is built into Michigan's legislative apportionment scheme, and typically—at least of Northern states—rural areas tend to be Republican. As a result, the Michigan Senate is heavily Republican. Democrats have controlled it only once in the last forty years. The House is more evenly divided but overall figures for 1951-62 indicate a Republican majority of 362 to 277. Table 3 illustrates the nature of Michigan's apportionment system. Senatorial district boundaries are fixed in the constitution, and are therefore exceedingly difficult to change.

TABLE 2

COMPOSITION OF MICHIGAN LEGISLATURE,
1951 to 1962

	House		*Senate*	
	REPUBLICAN	DEMOCRAT	REPUBLICAN	DEMOCRAT
1961-62	56	54	22	12
1959-60	54	55	22	12
1957-58	61	49	23	11
1955-56	59	51	23	11
1953-54	66	34	24	8
1951-52	66	34	25	7
	362	277	139	61

TABLE 3

MICHIGAN APPORTIONMENT SYSTEM

County	*Population (1950)*	*Population (1960)*	*Representatives*	*Percent of total*	*Senators*	*Percent of total*
Wayne	38.2	34.2	38	34.5	7	20.6
Oakland	6.2	8.8	6	5.5	1	2.9
Macomb	2.9	5.2	3	2.7	1	2.9
Kent	4.5	4.6	5	4.5	2	5.9
Genessee	4.3	4.7	4	3.6	1	2.9
Others	43.9	42.4	54	49.1	22	64.7
			110			

While Democrats accuse Republicans of insuring their position in the legislature with outstate Republican majorities, Republicans point to Wayne County and charge that "if all 38 legislators were chosen from equitably drawn, single member districts, their 30 percent of the total vote in Wayne County would give them between 5 and 10 of the representatives." To at least one observer, "It seems apparent that 'gerrymandering' . . . is not the exclusive province of one party."[8]

Fourteen years of Democratic governors and a Republican-controlled state legislature have served to aggravate, if not freeze, political disputes into such rigidities that it is now difficult for this large, diverse, and prosperous state to enact changes in public policy, especially in the much publicized area of taxation. While Democratic governors are cordial to school interests, education bills have trouble passing the legislature.

As in Missouri, the school men in Michigan, seeking favorable consideration for public school bills, have found the House of Representatives to be more receptive than the Senate in the eyes of the education lobby. The House has three or four members who qualify as experts in the field of education, one of whom is a member of the House's powerful Ways and Means Committee. Over the years of bitter partisan fights, the education interests have been able to maintain bipartisan support in the House Education Committee for most of their proposals and generally, as one representative of the MEA said, "we get a fair shake from the entire House."

During the past twelve years, the Republicans have been in the majority on the House Education Committee. On the whole, education groups in the state feel that this committee gives their needs a reasonable hearing, as well as support. One variable bearing on this may be the considerable number of committee members who come to this post with previous experience in educational affairs, either in some professional capacity or as an elected local school official. Five of the current nine members of the Education Committee have such experience, one as a local board president for twenty-three years. Another variable may be the continuity of serv-

[8] Joseph LaPalombara: *Guide to Michigan Politics* (East Lansing: Bureau of Social and Political Research, College of Business and Public Service, Michigan State University; 1960), p. 35.

ice on this committee. Normally this is a nine-member body (Ways and Means is the largest committee with 13). From 1953-54 through 1961-62, only 20 legislators, 14 Republicans and 6 Democrats, have served.

In contrast to the House, the legislative representative of the state superintendent's office maintained that the Senate was the "toughest to crack." During the late 1950's and early '60's, the Michigan Senate Education Committee was chaired by Republicans who were self-designated conservatives. The most recent chairman, Lynn Francis, says that the "state spends too much money on schools," and believes that "most educators are Democrats." Education lobbyists do not regard anyone in the Senate as an education expert or public schools' champion in the way some members of the House are. Each particular interest has its own "friends in the Senate," but the main job, according to those who make the demands, is "to persuade the Republican Senate leaders to support their position." "This is no easy task," an MEA official commented, "and in recent years the fight with the governor has caused the Republicans to stand firmly together against further appropriations."

Republican leaders insist that they are not opposing the schools, but that unless the school groups can demonstrate a real need and gain responsible support on a state-wide basis, the lawmakers will not go along with education bills that involve expenditures of state funds or disturb local school district autonomy. To sum it up, the Senate Education Committee has been the burying ground for much school legislation sent over from the House.

Although there is nothing comparable to the "local unity norm" found in Missouri, area delegations do bargain with other area groups within the legislature, and education matters are frequently the subject of the negotiations. For example, the Detroit-Wayne County Democratic delegation in the House and Senate bargained for the "aid to distressed schools" law which helps out particular schools within a metropolitan district. Of even greater importance, the broad concerns of the Detroit school system have been protected and enhanced largely through bargains arrived at between the urban and rural delegations. And, like the pattern in Missouri and Illinois, in return for the bargain Detroit school men have not played an active role in other state public school matters. As previously indicated, however, this pattern is undergoing a change. What is "given up" in these bargains depends on the issue, but "it is certain," one legislator said, "that the city bills would not pass without some concessions being made at the time or promised for a later date." In brief, schools are the objects of informal legislative negotiations in much the same way as other issues are.

CONSTITUTIONAL CONVENTION: MICHIGAN'S "SOLUTION"

After years of agitation on the part of Michigan citizens who are aware of impending disaster if the state continues to operate under the provisions of an archaic and restrictive constitution, Michigan has just finished watching the efforts of a 144 delegation Constitutional Convention. A considerable number of issues relating directly or indirectly to the state's educational systems were debated. On the surface, expectations of striking changes in the school picture appear reasonable.

As we have noted, Michigan elects its state superintendent of public instruction on a partisan ticket. Considering the fact that the Democrats have controlled most state offices since 1956, positions on whether the superintendent should be elected or appointed may reflect either individual concern for sound educational administration or partisan desire for control of important posts—or both. Arguments over the desirability of an appointive rather than elective state board of education and superintendent of public instruction follow two lines of reasoning: one concerned with the "model" or idealized approach to the question, and the other thoroughly enmeshed in partisan power strategies.

State Politics and the Public Schools 226

Those in favor of changing the current status of the superintendent and board put forth arguments which have been summarized by the Citizens Research Council of Michigan in the following manner:[9]

1. Separation of these offices from the requirements imposed by running for popular election would broaden and enrich the field of candidates for the offices.

2. The requirements and functions of the offices are such as to provide little effective basis for qualified voter judgment.

3. The office of the superintendent of public instruction in particular is administrative rather than policy-forming in nature and thus should be appointive.

The other side takes the Jacksonian view that these positions are "too vital to place beyond the control of the people as exercised by direct election."[1]

The example of debate in the convention over the school superintendent's office cannot be separated from debates over the power and authority of the governor. In fact, it can be used to mask the debates over the crucial question of whether to provide for a strong or weak chief executive. And in its turn, the struggle between administrative and legislative branches relates to bitterly conflicting fiscal and economic policies. For example, constitutional provisions pertaining to earmarked funds, sales tax diversion, Michigan's 15 mill property tax limitation, and a state income tax, were all in issue at the convention. So were the short (two year) terms of the governor, the dispersal of authority in a plural executive, the myriad responsibilities of an elected superintendent of public instruction who also serves on numerous state boards and committees, and a state governmental organization which "exhibits all the weird confusion of a

---

[9] Citizens Research Council of Michigan: *Michigan Constitutional Issues,* Report 201 (Detroit, June 1960), p. 35.
[1] *Ibid.*

twenty-mule team harnessed in the dark by a one-armed idiot." [2] And of course, all of these issues were part of the conflict between the two major parties and the interests behind them.

A number of changes in the Michigan constitutional set-up may have important implications for the public schools. Perhaps of greatest significance is that the state superintendent will no longer be elected but rather appointed for an indefinite term by an eight member *partisan-elected* state board. Also, the apportionment formulae in the House and Senate have been changed to give greater weight to population.

Despite these changes, pessimists in the state are convinced that the status quo will persist, except for the means of selecting the state school superintendent; and they believe the school lobbies will continue to operate in their traditional fragmented fashion while problems of finance and reorganization remain unresolved. That is, if constitutional revision does not lead to improvements, Michigan school interests will probably be forced to continue along the difficult but not unfamiliar road of temporary alliances, search for friendly legislators, and attempts at piecemeal amendment of existing school policies.

Thus far we have discussed the role of the major interests in the total political system and some of the prospects for the future. The absence of a stable power structure suggests that in order to understand education and politics in Michigan we need to examine major conflict issues. The remainder of this chapter is devoted to such an examination.

STATE AID AND SCHOOL DISTRICT REORGANIZATION: TWO CASE STUDIES

Two basic demands concerning public elementary and secondary schools were made on the Michigan legislature dur-

2 "Miracle in Michigan," *National Municipal Review*, XLVII, No. 7 (July 1958), p. 318.

ing the period of survey: one was for increased state financial aid to schools, and the other for the reorganization of local and county school districts. There have been numerous other education claims—proposals for changes in teacher retirement, certification, and tenure, and local district fiscal policies—but none has been as vital or received as much continuous attention as the state aid and school district reorganization issues.

In 1961 increased state aid and local and county school district reorganization were the key items on the public school legislative agenda; but in that year the legislature defeated all proposals dealing with these subjects. However, the reasons underlying the refusal of the state legislature to authorize the reorganization of either local or county school districts were essentially different from those that defeated proposed changes in the state aid formula. Therefore an analysis of these two issues and of the reasons for the legislature's unfavorable action should provide an assessment of the functions of the public school lobby in specific situations.

A note of caution is in order here. Since governmental action is a continuous process, no situation or series of decisions can be viewed as wholly typical. The conflict patterns that emerged in Michigan in 1961 will in all probability never appear again in *exactly* the same form. Thus an analysis of recent events, however illuminating in itself, will not suffice to bring *all* of the power relationships and influence patterns into proper perspective. Nor can we argue that the 1961 decisions will have long-term significance, more sweeping in character and more important in impact than previous or future decisions. We would severely strain the data if we used them to account for past or future situations.

Our purpose then is more modest. It is to discover what demands were made and who made them; who within the political system made the choices among various alternatives; and what were the perceived consequences on those making demands. By approaching the study of public school matters in this way, we can compare the potential influence of the public school lobby with its actual influence and account for some of the variations among the three states.

No Increases for the Schools

In the final hours of the 1961 Michigan legislative session, the House of Representatives defeated a last ditch demand for increased state aid to public elementary and secondary schools. Every Republican in the House voted against the proposal; every Democrat voted for it. In the week immediately preceding the final vote, the major public school interest groups and the State Department of Public Instruction engaged in an intense struggle to gain support for the bill. Such support failed to materialize. Despite the fact that many representatives of public school interests were known Republicans and that a conscientious effort had been made to prevent the state aid issue from becoming a partisan question, a straight party-line split developed with the Republican majority opposed to any increase. Before we look at the reasons for a partisan division on this issue, we must survey certain developments in state aid legislation just prior to the 1961 session.

In 1959, the state legislature passed an act guaranteeing that each year a minimum level of financial support would be given to every public school in the state which met certain minimum qualifications. The continuing appropriations act passed by substantial majorities in both the House (73-13) and the Senate (25-6). Thirteen Republicans from small rural districts who viewed the bill as a threat to local district autonomy opposed it in the House. The five Democrats and one Republican who opposed it in the Senate had based their votes largely on the ground that the bill would set a bad precedent. At the time it was adopted, all the public school interests hailed the act as the most significant step ever taken to insure a sound, minimum level of education for every child, regardless of the school district in which he resided. Prior to the passage of this law, the public school interests had been forced to vie each year for a portion of the state budget, "although," as one professional educator stated, "we [meaning the schools] didn't do too badly under the old arrangement."

The continuing appropriation act was due to a strong bipartisan effort both within the legislature and between Republican legislative leaders and Democratic Governor G. Mennen Williams to find in a period of fiscal crisis and uncertainty "as nearly a permanent solution as possible to the state aid issue." The basic idea underlying the passage of this act, aside from its obvious objective of financing schools was, according to one MEA representative,

to separate public school finance from other state issues. The theory was that this bill would get education out of politics and keep it from being a source of controversy between the governor and the legislators. But frankly, I think the bill was needed and supported as a solution to the fight between the large and small school districts. It's hard to say what everyone's reasoning was at the time, but one thing is clear, no one wanted to fight about schools.

If this were the case, then the objectives of Michigan educators and legislators were essentially the same as those of their counterparts in Illinois and Missouri: i.e., the removal of education issues from political conflict. The difference among the states is that in Michigan, attempts at separation have constantly been obstructed by forces which the public school interests have, thus far, been unable to contain.

Returning to the 1959 act for a moment, it provided $205 minimum for each pupil in average daily attendance and was to be financed by a two-cent sales tax earmarked for education and such additional funds from the general treasury as were necessary to insure the $205 minimum. The year this act passed was a golden one for the public school interests. They had worked long and hard to achieve unity among themselves on a specific bill. They had carefully built widespread public support for their cause. The Education Council had voted to let a nonprofessional group—the State Association of School Boards—lead the fight for its passage and the organization had carried out its task, according to one legislator, with "speed and dispatch." But the key group backing the proposal and the one responsible for much of the behind-the-scene negotiations in the legislature was a seven-member legislative committee of the MEA-MSSA organizations composed of veteran school superintendents. Support from both parties was cultivated, encouraged, and ultimately received by this group. "When the bill finally passed," said one lobbyist, "everyone seemed to be satisfied." Legislators were saying that at least one potentially explosive problem had been removed from the executive-legislative battle front. " 'What more could anyone ask for' was the general feeling I detected," said a former member of the governor's staff.

Representatives of all groups—the MEA, MASA and the MASB, etc.—were jubilant. They believed that largely through their efforts "public education had once again been removed and placed above politics." "We did it," one lobbyist asserted proudly, "and the kids in the schools throughout the state were the beneficiaries."

Operating under the assumption that "everything was now all right" and apparently without a worry about the future, the public school interests closed their legislative shops and quietly stood aside to listen to the thunder from other battles over fiscal policy. The public school lobby was soon to return to the practical world of competing for scarce resources, however. According to one group representative, "Our breathing spell certainly didn't last very long." In less than two years, educators throughout the state were asserting that $205 was totally inadequate and that unless something was done immediately, present educational programs would be placed in serious jeopardy. The pleasant vision of long-term settlement of a crucial school issue had faded quickly. Rapidly increasing operating and maintenance costs, expanding enrollments, demands for teacher salary increases, the need for capital expansion, inflation—all were cited as major reasons for more state aid. Each group, almost in turn, yielded to the crisis syndrome and began to clamor for action.

The Education Council, which included all the major groups, meeting in the conference room of the state superintendent's office late in 1960, decided unanimously to recommend an eight percent improvement factor in the state aid formula to the 1961 legislature in order to alleviate the situation. The Michigan Educational Association and the state superintendent's office did the basic research and formulated the proposals. The primary function performed by the other groups was to endorse and support their recommendations. What did this decision mean? How much money was involved? What were the expectations of the various groups? How was it to be handled? Would the governor support their position? What effect would this action have on other recommendations?

The "educators' proposal" (House Bill 407) provided an improvement factor of eight percent in the state aid act that, if adopted, would raise the guaranteed minimum for each child to approximately $221 per pupil in average daily attendance and would cost the state approximately $22,-500,000. Proponents of the bill contended that the eight percent increase was designed to bring about needed improvements in the quality of education throughout the state. The proposed measure was not designed to expand the school systems or to meet additional costs resulting from rising enrollment. Other steps would have to be taken to meet these contingencies. However, no provisions were included to alter the state aid formula in any basic way. Although the proponents agreed that some basic revisions might be desirable, to propose any would only aggravate the longstanding controversy between the wealthy and poorer districts over equalization and flat grant provisions. "In the context we had to operate, to demand a change in the equalization and flat grant formula would have meant sure defeat. We were in bad enough shape as it was," one group leader said.

In addition to the eight percent improvement factor proposal, some of the other major changes suggested were: removal of the maximum of $650,000 from the county school district section, and allowances of $5,125 for professional employees; removal of the maximum $12,000,000 for transportation; provisions for reimbursement of teachers of the emotionally disturbed; and extension of state aid to county districts that operate juvenile schools.

The bill was introduced by Representatives Wurzel, Buth, McCullough, Montgomery, Morrison and Jacobetti (six of the nine-member Education Committee), but the various groups relied most heavily upon the chairman of the House Education Committee, Raymond C. Wurzel, Republican from the St. Clair District. The chairman was regarded as a strong supporter of the public schools and, as one group leader put it, "not quite as conservative as some of the other Republicans—at least in this area." Representatives of the MEA felt that the ranking Democratic member of the committee, George Montgomery (Wayne County), was also their ally and could be relied upon to give them strong support from his side of the aisle.

They encountered opposition immediately. A few Republican legislators on the Education Committee suggested that the bill was merely a "teacher welfare" proposal designed solely to increase teachers' salaries. Proponents challenged this interpretation of their proposal, indicating that money for salary increases was only one of many purposes for which additional funds would be utilized. However, major opposition was expected to come from the formal Republican leadership: namely, the chairman and the ranking Republican members of the House Ways and Means Committee and the Speaker of the House, who had threatened several times to use his power over committee assignments to penalize Republicans who supported "big spending," whether such proposals came from the governor or some other source.

The public school interests knew they would encounter stiff Republican opposition to their proposals. They did not anticipate the governor's position. Despite extensive preliminary negotiations between Governor Swainson and the Democratic Superintendent of Schools, Lynn Bartlett, the governor refused to endorse and support the educators' proposal. Swainson submitted a 477 million dollar budget to the state legislature which called for only a three percent improvement factor in the state aid formula, which would cost approximately nine million dollars. The governor defended his budget request for public education as well as other items on the grounds that it was sufficient income to meet only the increases he recommended.

The governor had additional reasons for not supporting the education proposals. He was under pressure, both from within and outside the governor's office, to operate differently from his predecessor, G. Mennen Williams, who had in the past taken what politicians call the "service route." That is, Williams would propose what he thought was needed, with only a minimum initial concern for fiscal soundness, and expect to work out the compromises later on. One school lobbyist characterized the Williams viewpoint on educational problems as "excellent." He recalled occasions when the school groups brought finance proposals to Lansing and were told by the governor that they were not asking for enough. Of course, Governor Williams' recommendations often fell on deaf ears in the legislature.

Swainson, on the other hand, had been a member of the Michigan state Senate. He felt he knew the legislature and what it would and would not do. In his term as governor, he proposed not what the various groups wanted, but what he considered a "reasonable" or "compromise" program in advance. Thus not only did he refuse to support the education proposals, but he also cut substantially the requests made by other groups and state agencies, especially in the area of higher education, where he whittled a 40 million dollar request to 8.1 million.

The initial failure to obtain gubernatorial support for their proposed increase "hurt our chances," a representative of one group contended, "but with legislative-executive relations strained some of us felt that we were better off not to be involved in a partisan struggle." But the Republicans still accused the governor of being unrealistic and of recommending more than the state could afford, which complicated the situation for the school interests. Their recommendations called for greater expenditure amounts than even the governor had recommended. Early in the session, the fate of both proposals became clear. As one group representative put it, "It was evident from the start that it was going to be a 'hold that line' year."

The educators' proposal and the governor's bill were both sent to the House Committee on Education. The political grapevine indicated that a compromise proposal would be written in committee allowing for a five percent improvement factor, that this proposal would receive bipartisan committee support, and that after it was introduced, the House Ways and Means Committee would kill the bill. All of these things happened in that order. The burial of the five percent bill in Ways and Means came as a shock to practically no one.

There were numerous explanations for this initial setback and it might prove useful, at this point, to examine the ones that are usually advanced. Governor Swainson, for example, defended his total budget request on the grounds that there would be sufficient income from existing taxes to meet the increases he recommended, but no more. Republican leaders, on the other hand, strongly disputed his analysis of the state's revenue picture and opposed his proposals not only on an ideological and partisan basis, but also because they felt realistic revenue estimates were nearer a 462 million dollar figure. If the Republican estimates were correct, and the leaders were certain they were, then there would be no money available for any increases in any area.

The governor, though confident that his earlier estimates were correct, quickly realized that he would be unable to convince the legislature that his program fitted a balanced budget. He then proposed an alternative; he recommended establishing a public building authority to finance by long-term bonds all capital expansions that were currently being financed through annual appropriations. This measure, he maintained, would release twenty million dollars to be used for requested budget increases. The Republican leaders flatly refused to adopt such a proposal on the grounds that such deficit financing was fiscally irresponsible. The measure was promptly sent to the Ways and Means Committee and there it died with no vote being taken. Neither house of the Republican-controlled legislature at this halfway stage of the legislative session supported any of the governor's recommendations, those pertaining to the public schools included.

The education groups had foreseen the defeat of their proposal for some time. The reasons, they felt, were obvious enough. One tough-minded representative asserted:

Nothing we could have done would have changed things very much. The governor and the legislature were at odds over his budget and the Republicans had committed themselves to the position of adamant opposition to any increases. Our proposals as well as those of other groups were all pushed aside when the Republicans decided on a policy of no increases over last year.

The strategy employed next by the education groups, particularly the MEA, the State Association of School Superintendents, and the state superintendent's office, was designed to gain commitments from various key Republican legislators so that if increases were provided for any state services, the public schools would be given highest priority. All agreed that they had been successful in obtaining such promises, but they also felt that they didn't mean very much, since it was unlikely that any other services would be increased. In addition, the State Association of School Superintendents increased efforts to mobilize grass-roots support. They urged local school superintendents to contact their legislators and those who supported public education were encouraged to write, wire, or phone their representatives.

Although we made no attempt in this study to quantify the results of these efforts, interviews with legislative leaders of both parties indicated that the results were not impressive: that is, no widespread public concern was perceived to exist. It seemed readily apparent to all public school interests that despite the existence of a potential source of support, their efforts had produced only nominal interest on the part of their grass-roots contingents.

Towards the final third of the session, sometime in May to be exact, a group of Republican insurgents in the Senate, promptly tagged the "Young Turks" [3] by the old guard Senate Republicans, offered the pro-school groups a ray of hope. Striking out on their own, the Young Turks proposed to appropriate additional money for public schools, higher education, mental health, and a few other state services. These increases were to be financed by an extension of certain temporary excise taxes on liquor and tobacco that had been enacted the previous year. The Senate group claimed that the excise taxes would yield approximately 12 million dollars, of which five million would be used to provide in-

---

[3] This group included eight of the Republican majority's twenty-two senators. They were: John W. Fitzgerald, Grand Ledge; John F. Stahlin, Bedding; Harry Litzwich, Benton Harbor; Stanley G. Thayer, Ann Arbor; William G. Milliken, Traverse City; Thomas F. Schweigert, Pitoskey; Frederick Hilbert, Wayland; Farrell E. Roberts, Pontiac. All were first or second term senators.

creases and the distribution of the remainder left to the discretion of the legislature, which presumably would authorize its use for debt retirement.

At first the governor would have no part of this proposal. In his campaign the preceding fall, Swainson indicated that if elected he would vigorously oppose further extension of the nuisance taxes. But later, early in June, he amended this position when he felt there was no other alternative left open. He offered to compromise with the Young Turks, indicating that he would be willing to support an extension of the nuisance taxes if the Senate group would guarantee in return that the full amount of additional revenues would be used for increased appropriations. The Young Turks, however, refused to alter their proposal, and consequently the governor urged the Senate Democrats to vote against them, which they did. The Democrats in coalition with the old guard Republicans defeated the measure, once again proving the axiom that politics produces strange bedfellows. Hopes for an increase for the public schools via this route were wrecked on the Great Barrier Reef existing between the governor and the state legislature.

There were only six weeks left in the session following the Senate vote. At this point, Governor Swainson decided to realign his forces and attempt to expand his support in another effort to get through his original legislative program. This effort was also to fail, but not before most of the major public school interests had swung over to his side.

At this time, the representatives of all the public school groups were firmly convinced that they did not have sufficient influence to reverse the legislature's earlier decisions. On the basis of their assessment of the prevailing political setting, they believed that the only strategy open to them was to support the governor's proposals. In order to obtain gubernatorial support, the representatives of the various interests had to agree to support the governor's entire program. Faced with an unambiguous rejection of their claims, the public school interests moderated or changed goals and altered their basic strategy to become part of a coalition with the governor and other groups. The Educational Council provided the formal mechanism for the agreement.

Tying their fate to the governor's program required a major concession. Education groups had to agree that in the forthcoming negotiations between the governor and the state legislature, any proposal for increases in state aid for public schools would have a lower priority than proposals for increases for mental health and the state universities and colleges. The governor and his advisers felt that a more substantial case could be made for the latter two items because the public, as they perceived it, had demonstrated a greater concern about these areas. Governor Swainson also reasoned that the continuing appropriation act "guarantee" prevented any irreparable damage to the state's public school program, even if no increases were approved. The public school interests conceded most reluctantly. They were willing to join forces as a last resort on the sheer chance that an increase for the public schools would be swept in with the entire program.

For groups unusually sensitive to the important consequences of identifications and alliances, this strategy represented a radical departure from the usual course. Each group worried about the effect it would have on future relationships. In brief, the public school interests had now done three things they had never intended to do. First, they reduced their earlier demand for an eight percent increase to the governor's three percent; second, their proposal, now the same as the governor's proposal, was introduced by Democratic legislators, which identified the public school groups with a Democratic governor in a highly charged partisan atmosphere; and, third, in agreeing to support the governor's entire program, they had extended their activities into policy areas which they had carefully avoided in the past.

This departure from usual policy produced aggravated disunity within the public school lobby. Not all groups felt obliged to follow the agreement with the governor in its entirety. Interviews with legislators of both parties indicated that the representatives of the various interests, such as the MEA, gave no more than lip service to their endorsement of the governor's entire program. "We knew they were not committed to it and they knew we knew it," one legislator remarked. Furthermore, representatives of the State Association of School Boards, apparently anxious to relieve the pressing financial problems of many local districts, continued to press for a five percent improvement factor. The PTA, a major supportive group, but not a party to the alliance, held out for an eight percent figure. The total situation was summarized rather pointedly by one pro-school Republican legislator. He said, "Hell, they didn't know what they wanted or where they were going. First, someone would say eight percent, then next someone would say five, and lo and behold someone else would come along and say we support the governor's whole program. Now who would you believe?"

In the end, the one thing the public school groups feared most happened: the Republicans in the House, many of whom had previously supported bills for increased state aid for schools, voted unanimously against the proposal when it was presented as part of the governor's program. Many Republicans claimed that they had little choice since the speaker and the party leader threatened to use all of their discretionary powers to punish any bolters. As a result of a complex of factors, the public school interests were drawn into a partisan fight and their loss in this instance was directly tied to a defeat of a Democratic governor's program.

It must be said that throughout this legislative session the existence of a continuing appropriation act severely hampered the public school interests efforts. Most Republicans claimed that much more than partisanship was involved in their refusal to support an increase. They said that the schools would receive more aid anyway because the law required a $205 minimum for each pupil in average daily attendance and enrollments had risen. They also pointed out, time and time again, that it was the educators themselves who had engineered the present act and decided on the present figure. They should, therefore, be prepared to live with it.

Thus we see in the 1961 session of the Michigan legislature the pattern of public school politics on appropriations legislation. The education lobby, plagued with disunity in its own ranks and unable to devise a strategy to keep education a matter for separate or special attention, was drawn into partisan conflict and suffered defeat.

It is clear from an examination of circumstances in Michigan in 1961 that education appropriation measures are not self-enacting or immune from controversy. To pass from idea into reality they require skillful use of numerous resources. Neither the public school groups nor the governor could find the formula for success. Spokesmen for the school groups apparently had no difficulty in convincing the House Education Committee members from both political parties that more money was needed. Here considerable credit must be given to the representatives of the MEA and the state superintendent's office for their skillful presentation of data. But information alone, even though skillfully presented, did not sway the Republican leadership and the Republican members of the House Ways and Means Committee. It is only a slight oversimplification to say that the conservative Republicans had their eyes solely on the total revenue picture and believed the public, as they understood it, would not support any additional drains on the state treasury. The groups whose principal resource was an active and articulate membership had from all outward signs failed to convince these legislators that their memberships and the remainder of the public were more concerned about schools than about taxes and a balanced budget.

Consequently, school politics in Michigan in 1961 contrasted sharply with school politics in either Illinois or Missouri during that same year. No group in Michigan could boast of the close and effective relationships with the state legislature that were enjoyed by the MSTA in Missouri. There was no Everett Keith to represent "the total thinking" of education groups and to agree quietly to the necessary compromises to push a program through. There was no School Problems Commission which had the legislature's complete confidence and upon which it could rely to present a sensible program. In this fight, the pro-school people could offer few inducements to the legislators. The MSTA and the SPC both provide services and act as a buffer between legislators and their constituents; there simply was no counterpart in Michigan to keep education apart from the other conflicts. And when there is conflict and people choose sides, someone wins and someone loses. In 1961, the pro-school people lost out.

School District Reorganization—Two Proposals

An entirely different set of circumstances contributed to the defeat of the 1961 school district reorganization in the legislature. Since many of the same personalities and organizations were involved in the fight for the reorganization as were involved in the appropriations conflict, the issues, of course, cannot be completely separated. The results of the appropriations fight definitely effected the reorganization proposals. But three factors involved in the battle for reorganization made the issues fundamentally different from the appropriations fight. First, there was continuous well-organized opposition to the reorganization proposals from outside the legislature. Second, a tightly knit group of legislators fought all proposals, taking its cues from the opposition force. And third, the public school interests were clearly split, some for, some against, which contrasts with their positions on the state aid proposals where all groups were at least in favor of an increase.

Let us look first at the two reorganization measures themselves. One proposed to reorganize all school districts in the state into systems that offered at least grades kindergarten through twelve, and the second proposal recommended the consolidation of small county school districts into new intermediate school districts.

Michigan has no provision for the general reorganization of local school districts. School districts may change their boundaries through locally initiated annexation or consolidation. At this writing, such annexations and consolidations occur at the rate of one every forty hours. These changes are not, however, presently governed by, or geared to, any state-wide plan for reorganization.

In recent years, the State Department of Public Instruction, with the formal support of MEA, has sought the adoption of a state-wide plan for reorganizing school districts. This plan, formulated by the Department, would require all school districts in the State to operate grades kindergarten through twelve, or, to state it differently, would require districts of fewer than the twelve grades to reorganize into kindergarten through twelfth grade (K-12) districts. This would mean that approximately 1,300 of the state's 1,800-odd school districts would have to be reorganized. Even this drastic a reduction in school districts is not enough for some professional experts who feel that the ideal number is around 250.

A school district reorganization bill introduced with bipartisan support into the 1961 legislature provided for the mandatory K-12 reorganization to be handled by a seven-member State Reorganization Committee appointed by the governor. This committee would be responsible for establishing the policies, principles, and procedures for the reorganization of school districts. The committee would transmit these policies to the county committees, each with 15 members representing large districts, small districts, and the general public.

The county committee in each county, within nine months after receiving the standards from the state committee, would devise a plan to place all areas of the county into a K-12 school district. If approved by the State Reorganization Committee, the county plan would be submitted to the electors in the affected school districts. Adoption of the plan would require a simple majority of those voting on the question.

If the electors rejected the plan, the bill provided that the county committee, through a series of public hearings, would draft a revised plan to be voted upon within ninety days. If the electors rejected the revised plan, the county committee would then present its plan to the state board of education. The state board of education would be required to take action on the adoption of a school district reorganization plan for the county and its decision would have the same effect as an affirmative vote by the electors of the local districts involved.

The school district reorganization proposal would establish the means to reorganize all areas within the state within one year after its adoption. In brief, if such a bill became law, all school districts not offering grades kindergarten through twelve would have to reorganize. Any noncompliant local district would be reorganized by the state board.

The second proposal before the 1961 legislature, one to create intermediate school districts, sought a type of reorganization of county school districts not totally dissimilar from the proposal to reorganize local districts. This proposal, sponsored by the Michigan Association of County School Administrators, would require all county school districts with school membership of less than 5,000 to consolidate with or annex contiguous county districts until the intermediate district would contain at least that number. This would constitute a major departure from the present provision for reorganization which allows, but does not compel, contiguous districts with a total population of less than 15,000 to consolidate into a single district.

In addition, the proposed intermediate school bill, termed the "structure bill" by the educators, would give fiscal independence to the intermediate district by guaranteeing one-fourth mill of the 15 mill tax allowed by the constitution. This one-fourth mill would be within, and not in addition to, the 15 mill limitation. At the present time, county districts submit their budget to the County Board of Supervisors who in turn decide the amount to be allotted to the county school district.

The structure bill also provided for the popular election of the county school board. The five-member county school board is currently chosen for staggered six-year terms by the presidents, or designated representatives, of the school boards of all school districts within the county.

Both bills were introduced in the House. The K-12 local school district reorganization bill was considered first and encountered stiff resistance, both in the committee and on the floor. Opposition came from various quarters. A group officially known as the Friends of the Michigan Schools or the Little Red School House group offered the most vocal and perhaps most vigorous resistance. According to one of its principal spokesmen, this group saw itself as "fighting to keep control of our local schools because they are vital if we are to preserve our form of government, and we do not want our grandchildren to grow up and live under socialism as predicted by Khrushchev."

Though such a term as "well-organized" is difficult to define, the Friends of the Michigan Schools group—which boasted of a membership exceeding 5,000—appeared to all members of the House and Senate Education Committees to have this characteristic. "More members or representatives of this group have contacted me in connection with this issue than any other we faced—they are certainly here in force and well-organized." The chairman of the House Education Committee made this comment: "The Little Red School House people are *very* vocal, the most vocal group of its size and they are extremely well-organized. In my opinion, the fact that membership is noisy and scattered over the rural areas where the majority of the legislators— and frequently the most influential ones—come from has made it a highly successful group on this issue."

The political resources available to the Friends of the Michigan Schools group were relatively limited. It had little money, and even less social esteem; it made no claim to have control over information, credit, or wealth and it had no jobs to offer. Its principal resource aside from solidarity was a capacity to evoke support from legislators who identi- fied with it because of similarities in background and broad ideological commitment. The issue of school district reor- ganization touched a very sensitive spot in the minds of many legislators. They felt that a change in the pattern of school organization, particularly a change that the state government initiated and directed, would destroy an in- tegral part of rural life.

In many small communities, the school is much more than a place to send children for an education. Beyond its edu- cational functions, the school is the center for almost all civic and social activities. Athletic contests and dances held on school property provide entertainment for local citizens; the school assembly hall is a convenient place for discussions on public questions affecting the area and the local branches of the Farm Bureau frequently meet in the school house. In addition, the teachers and administrators have become, in perhaps the majority of cases, thoroughly integrated in the community they live in and they are frequently regarded as pillars of the community. Reorganization would threaten or perhaps destroy community life as these people know it. The Little Red School House group relied heavily on the fact that a large number of rural legislators would be pre-disposed to share these views. Moreover, even those legisla-tors who personally disagreed with the group's position but who were from areas where the group had demonstrated some strength regarded its views as representative of the prevailing set of attitudes in their home communities. "I don't like this group," one legislator said, "but I can't afford to ignore it. Most of the people back home feel the same way they do."

It would be misleading to attribute the ultimate defeat of the reorganization proposals solely to this group. The Farm Bureau also lined up against reorganization. In com-parison with the Little Red School House group, the Farm Bureau obviously had at its disposal more potential resources with which to work for the defeat of the proposals. The Farm Bureau had long been a powerful force in Michigan politics. It had an active and well-organized membership, established lines of contact with legislative leaders, money, and a per-manent division within its central bureaucracy that dealt ex-clusively with pending legislative matters. But the position taken by the Farm Bureau was considerably more moderate than that one taken by the Little Red School House group. The legislative secretary of the Farm Bureau summarized the organization's view as follows:

Reorganization should not be forced upon the local school dis-tricts. We are against the current state-wide plan that would re-quire this. Reorganization is a matter for local decision and the door should be left open for whatever the local districts want to do. In short, reorganization should be entirely voluntary.

The Farm Bureau did not intervene strongly on this issue. It made no attempt to cash in on favors owed; it offered no rewards to legislators who supported its position. The bu-reau's limited use of its resources resulted largely from what an organization's spokesman described as "member-ship inertia." "Our membership isn't as concerned as it used to be about reorganization; the Farm Bureau's position hasn't changed, but the members who were once very much against this, now show no feelings on this issue, pro or con. Of course, this restricts how much we do." Taken together, however, the Farm Bureau and the Little Red School House group constituted what may be loosely described as the rural bloc against reorganization.

Anti-reorganization forces were not confined solely to the more rural areas of the state. Direct and intense opposition to the K-12 bill came also from groups representing the cities and large wealthy school districts. The Michigan Municipal League, a group composed of mayors and various city officials, was considerably stirred up over the K-12 bill. Like the Farm Bureau, the league had ample potential resources at its disposal. Many of its members could claim to control large blocs of votes in a number of legislative districts. The group could and did make claims on enough legislators so that the legislative leadership, including the speaker, the majority leaders in both houses, and the chairman of the House and Senate Education Committees, would not ignore its views. Although the league had no continuous concern over the details of public school organization, it vigorously opposed the bill because of a provision in the constitution which required, according to a decision of the state Supreme Court, that all component parts (school district, water district, etc.) within a governmental unity (city or county) adopt a uniform tax rate, equal to the rate of the lowest component part of the governmental unit.

What would this bill mean to a city such as Saginaw with a 10 mill tax levy for schools? If forced to reorganize its school district to include a school district within a township that had only a 9 mill tax levy for schools, the city would have to lower its school tax levy to 9 mills unless the entire area of the school district were annexed to the city. Following through on this example, in dollar terms Saginaw would suffer a school revenue loss of almost $200,000 per year. In brief, the Municipal League's position was based on the obvious assumption that no mayor was anxious to have the tax base of the city schools adversely affected by required school district reorganization.

It is virtually impossible to measure the extent of Municipal League influence on this issue, since legislators had so many reasons to vote against it. Unquestionably, much of the opposition that came from the representatives of areas in which large school districts would be affected was almost directly traceable to the efforts of this group. One legislator from such an area put it bluntly: "I'm not going to alienate city hall merely to help out a few small districts."

The school districts that would themselves be hurt by such a change came down against reorganization. The representatives of school districts which had boundaries entirely within a city and a higher tax levy than surrounding areas pounced hard on their legislators. This signified a major break in the education front. "As usual," one legislator said, "the school people couldn't get together on this issue either." Even the proponents of reorganization had to agree that the city school interests made a substantial and reasonable case against the proposal. The only counter argument was that the state Supreme Court might reverse its earlier interpretation of the uniform tax provision. "We just couldn't say their position was untenable. Unfortunately, they were right," a group leader admitted.

In the face of such opposition, "a positive force of substantial strength was desperately needed," representatives of the MEA and state superintendent's office asserted. But such a force failed to materialize. "There was little widespread citizen interest in our proposal," an MEA official said, "and although it was the kind of proposal that a few citizens' groups such as the PTA were in favor of, none gave it very active support." Moreover, the resources at the disposal of the state superintendent and the MEA were being spent on the appropriations fight; reorganization of the K-12 districts had only second priority. "Reorganization is needed and needed desperately," an education lobbyist said, "but it can wait. In this fight our hope was that the reorganization proposal could be used as sort of a bargaining weapon for increased state aid. Our strategy obviously did not work." Again, as had been the case in the state aid fight, information about school needs backed by the trust and confidence legislators had in the MEA and state superintendent's reliability was the only effective resource.

The other major education group supporting K-12 reorganization was the Michigan Association of School Boards, but this group did not back the bill enthusiastically. As one representative of a public school group described the MASB's position: "They didn't oppose the bill; they just didn't fight for it." Representatives of the group frankly admitted that this was indeed an accurate appraisal of the association's position. "Our reluctance to get behind reorganization vigorously was based on the fact that districts of some of the member boards would be sharply altered by this plan and some of our boards are opposed to any forced reorganization." The group's representative went on to say that the association had backed a comparable plan a few years earlier, and after having received considerable criticism from within the organization, had adopted the general policy of favoring such plans in principle only.

Despite evidence of a split in the public school lobby and strong opposition from outside groups, the House of Representatives passed the K-12 bill (House Bill 531), but the vote was relatively close. Forty Democrats and 17 Republicans lined up against 36 Republicans and 6 Democrats. The consensus among the advocates was that Chairman Wurzel performed yeoman's service in keeping the K-12 bill and the Structure Bill clearly differentiated in the minds of House legislators and in House procedures. We have already mentioned the factors acting on the K-12 bill from outside the House. Certainly an important variable operating inside the legislative body in this instance was the force of Representative Wurzel's personality. Wurzel's position regarding H.B. 231 obviously carried considerable political weight, since the bill was passed despite the heavy pressures against it.

The vote was not simply partisan, however, and an analysis of its composition suggests the conflicts that have existed over public school questions in Michigan. Although the Democrats overwhelmingly voted in the affirmative, the vote was by no means a strictly partisan split. Republicans were not united in opposition, although two thirds of them voted against passage. Perhaps the key lies more along the lines suggested earlier in this study: i.e., the discrepancy between wealthy, average, and poor school districts in terms of revenue. Some urban districts are not wealthy and all rural districts are not poor when it comes to school financial supports; however, there is some justification in fact for looking at this vote to see how urban and rural representatives lined up.

According to United States Office of Education classifications of rural counties, which are based on census data, Michigan contains 36 rural counties out of its total of 83. The K-12 bill brought forth the following votes from urban, rural, and mixed representatives.

TABLE 4

VOTE ON K-12 REORGANIZATION BILL (H.B. 231)

Representatives analyzed by counties	Yes	No
Urban	37	16
Rural	5	21
Mixed (2 or more counties—1 urban, 1 rural)	15	5

Both urban and rural members were split over this issue. But most of the rural legislators were against passage. Significantly representatives from *both rural and urban* areas were opposed but for substantially different reasons. Most of the urban legislators who opposed did so on principally the grounds that it would damage the tax status of the local districts in their respective constituencies; whereas the majority of rural legislators who opposed did so on the grounds that state reorganization interfered with local autonomy.

Meanwhile, the county school district reorganization (structure bill) cleared all of the legislative hurdles in the House with only token opposition. The proposals had the endorsement of all the major educational groups. It was reported out of committee favorably and passed the House April 14, the day after the K-12 bill, by a vote of 92 to 5. The chairman of the Education Committee had made a deliberate effort to help the two reorganization proponents get separate consideration of their bills, and he succeeded.

The real test for the two proposals came in the Senate, however, where the proponents knew they had few friends. Both bills were immediately assigned to the Senate Education Committee. It was known well in advance that the chairman was generally opposed to both bills, but particularly the K-12 bill. The chairman, strongly supported by the ranking majority members of the committee and several senators who were not on the committee, made no effort to keep the two bills separate.

After considering each bill for several days, the committee reported both out on the same day. Both proponents and opponents of the bills agreed that many, if not most, senators were confused, not knowing which bill was which. The structure bill was amended extensively (an amendment was introduced to continue certain features of the county school district organization) and before the final vote on the structure bill could be taken, the Michigan Association of County School Administrators suddenly withdrew its support and persuaded its allies in the legislature to have the bill killed by a motion to refer it back to the committee. This was accomplished without a recorded vote.

The K-12 bill was dealt the same death blow when it became clear that neither the large, wealthy school districts nor the small rural poor districts were behind the bill. In this case, the interests ended up on the same side, but for entirely different reasons. The large school districts which operated within incorporated cities feared a loss of revenue; otherwise, they might have supported the bill. On the other hand, the small rural districts based their case more on ideological grounds, viewing the bill as a threat both to local autonomy and, in some instances, community life. Opposition from both sides made it easy for the Senate to kill the bill. The state superintendent, acting through his legislative liaison and the representatives of the MEA, made a last-minute appeal to secure favorable action; but by this time the senators who were opposed to the bill were able to capitalize on the obvious split among public school interests and the confusion between the structure and the K-12 bills. The Senate approved a motion to refer the K-12 bill back to the committee, where it died.

What does the K-12 reorganization fight suggest about school politics in Michigan? Several things. First, the groups that led the fight—MEA and state superintendent's office —were not completely committed, partly because of a greater concern for increasing state aid and partly because of the uncertainties of applying the uniform tax rule. Yet these two groups had supplied the initiative for the program. There seemed to be a great gap between the potential influence of these groups and their actual influence. Their effectiveness was limited to the House, where they relied on the efforts of a strong and vigorous chairman to lead the fight.

Second, the split between the wealthy and poor districts affected the outcome of the decision. The two principal interests—the wealthy and the poorer districts—were not split on the issue; they were, in fact, on the same side, both against. But the wealthy districts, particularly those in the large cities, were not about to approve of any plan, regardless of its alleged merits, that would affect their tax base adversely. Their position was, as one legislator said, to "let the small poor districts organize on their own. Why include us?" The small poorer districts wanted state aid in the form of equalized grants, not state interference in their internal organization. They were suspicious of large school domination if such a plan went into effect. The Little Red School House group capitalized on this attitude, particularly in its attempt to influence the Senate, and was able despite limited resources to convince many legislators that its views were indeed representative of the prevailing set of attitudes in many areas of the state.

Third, the K-12 bill incurred the opposition of a group with powerful political resources at its disposal, the Michigan Municipal League.

Finally, except for the MEA and state superintendent's office, the groups which comprise the public school lobby shunned direct involvement in this issue. The Michigan Federation of Teachers displayed no concern at all beyond endorsing the idea. Reorganization would not affect the Detroit school system where the bulk of its membership is concentrated. The State Association of School Boards and State Association of School Superintendents felt themselves to be in a weak political position because of the anticipated effect that reorganization would have on some of their members and because they felt that a large number of members would not support or tolerate a strong pro-reorganization position. In brief, the preferences of the MEA and state superintendent were clearly in favor of reorganization but they were not too strong, while the preferences of the other groups were equally clear in favor of reorganization, but were extraordinarily weak.

The structure bill failed simply because it was too closely tied to the K-12 bill. In all probability it would have passed had it not been considered on the floor at the same time as the K-12 bill. Everyone involved agreed it had been struck down because of the confusion between the two.

Public school politics on the state level in Michigan appears to be analogous to the pattern of public school politics in Illinois *prior* to the creation of the SPC. The interests are fragmented; each tends to have its own design for public school improvement or acts independently of the others. In going their separate ways, the various interests follow the procedure that was so characteristic of Illinois school politics a decade or so ago. That is, each seeks out a friendly legislator or group of legislators, persuades him to introduce its bills, and then adopts whatever strategies and tactics that seem appropriate. Moreover, the state superintendent's attempts to build a united education lobby have been only moderately successful. The partisan nature of the state office, the desire of certain groups to be *the* major innovators, the overcrowded agenda—all are cited as major reasons for the educational councils' ineffectiveness.

Michigan differs from Illinois prior to the SPC in one important respect. Education leaders view the political environment in which they operate as riddled with partisan conflicts, which makes it impossible to depoliticize crucial public school issues, particularly those relating to finance. Education leaders confess that they have been markedly unsuccessful in their campaign to separate public school issues from the conflicts that rage over other issues. Education leaders also argue that stable and durable structures are needed for decision-making in the public school field. But thus far all movements in this direction have failed.

A VARIETY OF BILLS

To round out the public school picture in Michigan we should mention the variety of school bills considered in that state. As in Missouri and Illinois, bills introduced affecting the public school in the 1961 session dealt with diverse subjects (see Appendix IV), and although particular bills are not necessarily significant, their diversity is. In total, 65 bills were introduced in the House and 35 in the Senate (six of which were either substantially or exactly the same as those introduced in the House). The Department of Public Instruction sponsored actively ten of these measures and the Educational Council reviewed each proposal, but took an active interest in only a few.

The wide range of issues these bills covered merits at least a passing comment. The subject matters ranged from a proposal to distribute the money from a tax on mining companies of low grade ore to school districts proportionately according to actual mileage levied, to a bill increasing the professional requirements for the certification of consulting psychologists. A few bills applied to exclusively local situations, such as the proposal to require the Detroit Board of Education to submit its annual budget to the Detroit City Council for approval (which did not pass). Others dealt with relatively procedural matters, such as the regulation of bonded indebtedness, school board election practices, the amount of sick leave for teachers, and recodification of certain provisions of the school code. Most of the bills did not pass, and of those adopted, none altered school procedures in any basic way.

More specifically, of the 100 bills introduced, only 22 passed, and of these, 19 originated in the House. At least two were of special concern to the state's major educational interests and therefore should be mentioned here. One was Senate Bill 1357, more generally known as the "school lobbyists" bill. Six Republicans, including the chairman of the Senate Education Committee, and one Democrat introduced a measure that would prohibit the use of public funds to pay dues, membership fees, workshop fees, or travel expenses to any convention or meeting of any private organization or nonprofit corporation. The bill also provided that no employee of a school district shall be given a leave of absence unless he pays for a qualified substitute and that *no public funds shall be expended for the activities of an employee in any legislative matter,* unless requested to testify by the legislature itself. Every group was bitterly opposed to this bill, which was described by one member of the Educational Council as merely an attempt "to show that a lot of money is spent in lobbying. It illustrates again the hostility some of the senators have toward the efforts education groups in this state are making to improve the schools." The bill never came out of the Senate Education Committee to which it had been referred and there is no record of any type of deliberators ever held in connection with it.

But the mere fact that such a bill was sponsored by 7 out of 34 senators, at least 2 of whom hold leadership positions, and that it had some bipartisan support suggests how severely strained were the relationships between professional education groups and the state Senate. It would probably stretch any analysis of this bill to the breaking point to suggest that its introduction indicates a great deal more than annoyance or irritation with the education lobby. But it is conceivable that if such a bill were to pass, the power position of education groups would be restricted in such a way as to hamper attempts to secure the allocation of greater resources for public schools. Perhaps more important, it also suggests that at least some senators do not visualize that support for the MEA—and this bill would obviously restrict the MEA—may serve as a means for preventing the unionization of teachers. In any event, education groups in Michigan were either powerful enough to prevent the enactment of this bill or the majority of legislators were not inclined to support any measure that might drastically curtail the efforts of the public school interests.

Another measure of considerable consequence to Michigan school interests was a proposal for a minimum teacher's salary law. It was generally known that the MEA was the originator of this proposal, which is consistent with a trend in other states for NEA affiliates to initiate more teacher "welfare" proposals at the state level. House Bill 549, introduced by five Upper Peninsula Democrats, required that a fully qualified degree teacher receive a minimum salary of $4,800 per year, with increments of at least $200 per year for ten years. The Educational Council endorsed the proposals, although within the council there was some question as to its merits. On the positive side, the MEA claimed Michigan was in a poor bargaining position with neighboring states in the recruitment of teachers and that the people would pay for the necessary increases once the facts were brought to light. On the negative side, other members of the council suggested that $4,800 was too high, particularly with the guaranteed $200 a year increments for teachers with a bachelor's degree, $240 a year for those with a master's degree, and $50 a year for those without degrees, and thus beyond the reach of many districts. The legislative representatives of the Detroit public schools suggested that if the $200 increment were dropped, chances for passage would improve, claiming a "half a loaf was better than none." The state superintendent objected to the $50 increment for non-degree teachers on the grounds that this would encourage too many non-degree people not to finish. Despite these objections, which were offered and taken seriously, the MEA stuck to its original proposal, once again revealing the dissension within the educational lobby. Meanwhile a somewhat similar version was introduced in the Senate.

Despite MEA's intense interest in these proposals, particularly the House bill, neither progressed very far in either the Senate or the House. In both bodies, the bills were referred to the Education Committees and they stayed there, with no record of any deliberations ever being held. Again the reasons the minimum salary proposals never got anywhere, not even to a vote, are due to Michigan's political climate in 1961. As one group representative said, "We were fighting a losing battle all along the line, we could not afford to try to *force* a vote on this issue." Or, as another put it, "our timing was off. This wasn't the time to raise another issue that obviously would cost the state more money. It is impossible to tell whether these proposals would have encountered additional roadblocks in the event that other issues were not at stake, such as opposition from school administrators' or school board associations. Although some felt that these organizations would oppose if left entirely to their own devices, there was apparently no need to express such opposition openly at this time.

This brief reconnaissance of school politics in Michigan reveals how difficult it is for the majority of professional education interests in a high conflict and partisan atmosphere to contrive working arrangements that will meet the practical necessities. The political style and strategies of the education "establishment" (with the possible exception of the teachers union) are based on certain values or attitudes about how education issues *should* be decided. Consensus and avoidance of conflict are essential ingredients of these values, which results in the policy neutrality and objectivity as well as a bipartisan approach in the presentation demands. Strategies based on these attitudes have in the past in Michigan proved satisfactory to the interests concerned, much as they do in Illinois and Missouri. But when the *parties divide* on issues that directly affect schools, the education interests tend to lose their initiative; they are, so to speak, boxed in by the very tactics that in the past may have been effective. Emphasis on consensus and avoidance of open conflict are advantageous only when the strains and divisions within the political system do not erupt. We do not mean to imply that partisan divisions require partisan identifications. Rather in such situations it seems that the political style of education interests is not geared toward bringing the type of pressures that will break deadlock or stalemate. Yet well-posted informants agree that these myths are so deeply

pervasive that the education interests have an inherent in-
capacity to act effectively when open eruptions occur. In
fact, despite the political sophistication and insights group
leaders may possess, these commitments have frequently
made it difficult for them to broaden their perspective and
take more practical positions. Such was the case in Michigan.

CHAPTER V

❀ ❀ ❀ ❀

Conclusions

The purpose of this study has been to determine how and
by whom power is exercised when decisions are made concerning public schools at the state level in three midwestern
states, without implying that they are typical or atypical.
The book deals directly with only certain aspects in the political process where education and politics meet. We excluded decision-making concerning higher education entirely
because, in that policy area, different groups initiate demands
which are handled in substantially different ways. A large
part of the politics that inevitably surrounds state administrative decisions, particularly in the areas of teacher certification, school accreditation, textbook selection, vocational
education, and the administration of federally supported programs, was left virtually untouched and remains virgin territory for future inquiries. The influence patterns that emerge
in negotiations between the city school systems of St. Louis,
Kansas City, Chicago, and Detroit, and state officials, were
only tangentially discussed. We designed this project assuming that each state should be examined as a separate
entity before we could make any meaningful generalizations
or comparisons.

Of necessity, we restricted the project to selected aspects of state politics, mainly those decisions that must ultimately be approved in the legislative arena. Attention was focused on the 1961 sessions in the three states. The dramatic contrasts among the states we studied illustrate the importance of discussing the politics of education with a clear understanding of the variations in policy processes that occur from state to state. Our efforts reveal that there are almost as many variations as there are uniformities.

In view of the massive effort that is made today to provide educational opportunities, the obviously increasing role which the states play, and the demands for uniform standards and equality of educational opportunity, we need to know who is doing what, how. It is more evident now than ever before that educators must face political realities, as well as problems concerning the improvement of educational instruction. For they, too, as this study has attempted to show, *must compete for scarce resources*. However, this book is not designed as a guide for political action or as a source for answers to political complexities. Our study has been exploratory and our conclusions are explanatory rather than prescriptive.

SOME HYPOTHESES

At this point we should like to set forth certain *a posteriori* hypotheses with the understanding that new data must be collected to test them. In this chapter, we have focused on generalized statements in order that our findings may have wider applicability. The points we wish to emphasize are not mutually exclusive so some repetition is necessary.

THE POWER STRUCTURE

Public school decisions are made within a clearly identifiable power structure in which the influence relationships are clearly established, or in a political arena where power is fragmented, resulting in a high degree of uncertainty for the particular interests which are making claims.

The routine way in which most state public school decisions are made and the regularity with which certain procedures are followed in Illinois and Missouri clearly indicate the existence of a power structure in each of these states. The existence of such structures is one thing, what makes them "work" is another matter. Our data suggest that the key to understanding the Illinois and Missouri patterns, although they take different forms, lies in an appraisal of how these structures fit into each state's total political system. Although it is true that the School Problems Commission in Illinois and the MSTA in Missouri are the focal points of power, their power is exercised within the bounds imposed by their respective state's political system. In essence, these two agencies have become such integral parts of the systems in which they operate that the personal judgment of their leaders or members, as the case may be, frequently become the policies.

In Michigan, we found only the remnants of power structure in public school matters, although attempts were being made to forge a new one. The strains and stresses within this state's political system, coupled with the emergence of *strong independent* groups directly concerned with public school policy (the two phenomena are not unrelated), have destroyed any semblance of continuity and predictability in Michigan as to final policy outcomes, especially in the area of finance.

Given these influence arrangements, then, what additional characteristics of the process may be cited to explain the nature of public school decision-making? The following general statements are designed to highlight these characteristics.

THE ROLE OF RESPONSIBLE LEADERSHIP IN THE POWER STRUCTURES

Those who seek to influence public school policy work within a framework or "an area of permissible negotiation" established or set by the "responsible leaders"—a leadership that includes both legislators and the governor. In Illinois and Missouri the responsible leaders, those with the power to say "You can go this far and no farther," work together and enjoy highly developed and long-established interrelationships, although they may occasionally disagree. The responsible leaders include in both states the governor and "key" members of the legislature. In both Illinois and Missouri, the education interests are, for all practical purposes, a "part" of this leadership, having sufficient influence and resources to help design and shape the total political climate in which final decisions are reached or the proposals for change are judged and acted upon. In both states, the claims of the majority of education interests are given a high degree of legitimacy, but it is a legitimacy that is constantly in jeopardy.

In Michigan, as we have seen, the "responsible leadership" itself is fragmented, with the governor and legislative leaders frequently being at odds. In the period we observed, the public school interests, divided among themselves, remained apart from the responsible leadership, almost as if they had to be deliberately excluded. Moreover, one segment of this leadership, the Republican leaders of the Senate, had sufficient influence to set boundaries on expenditures that left no room for negotiation. In brief, then, what we are saying is that public school interests encounter the "responsible" leadership which lays out the playing field and sets the rules of the game of competing for scarce resources; in order to be effective, school interests must persuade or become part of this leadership. To be sure, this is a nebulous concept, but it is designed to characterize nebulous situations.

ORGANIZED USE OF UNORGANIZED OPINION

Relatively few public school policy proposals entertained in the legislative halls of the three states studied result from general public pressures or from wave-like "public" protests. We observed none and no one suggested that any issues have ever come up this way. Normally, general concern or expression of opinion that is presumed to emanate from the public is significant only when the organized interests themselves *use it or are able to use it* as a key element in making their claims upon governmental agencies. Whenever MSTA tries to secure some major innovation, such as the adoption of a foundation program, it carefully cultivates and in fact creates committees composed of prominent Missourians from all walks of life to help build support. Such effort is largely behind the scenes. Similarly, in Illinois the IEA, with the assistance of various other interests, circulates petitions among the public for presentation to the governor or legislative bodies. It also arranges conferences composed of prominent Illinoisians to advocate solutions to school problems.

The situation in Michigan is slightly different, in that in view of the conflicts, generating public support or widespread interest has often appeared as the only alternative to deadlock. The passage of the continuing appropriations act in 1959 resulted from the education interests' successful efforts to mobilize widespread citizen support, an effort that was given considerable stimulus by the first Soviet Sputnik. Precisely what constitutes widespread support or what legislators interpret as public pressure not only varies with the individual legislators but rests to a large extent on how each sees the political world in which he must live. This latter point is, of course, true in all three states.

CONTROVERSY

Issues concerning public schools can and do become highly controversial, despite the fact that there are no organized anti-school groups.[1] Conflicts occur over how much additional money the states can afford to spend on schools, how reorganization of school districts will affect particular locales, the extent of state as compared with local responsibility for financial matters, racial integration, state responsibility for teacher welfare, transportation of parochial students, etc. The nature and extent of the conflicts will, of course, vary with the issues.

The very fact that education issues involve conflict, potential or real, is clearly illustrated by the pattern of decision-making and non-decision-making in each of the states studied. In Missouri, many potential conflicts are contained within a private group, the MSTA, but they are not allowed to escape into the legislative process. The SPC in Illinois was created largely as a result of chaos and continuous controversy over policy alternatives, and it too has found ways to contain conflicts or minimize their disruptive effects. In Michigan, the efforts have been made to create an analogous mechanism primarily through an Educational Council, but the major issues in that state are too broad in scope and affect too many decision-makers to be contained. In short, in Michigan, when the governor disagrees with the state legislature—or some effective veto element within it— the state has no machinery and no group has the resources (or the ability to use them effectively) to act as an intermediary to "ready" decisions for final approval by the powers that be. Approval may still be forthcoming, but it seems mainly to be a hit or miss proposition.

[1] Among professional educators in Michigan, the Friends of the Michigan Schools is often referred to as the public schools' number one enemy. But this group, as its title suggests, does not regard itself in this light and counts among its allies many professional educators from the state's small rural school districts.

THE RED FLAG OF FINANCE

Issues that involve basic changes in the revenue structure or involve substantially increased expenditures for education purposes, can activate groups that are capable of exerting strong counter pressures and manipulating strong consensus-building symbols in opposition to the proposed changes or increases in expenditure levels. Characteristically, such groups do not oppose the schools *per se.* On the contrary, they will frequently acknowledge that schools need additional funds, although such admissions do not necessarily temper the tone of the opposition. These groups, in the main, base their attack on political themes such as fiscal responsibility, balanced budgets, and that "taxes are already too high."

The politics of public schools in Michigan provides the most dramatic support for this generalization. In that state, for example, school proposals encountered stiff resistance from groups and individuals that were not opposed to the schools but which were opposed, frequently vehemently opposed, to *any* increased expenditures. In 1961 lobbyists representing General Motors, Ford, and Chrysler managements and conservative-oriented senators and representatives responding to their own personal ideologies, as well as to outside pressures, expended considerable time and effort to keep taxes down and expenditures at as nearly present levels as possible when the school groups, as well as others, were asking for additional funds.

The unity and effectiveness of the SPC in Illinois were almost destroyed by an attempt of some of the commission's members to increase substantially the expenditures under the state's foundation programs. The normal practice in Illinois has been to ask for only moderate increases, determining *in advance* how much opposition there might be.

Moreover, in a sense, the MSTA in Missouri operates tactically in the same manner as does the SPC. Representatives of that organization try to avoid proposals that might activate this type of opposition, and if they seek substantial changes, they start an elaborate process to obtain consensus before conflict arises. But despite its predominant position, the MSTA has not always been successful in containing the opposition. The initial effort to secure increases in state aid in 1959 through an increase in the sales tax earmarked for schools is a case in point. In that instance, opposition came from two normally conflicting sources—the state Chamber of Commerce which was opposed to any increase in taxes or expenditures and the state AFL-CIO, which was opposed to an increase in the sales tax.

PROPOSING THE PROGRAMS

The groups and individuals who articulate the policy proposals, the innovators so to speak, are those who have a direct or tangible stake in the outcome of the decisions.

In the three states we surveyed, however, no one single pattern emerged in this regard. In Missouri, policy proposals emanated primarily from a single interest group, the MSTA. In Illinois, the professionals shared the policy articulation process with SPC legislators and gubernatorial appointees who had achieved the status of experts in their own right. In Michigan, policy proposals emanated from various organized interests which often found agreement among themselves impossible.

Despite these important variations, in each of the states we surveyed the major group was the state affiliate of the National Education Association; namely, the MSTA in Missouri, the IEA in Illinois, and the MEA in Michigan. These groups have a relatively high degree of organization, a principal spokesman, a wealth of information about school needs, and generally favorable access to at least some points in the *formal* decision-making structure.

Education association representatives in each state assiduously try to prevent their organizations from being labeled political action groups. All regard the systematic presentation of information about school needs as the most useful manner in which to approach political officials. Professional expertise and "objectivity" are regarded as the most important resources of influence of each group. Each group expends a vast amount of effort to influence policy and calls upon some extremely able people to support their views. Each group would prefer not to activate its members or to pressure a legislator in any overt way. Whenever possible, all avoid identifying and allying with other groups that are not directly concerned with education and which compete in the legislative arena. Obviously, as we have attempted to demonstrate, each of these three principal interests has had to accommodate its policies and strategies to fit its own state's political system and thus in a sense, too, each group is similar.

The tactic of using information, of presenting the facts of their case in the best possible light, is based, in the main, on the assumption that groups that claim to be above politics, that claim to be neutral and objective and that as a matter of course refuse to take sides when other interests are battling, cannot go much further than this without taking the risk of being labeled political. Anything beyond persuasion is a strategy reserved for "desperate" or "critical" situations. By labeling these situations "desperate" or "critical" they indicate their desire that additional efforts not be regarded as merely politically inspired.

With the exception of the teachers union, other education interests—the School Board Association, School Superintendents Association, the PTA, etc.,—rely more heavily on other means to secure legislative objectives. But for the most part they leave it to the NEA-affiliated groups to determine and articulate the demands. Michigan is the exception. Explaining Michigan's more pronounced fragmentation presents a problem. The answer seems to be that each group in Michigan perceives itself as having a greater stake in the outcome than do the comparable groups in the other two states. But this may beg the question, "Why is each specific group more independent?" On the surface at least it appears that the state's greater role in financing public schools allows for a more comfortable independence and opens the way to each group to pursue its own special interest, which may be incompatible with other interests. Also the unambiguous refusals by the state legislature seem to create uncertainty as to where new efforts should be directed. In brief, failure to achieve results has its divisive effects. Of equal significance is the MEA's sensitivity to competition from the MFT. To meet the competition, MEA places greater emphasis on its teacher welfare proposals, which in turn alienates the school board and superintendents' organizations.

Even though the extent of fragmentation of interests varied in each state, with Michigan clearly on one end of the continuum, Missouri on the other, and Illinois somewhere in between but closer to Missouri, there is in each state a subtle pyramiding of power *in terms of who articulates the demands*. This power lies predominantly in the hands of the official spokesmen for the organized interests, the professionals, who are limited only by what the political system will allow or (just as importantly) by what they think it will allow. Exclusively lay interests have little to say about what is needed, although they may have a great deal to say about what is finally gotten. The Farm Bureau in Illinois and Michigan are active and concerned, but their concern lies in the area of school district reorganization and has diminished as reorganization has been accomplished. These groups repeatedly said it was "up to them to decide what was needed," and by "them" they meant the professional associations or groups. This may be distressing news for those who believe education should be the chief bulwark against concentrated power and may raise some knotty questions for those who believe that democracy requires a wider diffusion of responsibilities. But the grooves of influence are deep and have been carefully channelled out.

The interests are like a closed club, displaying a pattern of influence that constantly repeats itself. Yet, although the professionals pull the strings, they must pull people instead of puppets.

The Rule of Favorable Access

The extensive commitment of virtually all groups within society to the maintenance of a system of public education facilitates access of the public school lobby to decision-makers. In each state surveyed, legislators frequently singled out the education interests as the most powerful in the state. This image seems to rest largely on the single fact that education groups have a considerable symbolic advantage that virtually insures access. That is, the sentimental appeals used by education groups—"doing something for the children," "young people are the future of America," etc.— even if sparingly used, are most difficult for politicians to resist or counter, if indeed there is a desire to do so. It would be difficult to suggest that education is not operating in the public interest, even though some legislators may privately hold this view. Moreover, the presence of professional educators in every local community, coupled with the fact that many local superintendents and educators are prominent in their communities and are backed by fairly active and prestigious groups such as the local PTA, League of Women Voters, etc., insures the education groups to which they belong virtually guaranteed access to elected officials who represent these areas in the state legislature. *However, the lack of political sophistication, failure to recognize the realities of politics, or just plain inertia on the part of its members frequently prevents an organization from utilizing its maximum resources.*

Teachers unions, which enjoy relatively limited access on the state level, access usually confined to urban Democratic legislators, are a general exception to the favorable access rule. The developmental pattern of teachers unions indicates that they are primarily big city organizations with few locals in the less urbanized areas of the state. At least this was the pattern we observed in Illinois and Michigan and in an embryonic way, in Missouri. State legislators bring out the point that because teachers' unions are affiliated with other segments of organized labor, they enjoy less social prestige among their colleagues, particularly among Republicans and rural or outstate Democrats, than do the other education groups. The generally unfavorable position among the school interests of the Illinois and Michigan Federation of Labor, and their limited relationships with the state legislatures exemplify the widespread resistance to unionism of white collar and professional workers.

MINIMIZING CONFLICTS AND REDUCING GOALS

Based largely on the mythology that education and politics should be kept apart, a major goal of education interests is to have governmental decisions affecting public schools made in a routine manner; that is, they desire a process in which all decisions are highly predictable as to their outcome, even if this means the sacrifice of certain policy alternatives or acceptance of less desirable results. Efforts of the major education interests concerned with finance and reorganization are clearly in this direction. The high level of confidence the interests in Illinois have in the SPC, the efforts to form an effective Educational Council in Michigan, the dominance of MSTA in Missouri despite its clear policy of incremental gains and restricted demands, all suggest a desire not to engage in a process that would require competition with other groups each year in the legislature. Continuous competition and agitation for legislative action would make it appear that professional educators, including the representatives of organized interests concerned with legislation, have abandoned the high ground of professional neutrality. In short, the less direct and open involvement in *political* decision-making the better. This may seem to involve ordinary political bargaining, but it is more than this. It is a desire for *safety* that permeates the thinking.

In Missouri, for example, the predominant group, the Missouri State Teachers Association, *avoids* raising certain questions, particularly in the area of teacher welfare, in order to minimize conflict within its organization between teachers and administrators, and, by refraining from raising issues that rival legislators would oppose, to maximize its chances for gaining other objectives. The SPC in Illinois deliberately sets aside those questions that it regards as explosive and concentrates on areas where immediate results can be reasonably assured. With the possible exception of the Illinois Federation of Teachers, Illinois education interests have not only willingly and enthusiastically supported this approach, but are indeed an integral and official part of the machinery.

In Michigan, on the other hand, where the goals of education interests are similar, the results are not the same. A neat, clear separation of education from conflict is the ultimate aim of groups such as the Michigan Education Association, but several factors present in Michigan and not present to the same extent in either Illinois or Missouri, have thwarted this objective. First, all attempts at unity in Michigan have failed. Second, Michigan differs, and not insignificantly, because the state government has been more generous in the past in its support of public education in general and the public schools in particular than either Illinois or Missouri— or for that matter most other states. Affluence seems to have made education interests disagree about how hard to push for further improvements. It has also allowed legislators to refer constantly to "Michigan's favorable position among the states," whenever faced with new demands for greater appropriations. This factor was clearly evident in 1961, when several groups were advocating different proposals as the absolute minimum necessary for a sound public school system.

Third, in Michigan the education interests feed their demands into a political system rife with conflict, much of it partisan in nature. In Missouri, there is a relative absence of deep divisive forces, particularly those of party. In Illinois, the SPC is engineered in such a way as to weed out or reconcile the divisive forces in that state before there are any eruptions, particularly those of party or those that emanate from the historic Chicago-downstate division. In short, the pattern of decision-making involving most major state education decisions in Illinois and Missouri is set and locked. But in the Michigan political system, differences run deep over fiscal matters and consequently touch all policy areas. Thus, conflicts over education can hardly be avoided. It should be pointed out, however, that if the conflict in Michigan is an extreme case because the state's total activities are the subject of controversy, it is only the extreme of a conflict that may exist in any state political system.

GROUP LEADERSHIP

Direct participation in the decision-making process by the representatives of organized education interests frequently forces them to tailor or alter their programs in order to produce consensus or sufficient support for their adoption; or it may serve as means for such representatives to take positions that might otherwise be impossible because of internal dissension. In short, knowledge of the political process enhances the control a representative of a group has over the aims, direction, and priorities of the group itself. It would be a mistake in this study not to single out certain key individuals who are constantly adjusting group demands to fit their assessment of the realities of politics. In the states we surveyed it was Everett Keith (MSTA's Executive Director), Lester Grimm (IEA research director, emeritus, and SPC member), Dick Adams (MEA lobbyist) and Max Cochran (Legislative Representative of the Michigan state superintendent) who acted both as brokers and innovators, attempting to transfer organization ideals into reality. This does not suggest that these and other officials of organized interests operate as free agents, yet their knowledge of organizational views and membership desires, combined with their working relationships on a day to day basis with political officials, serve as a dual shield, allowing their independent judgment in effect to become the policy and strategy of their respective groups. We can reasonably suggest that certain discrete or personality variables play a crucial role in each state.

LITTLE POLITICAL CURRENCY

With few exceptions political officials feel that efforts in behalf of education offer few of the traditional prizes; therefore they avoid direct involvement. The only exceptions to this rule are those legislators who achieve the status of experts in this policy area and who count education interests among their principal bases of support. Although in this study we did not quantitatively measure legislators' attitudes on this subject, our fragmentary evidence strongly suggests that the overwhelming majority find advocacy of public school causes not particularly advantageous, or to use their own jargon, not to contain much political currency (voter appeal, patronage).

With even less evidence, we can suggest some reasons for this. First, education is itself a highly specialized area and most legislators feel that to deal with it substantively requires some background in and familiarity with an education enterprise itself. Few legislators have this type of experience. Second, legislators must be reëlected. In the states we covered, where racial and religious issues do not intervene to any disruptive extent, everyone is generally in favor of schools or is pro-school in attitude. Thus, a legislative candidate who is for better schools is not unique. Rather, he is expected to be so disposed. Third, education is a policy area that offers few payoffs. Education interests do not endorse candidates or contribute money, and they generally refuse to get entangled in any campaigns unless they are trying to defeat a perceived foe. Other groups engaged in the policy process are not so inhibited or restrictive in their activities and may and do offer private inducements to secure support. And lastly, patronage is largely unavailable to legislators whether they champion school causes or not. This is of special significance in Illinois where most downstate legislators of both parties view the patronage at their disposal as a necessary ingredient for a successful political career.

All this means that public school policy questions are handled in a different way from other policy areas. Legislative decision-makers who are experts on education are open to persuasion; they *do* pay attention *even though* there are few other inducements. The other legislators, recognizing that education must be financed and improved, will usually go along, *providing* the tensions among education interests themselves and within the larger political context are not so great as to make support inconsistent with their own and their constituents' views, as was the case in Michigan during 1961.

Role Specialization

Because of the limited political opportunities education seems to offer to ambitious politicians, role specialization within the legislative branch has become a vital aspect of state politics as it relates to the public schools. In each state, several legislators, usually one from each party in each house and several more, have become the recognized experts and the ones upon whom education interests rely most heavily to carry their proposals through. Insofar as we have studied it here, the extent of role specialization varies. It was much more pronounced in the Illinois legislature than in the Missouri legislature, largely because ten Illinois legislators were also members of the SPC. Missouri and Michigan relied on fewer legislators, but in Michigan the absence of an expert or a legislator committed to representing school needs in the state senate greatly hampered all attempts to influence that body. "We didn't have anybody to carry the ball," was the way one group official put it.

INEFFECTIVE STATE SUPERINTENDENTS

The politically-elected state superintendent departs too widely from the norm of professional neutrality to be an effective, independent force, except perhaps in a state such as Florida, where the elected superintendent is a member of the state cabinet system and has political bargaining powers far beyond those of his counterparts in Illinois or Michigan. The elected superintendents in Illinois and Michigan serve interests that are committed to "professionalism." Thus, whatever firepower they may have stemming from their political contacts is effectively muzzled. This was true in both Illinois and Michigan, where the state superintendent either was influential through SPC or attempted to be influential through an Educational Council established through his office. The situation in Michigan contrasts with Illinois, however. In Michigan, the elected superintendent, being a Democrat, has been closely aligned with the teachers union movement, which obviously strains his relations with the MEA. Nevertheless, this has not erupted openly because the entire staff of the Department, with one exception, is on permanent civil service tenure and enjoys close ties with the MEA regardless of who fills the top position. His elected status as a Democrat has also severely curtailed or limited his influence with Republican leaders who have controlled both houses of the state legislature. In Illinois, SPC membership has allowed the superintendent to exercise influence that otherwise would have been impossible. But whatever influence he does exercise is of little consequence to him politically; that is, a state superintendent cannot build a political record on SPC accomplishments. Yet in both states, the aim is to make the state education department or office appear to be professional and nonpartisan.

The political role of the appointive head in Missouri contrasts markedly with the roles performed by the elected superintendents. Hubert Wheeler, the incumbent since the office was created in 1945, does not attempt to influence either the legislature or the governor directly. He has no program to present to the legislature nor proposals to make to the public. The present incumbent conceives his role as that of a professional educator concerned exclusively with administrative duties. He contends that any attempt to participate openly would meet with strong disapproval, not only from the education interests he serves, but from the state board to which he is directly responsible. Instead he relies on his close connections with the MSTA as the way in which he can influence policy matters. The extent to which he exploits these ties rests upon certain discrete variables, primarily the incumbent's assessment of a situation and the reception he receives from the personalities who govern the MSTA.

The conclusions of this study are tentative. The study has attempted to demonstrate that here is no great distance between professional educators and politicians, and that political activity of education interests will probably increase as the need for resources increases. If the professional educators' article of faith that politics and education should be kept apart is ever taken literally, then professional educators will be totally unprepared for what awaits them. But this is not to argue that attempts to divorce school questions from politics are unrealistic. Quite to the contrary. It has been just such attempts that have led to the type of policies and decision-making structures that have been adopted. True, as long as public schools remain *public* schools, they cannot escape political decision-making. However, the *very desire* to place public school questions above any conflict is itself an integral part of the process of decision-making.

Our experience with three midwestern states reveals that the political issues which questions of public school policy generate become entangled in varying degrees with the

many processes and patterns of conflict and resolution in
the total state political system. When such studies as this
are made in other states, we anticipate that certain dimen-
sions of conflict not found in our states will affect education
policy. A cursory examination of other states suggests several
salient areas of investigation:

First, political scientists might investigate the degree and
nature of conflict between teachers' unions on the one hand
and state and national NEA groups on the other. Involved
here is the public school teachers' self-perception as a professional, and their attendant modes of behavior. Who is to represent the teachers? Are classroom teachers to be lumped, for
purposes of vocational identification, with school administrators? Or must the classroom teachers, on the basis of
shared attitudes and common occupational objectives, organize apart from the administrators, who do not share the
same attitudes and objectives as their staffs? If the latter, do
classroom teachers lose their status as professionals? Or do
they make their profession more cohesive and homogeneous?
In either case, what is the effect on their political influence?

Teacher's unions are not yet a significant factor in two
states we studied; Michigan is the exception. However, conflict between the unions and the NEA affiliates might be more
pronounced in states such as New York, Pennsylvania, or
California. In cases where such conflict is highly developed,
we would expect a greater emphasis on teacher welfare on
the part of both groups in an effort to attract and retain
membership. Such a situation would weaken or strain the
alliance between the state NEA affiliate and the state school
boards association, as is the case in Michigan and possibly
New York and Pennsylvania.

Secondly, political scientists might investigate the entire
web of conflict patterns in other substantive policy areas in
terms of their effect on educational policy and the way they
render futile educators' efforts to keep politics and education

separate. The controversial question of the separation of church and state still remains an unresolved issue in public school policy formation.

Third, political scientists might study the racial problem as a possible cause of further conflict situations for the NEA as it competes with teachers' unions for the loyalties of American teachers. As long as NEA support depends on affiliates which are segregated—as in Florida, Texas, Georgia, North Carolina—this may give the teachers' union movement greater currency in the North and Midwest. And, of course, de facto and de jure segregation in our public schools is a burning political issue.

Finally, political scientists might study the potential conflict—if indeed it is just potential—between higher education and the public schools in their competition for scarce resources. For example, are we to accept without scholarly investigation the explanation that NEA's last-minute, well-mobilized opposition to a college aid bill in the Eighty-seventh Congress was predicated on the fear that the bill would "establish a precedent for Federal aid to private elementary and secondary schools"? Or again, what is the nature of the political tension between community (as opposed to state-supported) junior colleges and state-supported institutions of higher education that maintain far-reaching extension programs?

This book has dealt with the question of the relationship of politics to education—a basic issue that affects all Americans. The problem has been most succinctly stated in these words of J. K. Galbraith:

Education, no less than national defense or foreign assistance, is in the public domain. It is subject to the impediments to resource allocation between private and public use. So, once again, our hope for survival, security, and contentment returns us to the problem of guiding resources to the most urgent ends.[2]

[2] *The Affluent Society* (Boston: Houghton Mifflin, 1958), p. 355.

Appendixes

Bibliographical Essay

Index

APPENDIX I

The Comparative Picture: State Involvement

Since this is a book about how three state governments formulate public school policies, and since it is based on the assumption that all policy decisions involve conflict over allocating scarce resources, it seems appropriate to comment here on the respective contexts of this competition as it relates to public school policy.

We begin with a quick over-all survey of the patterns of state involvement in public education in each state, as well as some of the more relevant social and economic characteristics. Though none of our three states is as thoroughly agricultural as Iowa or Nebraska, each has a large rural population and—with the possible exception of the Missouri senate—are more representative of this rural segment than of the large cities and mushrooming suburbs. They have many similarities in population characteristics. All three have about the same percentage of Catholics and Jews. The rapid influx of Negroes from the South has put a new cultural face on the cities of Detroit, Chicago, and St. Louis, posing difficult and at times excruciating problems with regard to public education, housing, welfare, and employment opportunities.

But despite these similarities, the current resources and developments in each state differ considerably, leading to different tactics and results in the battle for changes in public school policy. One important variation is the level of federal, state, and local support for the public schools. Each of the three states is below the national average of 3.7 in the per cent of its school revenue receipts from the federal government. Illinois receives

2.8 per cent from the federal government, Michigan 2.6 per cent, and Missouri 2.5 per cent. However, further analysis reveals that, against a national average of 40.2 per cent of public school revenue from *state* sources, Illinois falls to 22.8 per cent, while Michigan and Missouri are higher at 42.4 per cent and 35.7 per cent respectively. The tendency in Illinois is to gather the bulk of the revenue for schools at the local level. The Illinois figure in this category is 74.4 per cent, considerably higher than the national average of 56.1, and higher than Michigan's 55 per cent and Missouri's 61.8 per cent.

In terms of school district consolidation, Michigan and Missouri both rank in a select group of nine states that have reduced their number of districts at least 30 per cent since 1956-57. This was part of a national trend that resulted in a reduction of 15,000 districts since 1957, lowering the nation's total to 37,438. The reduction in Missouri was 48.1 per cent, from 3,234 to 1,679. Illinois trailed the national average of 29.2 per cent by reducing its districts only 22.3 per cent, from 1,993 to 1,548. The percentages on Michigan, however, are somewhat deceptive, for Michigan still has more districts than either Illinois or Missouri, and significantly, Michigan has never adopted a state-wide school district reorganization plan. Figure 1 presents graphically the reorganization trends in each state from 1945 through 1961.

Considering the number of students to be educated and the attendant financial tasks, Michigan has a slightly greater problem than either Illinois or Missouri. Figure 2 sets forth the details concerning the estimates of enrollment in 1961-62. In addition to this, in Michigan, 27.5 per cent of the civilian population is of school age, ranking the state fifteenth in the nation in that category. Illinois ranks fortieth with 23.8 per cent of its population of school age and Missouri is forty-first with 23.7 per cent. The school-age population of Michigan increased 15.48 per cent from 1957 to 1960 (see Figure 3). The increase in Illinois was 12.65 per cent and in Missouri it was 9.52 per cent. During the decade 1951-52 —1961-62, school enrollment in Michigan increased by 52.1 per cent; the Illinois increase was 53.8 per cent, while in Missouri it was only 27.6 per cent.

Of the three states, Michigan was the only one in 1960 to have a per capita revenue of state and local governments above the na-

FIGURE 1

NUMBER OF SCHOOL DISTRICTS (1945-1961)

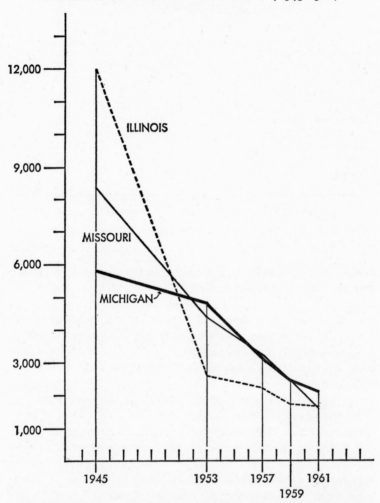

Data obtained from *School District Reorganization, Journey That Must Not End*, published by the American Association of School Administrators and Department of Rural Education of the National Education Association (Washington, 1962).

FIGURE 2

ESTIMATED PUBLIC ELEMENTARY AND SECONDARY SCHOOL ENROLLMENT (1961-1962)

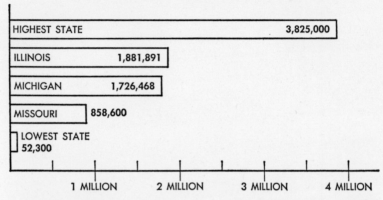

HIGHEST STATE	3,825,000
ILLINOIS	1,881,891
MICHIGAN	1,726,468
MISSOURI	858,600
LOWEST STATE 52,300	

1 MILLION 2 MILLION 3 MILLION 4 MILLION

Source: *Rankings of the States, 1962*, Research Division, National Education Association.

tional average of $280.62. The Michigan figure was $288.74. Illinois was not far behind with $272.83, but Missouri trailed the other two considerably, with $225.86.

If Missouri school men need to prove to the residents of the "show me" state that Missouri public schools are not faring as well as leading U.S. public schools, they can do so with little difficulty. Financial aid for schools in Missouri differs significantly not only from our two other states in this survey, but from the nation as a whole. Missouri's estimated expenditure per pupil in average daily attendance (ADA) for the school year 1961-62 is $386.17, compared with a national average of $414. Missouri ranks thirty-eighth among the fifty states, spending $229 less per pupil than top-ranking New York. Of this total amount, 35.7 per cent or $137.86 per pupil comes from state sources. In this category, Missouri ranks thirtieth among the fifty states, $28.57 below the national average.

Admittedly these are neither precise nor altogether fair methods for evaluating a state's effort in terms of its capacity. One common measurement that seems about as fair as any is the per cent of personal income spent for public education. In terms of both

FIGURE 3

PER CENT OF CHANGE IN PUBLIC ELEMENTARY AND SECONDARY SCHOOL ENROLLMENT

(1951-1952 to 1961-1962)

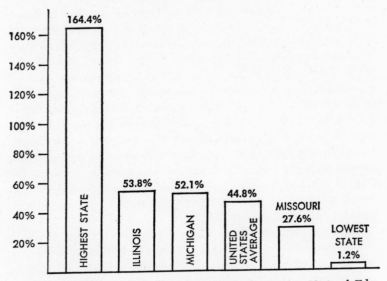

Source: *Rankings of the States, 1962*, Research Division, National Education Association.

state and local public school revenue, Missouri, in 1960, spent 3 per cent—the highest it has ever spent—of its personal income for the public schools, ranking forty-eighth against a national average of 3.7 per cent. In terms of only state revenue for the public schools, Missouri spent 0.9 per cent of its personal income, ranking thirty-eighth among the states, behind a national average of 1.5 per cent. These percentage figures, moreover, conceal as well as reveal, since Missouri ranks twentieth in per capita income. New York, for example, which spends $615 per pupil in average daily attendance and ranks first in the nation, spends only 1.6 per cent of its personal income on the public schools, and ranks twenty-sixth among the fifty states.

Rudimentary information on public school finances in Illinois paints a different picture, and indicates that a more complex explanation is required. In the school year 1961-62, the state provided 22.8 per cent of its public school expenditures. (The remainder was provided by the local school districts.) Expressed in terms of dollars, this amounted to approximately $114.46 per pupil in average daily attendance. In this regard, Illinois is well below the national average, ranking forty-fourth, and is below both Michigan and Missouri *in terms of state participation*. In terms of per capita income expenditures for public elementary and secondary schools for 1960-61, Illinois is very close to the national average, spending about $77.23 per capita and ranking twenty-third in the nation. This places the state well above Missouri, which is thirty-eighth, but substantially behind Michigan. Among the three states, Illinois outranks both Michigan and Missouri in terms of per capita income, being eighth in the nation. However, the state ranks forty-fourth in terms of public school revenue as a per cent of personal income, spending only 0.7 per cent of personal income for the public schools. Yet Illinois is fourth in terms of amount spent from state and local sources, spending $502 per pupil in ADA.

Michigan presents still a different picture. In terms of effort, it does much better than either Missouri or Illinois, spending 1.9 per cent of personal income on the public schools and ranking twenty-first in that regard. Combining state and local expenditures, Michigan ranks fourteenth, spending 4.2 per cent of personal income on the schools. In per capita state tax collections, Michigan is thirteenth with $123.50, compared to Missouri's $78.70 and Illinois' $86.45. This places Michigan above the national average of $106.03. In terms of public school revenue as a per cent of total revenue of state and local governments, Michigan ranks ninth with 37.6 per cent. Missouri ranks twentieth and Illinois ranks twenty-fourth.

The $440.13 that Michigan spends per pupil in ADA is above the national average of $414. The $186.61 of this amount that comes from the state is obviously greater than the $137.86 from Missouri and the $114.46 from Illinois. Figure 4 shows the percentage increases in current expenditure per pupil in ADA for the decade 1951-52 to 1961-62.

All three states are fairly close in terms of one criterion, the per cent of selective service registrants failing the mental test in

FIGURE 4

PER CENT OF INCREASE IN ESTIMATED CURRENT EXPENDITURES PER PUPIL IN ADA
(1951-1952 to 1961-1962)

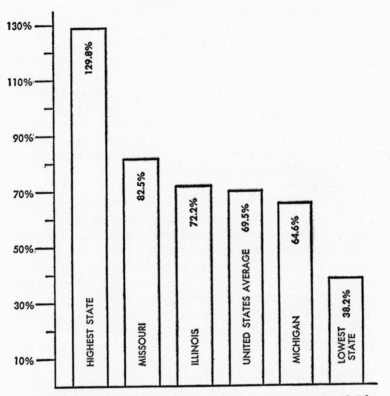

Source: *Rankings of the States, 1962,* Research Division, National Education Association.

1960. Of the three, Michigan, in twenty-first position with only 14.5 per cent of its registrants failing, rated the highest, but this was far behind leading Montana, where only 4.7 per cent failed. Illinois and Missouri shared the twenty-fifth ranking spot, each with 17.9 per cent failing the mental test.

Turning now to problems of teacher certification and salaries, we find that in 1961 only 0.2 per cent of Missouri's elementary school teachers had less than standard certificates, while 10 per cent of those in Illinois and 17 per cent of those in Michigan were in that category. In terms of secondary school teachers, 0.9 per cent of those in Missouri had less than standard certificates; 1.5 per cent in Michigan and 2.6 per cent in Illinois were not fully certificated. Of the three states, only Illinois reduced its number of substandard teachers from 1960 to 1961 by 2.9 per cent. The national average was an increase of 2.8 per cent in substandard teachers for that period. Both Missouri and Michigan experienced greater increases in the number of teachers with less than standard certificates. Michigan's increased 16.7 per cent and Missouri's 8.7 per cent. However, such figures may be misleading because each state defines a "standard" certificate differently.

All three states were fairly close to the national average in pupil-teacher ratio for 1961. The average was 25.6 pupils per teacher: Illinois had 23.7 pupils; Michigan, 26.1 pupils; and Missouri, 27.1 pupils.

Nationally, the average teacher's salary in 1961-62 was $5,527 (see Figure 5), which represented a 4.9 per cent increase over 1960-61. Although Missouri was the only one of the three states to fall below the national average in salary level with $5,080, it was also the only one to keep ahead of the average pace with an increase of 9.1 per cent over 1960-61. Illinois had the lowest rate of increase among the three, with 3.6 per cent, while Michigan had a 3.9 per cent increase, bringing the two states' salary levels up to $6,156 and $6,162 respectively. Figure 6 shows the increase in average salaries of classroom teachers over a period, from 1943 to 1962.

Despite recent efforts in all three states to equalize educational opportunities, there are wide variations in local school district resources and expenditures. The resources at the disposal of each district obviously affect the extent of its dependence upon the state government for funds, and the variations among the districts affect political alignments in each state legislature when state aid is the issue. For example, in Missouri the school district of Clayton (a wealthy suburb just outside St. Louis) has a total assessed valuation of $75,991,180 and a tax levy of $2.37 per 100 of assessed valuation. In 1961, Clayton, a district of triple A rating (the state's highest accreditation) had 1,993 pupils enrolled in kindergarten

FIGURE 5

AVERAGE SALARIES OF CLASSROOM TEACHERS IN PUBLIC SCHOOLS (1961-1962)

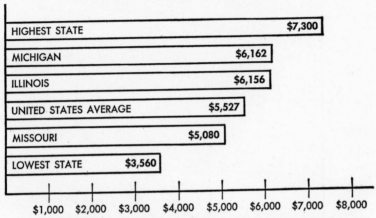

Source: *Rankings of the States, 1962,* Research Division, National Education Association.

through twelfth grade and therefore had an assessed valuation of $39,312 per pupil in average daily attendance. The Clayton district spent $2,400,504 (approximately $906 per pupil in ADA), of which less than 10 per cent[1] came from state sources. In that year the Clayton district employed 157 teachers, giving it a pupil-teacher ratio of 13:1.

The Valley Park school district (which lies a few miles southwest of St. Louis) stands in marked contrast to the Clayton district. For 1961, Valley Park had a total assessed valuation of only $4,434,530 or $5,488 per pupil in ADA. Valley Park spent $297,406 (approximately $280 per pupil in ADA), despite a higher tax levy of $3.90 per $100 assessed valuation. This district, maintaining an A rating, employed 39 teachers for 761 pupils in ADA for a pupil-teacher ratio of 20:1. Forty-four per cent[2] of the district's expenditures was derived from state sources.

[1] Clayton received $237,400—$180,025 in flat grants and $57,375 in teacher incentive—from the state.

[2] Valley Park's receipts from the state totaled $132,391, including $38,899 in equalization grants, $9,990 in teacher incentive, $77,961 in flat grants, and $5,441 for transportation.

FIGURE 6

AVERAGE SALARIES OF CLASSROOM TEACHERS IN PUBLIC SCHOOLS (1943-1962)

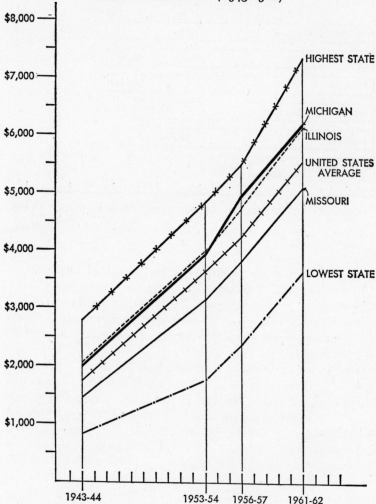

Data obtained from Illinois School Problems Commission Reports.

Figures for school districts in Illinois and Michigan are similar. The School Problems Commission Report for 1961 indicated, for example, that Marshall County in Illinois, encompassing nine local school districts, has maintained an average school expenditure of $557 per pupil in ADA, of which 95.6 percent is raised from local property taxes. The average amount of state aid paid to this county for the 1948 to 1958 period was $30 per pupil. Its assessed valuation per pupil for this same period increased 27.3 percent, its school taxes increased 131.6 percent, and its average attendance increased 25.7 percent. In contrast to Marshall County, however, is Pulaski County, encompassing fourteen local school districts, which has spent $263 for school purposes for each pupil in ADA. Of this amount, only 43.5 percent is raised from local taxes. As a result, Pulaski receives $149 per pupil in state aid each year. During the 1948-58 period, Pulaski County's assessed valuation increased 20.1 percent, its school taxes increased 68.0 percent, while its average attendance actually decreased 20.7 percent.

The pattern repeats itself in Michigan. In a random sample of Michigan school districts, we found one district of 212 pupils spending $581 per pupil in ADA each year and maintaining a pupil-teacher ratio of 21.6:1.

This cursory glance at the situation in all three states indicates some similarities and differences, but our purpose is not to evaluate and analyze performance levels. The question we are concerned with is how and why and in response to what forces the policies are adopted: that is, why does Illinois take one position on one thing and another position on something else, while just the reverse may be true in Michigan or Missouri. The three states are suitable subjects for analysis largely because none is extreme or atypical with regard to what the majority of states are attempting to do in the public school field.

APPENDIX II

Special Legislative Commissions on Education
in Illinois (1900-1947)

Commission	Recommendations	Adoptions
Education Commission of 1907	Issued series of bulletins calling for: state board of education to give continuous research and leadership to Illinois education system; county boards of education in each county; certification of teachers by superintendent of schools and county superintendents; revised, simplified, condensed, and codified school law; and increased teachers salaries.	Recommendations produced little immediate substantive action in General Assembly. They did set pattern for recommendations made by subsequent commissions.
Illinois Education Commission of 1921	Recommended school fund be distributed to elementary schools in the following way: .70 for each school day; grant from $2.50 to zero, depending upon	Recommendations were embodied in bill to provide new basis for distribution of State School Fund which was passed in 1923. When operation of law

	amount of teacher training and length of school term up to 36 weeks; 1½¢ per pupil-attendance-day; $100 for each one-room district employing normal school graduate for nine months term; involved equalization plan for weak districts.	proved unsatisfactory, Illinois State Teachers Association initiated studies which resulted in new law passed in 1927, which completely altered the 1923 act.
Illinois Education Commission of 1923	Concluded that district organization was not satisfactory but suggested little immediate improvement and recommended constitutional changes in revenue; recommended a state board of education and increased state aid for the education and training of handicapped children.	Bill to establish state board was introduced in General Assembly in 1925 but was defeated. Other recommendations favorably received.
Illinois Commission on Taxation and Expenditures of 1931	Recommended creation of state board of education, drastic consolidation of school units in downstate areas, and elimination of county superintendents.	No immediate action on any recommendations although some were eventually adopted (consolidations in some areas were effected along lines proposed by this commission).

APPENDIX II (*cont.*)

Commission	Recommendations	Adoptions
Illinois Education Commission of February 1935	Issued only brief preliminary report whose main recommendation was creation of state board of education.	Produced no immediate action in General Assembly.
Illinois Education Commission of July 1935	Re-emphasized the need for state board of education, nonpartisan county boards of education, additional state aid to schools, closer financial control, more rigid budgeting and accounting standards, and required audits of school treasurer's accounts. Most of latter suggestions could be delayed until after formation of state board.	Main recommendation of state board not acted upon. Some recommendations were implemented but not under terms suggested.
Some aspects of school administration in Illinois prepared by the Illinois Legislative Council, 1938	Recommended an increasing rate of taxation without referendum by unit districts; reducing aid to inefficient units; eliminating equalization aid on basis per	Most recommendations were subsequently enacted or influenced later legislative thinking.

Special study of the Department of Finance, 1939	teacher; eliminating aid to very small enrollment districts and providing for transportation to other districts; consolidating non-high districts; reducing qualifying rate for equalization aid; eliminating township treasurers. Recommended program of aid to school districts fulfilling minimum requirements for efficient operation, thus encouraging reorganization; adjusting present program of special aid to consider different assessment rates of property throughout state; and increased equalization provisions. It opposed expansion of flat grants.	Most recommendations were accepted, at least in principle.
First Report of Governor Dwight H. Green's Advisory Committee on Taxation, 1941	Recommended: creation in each county of school survey committee to recommend adjustments of school district boundaries; major changes in school law to	Recommendations provided basis for subsequent legislation, although immediate legislative action did not result.

APPENDIX II (*cont.*)

Commission	Recommendations	Adoptions
	operate to encourage continued formation of districts with adequate areas and resources; elimination of state aid to elementary school districts with average daily attendance of less than 7 pupils; minimum requirements of new high school districts of 100 pupils and assessed valuation of $1,000,000; withdrawal of recognition from each high school with less than 10 pupils per high school grade; elimination of school township treasurers.	
Report and Recommendations of the Illinois Postwar Planning Commission, 1945	Recommended: establishment of state-wide foundation program of minimum essentials of education; extension of school program to include kindergarten, nursery schools, and junior colleges; greater attention to re-	Recommendations were generally implemented subsequently but not immediately.

cruitment, preparation, and welfare of public education workers; increased state aid to finance foundation program; uniform and fairer property assessments; state-wide compulsory accounting system.

School Finance and Tax Commission, 1947

Long-range goals: state should guarantee financial support for foundation program to all districts properly organized and intelligently administered; eliminate small schools, both elementary and high schools; major portion of state funds should go for equalization purposes rather than flat grants; encourage unit district form of organization; amend school code to direct county superintendents to dissolve districts which fail to maintain school for period of two consecutive years; better distribution of tax load between local and state revenue.

Goals provided basis for much future legislation and were instrumental in establishment of first SPC.

Membership of Illinois School Problems Commissions

SPC Number One	Two	Three	Four	Five	Six	Seven
Senators						
Merritt J. Little	Lottie Holman O'Neill	Mrs. O'Neill	Robert E. Cherry	John P. Meyer	William Lyons	Edward C. Eberspacher
Robert W. Lyons	Lyons	Homer Butler	George E. Drach	Drach	Drach	Drach
Robert J. Young, Jr.	Young	David Davis	Davis	Davis	Davis	Davis
		John J. Gorman	Egbert B. Groen	Groen	Groen	Groen
		Albert Scott	Marshall Korshak	Korshak	Korshak	Korshak
Representatives						
Homer Caton	Charles W. Clabaugh	Clabaugh	Clabaugh	Clabaugh	Clabaugh	Clabaugh
W. O. Edwards	Edwards	Edwards	S. O. Dale	Dale	Dale	Dale
Adam S. Mioduski	Harry W. McClintock	McClintock	McClintock	McClintock	Edwin R. Haag	Charles Armstrong
		Rollie C. Carpenter	Walter J. Reum	Reum	Eberspacher	Clyde Lee
		Fred J. Smith	Kenneth R. Wendt	Wendt	Wendt	Wendt

Gubernatorial appointees

John K. Cox	Cox	Cox	Cox	Cox	Cox	Cox
Lester R. Grimm	Grimm	Grimm	Grimm	Grimm	Grimm	Grimm
A. J. Doyle	Doyle	C. J. Schlosser	Schlosser	John R. Kinley	Kinley	Edwin R. Haag
Harold W. Norman	Norman	Norman	Norman	Norman	Norman	Norman
Mrs. Clifton Utley	Mrs. Utley	Mrs. Utley	Frank M. Whiston	R. Sargent Shriver	Shriver	William Caple
Superintendent of public instruction						
Vernon L. Nickell	Nickell	Nickell	Nickell	Nickell	Wilkins	Wilkins
Director of finance						
George W. Mitchell	Joseph Pois	Morton H. Hollingsworth	Hollingsworth	Hollingsworth	Hollingsworth	Ronan
Research director						
Richard G. Browne	Orville Alexander	Alexander	Alexander	Alexander	Alexander	Alexander
Chairman						
Edwards	Clabaugh	Clabaugh	Clabaugh	Clabaugh	Clabaugh	Eberspacher
Vice-chairman						
Norman	Lyons	Davis	Davis	Davis	Davis	Clabaugh
Secretary						
Nickell	McClintock	McClintock	Dale	Dale	Dale	Haag

APPENDIX IV

Summary of Acts Affecting Education in Michigan
1961 Legislative Session

Local Act 2   *Repeal local acts governing twelve school districts*
(Senate Bill 1088)

Repeals special act charters of 12 school districts in Michigan, and provides that they shall operate under the School Code.

Public Act 5   *Repeal physiology and hygiene texts*
(House Bill 135)

Repeals Section 16 of Act 194 of the Public Acts of 1889 (Section 390.416 of the Complied Laws of 1948) which is obsolete because, while it makes it the duty of the state board of education to examine and approve all textbooks in physiology and hygiene, it provides that approval is based on a statute specifying space required to be devoted to consideration of the nature and effects of alcoholic drinks and narcotics, which statute has been repealed (Act 9, P.A. 1877). The state board of education, therefore, has no basis for either approving or disapproving such texts.

Public Act 21   *Specific tax on low grade iron ore* (immediate effect)
(Senate Bill 1182)

Provides that all sums collected under the provisions of this act shall be distributed by the township treasurer to school districts and to governmental units in the same proportion as the general property taxes are distributed.

Public Act 29   *Uniform election date*
(House Bill 455)

Provides that all annual school meetings or elections in primary school districts and school districts of the fourth class shall be held on the second Monday in June; members of the board of school districts of the fourth class shall meet on the first Monday of July succeeding their election and annually on the same day thereafter, and shall organize by electing a president, a secretary and a treasurer; and the terms of office of all members of boards of education shall commence on July 1.

Public Act 61   *Settlement of bonded indebtedness—transfer of property*
(House Bill 133)

Amends section 466 of the School Code (Section 340.466 of the Complied Laws of 1948) to allow school districts to settle bonded indebtedness with respect to property transferred.

Public Act 91   *Self-liquidating act amendments*
(House Bill 658)

Permits borrowing of funds for construction of facilities, such as recreational fields; requires legislative approval as to the location and extent of the cost of land and structures or facility before the letting of any contracts.

Public Act 108   *School bond qualifying*
(House Bill 587)

Defines terms under which bonds may be qualified and school districts may borrow when unable to meet bond payments; and provides for mandatory loans by the state to school districts when money is not on hand to pay bonds when due.

APPENDIX IV (*cont.*)

Public Act
111

State school aid deficit appropriation (immediate effect)
(House Bill 7)

Appropriates money from the general fund of the state for the fiscal year ending June 30, 1961, in an amount necessary to fulfill all obligations of the state aid act for 1960-61. This act also includes supplementary appropriations for the fiscal year ending June 30, 1961, to certain institutions of higher education and governmental agencies.

Public Act
112

School bond program—state funds
(House Bill 588)

Provides for the issuance of bonds or notes by the state to obtain funds as needed for loans to school districts as provided by Section 28 of Article X of the constitution under Act 108 of the Public Acts of 1961.

Public Act
115

School bond loan program—amendment to Municipal Finance Act
(House Bill 586)

Provides that first maturities of serial bonds shall fall due not more than four years from the date of issuance and that no maturity shall be less than one-fourth of the amount of any subsequent maturity; and that all outstanding and authorized bonds of a school district payable out of taxes may be treated as a single issue for the purpose of fixing maturities.

Public Act
152

Recounts—school elections
(House Bill 238)

A procedure is established for holding recounts in school elections, except elections for board members in primary districts. Recount procedures are removed from the "Registration School District" chapter and placed in the chapter governing school elections in all school districts. Six days are allowed for the obtaining of necessary signatures to apply for a recount.

Public Act 155

Repeal—excise tax, cigarettes—State School Aid Act, and extension of "grandfather" clause—county school districts
(House Bill 674)

Amends Sections 16 and 39 of Act 312 of the Public Acts of 1957, as amended (Sections 388.626 and 388.649 of the Compiled Laws of 1948) by extending the "grandfather" clause for county school districts for one additional year; and by removing from the State School Aid Act provision for the collection of an excise tax equal to 1 mill on each cigarette to be paid monthy to the state department of revenue.

NOTE: The crediting of this money to the state school aid fund was provided for by Act 156 of the Public Acts of 1961 (House Bill 599).

Public Act 159

Tax Allocation Board
(House Bill 311)

Provides that in each year, not later than 10 days after the county clerk has received a certified transcript from the state equalization board, the board shall make a preliminary order approving a maximum tax rate for the purposes of each local unit and shall give written notice of such order to each local unit.

Public Act 162

Property transfer—joint county board action
(Senate Bill 1316)

Requires that action on the resolution or petition for transfer of territory between school districts shall be taken only at a meeting attended by at least a quorum of each of the county boards of education when the proposed alteration extends into two or more counties.

APPENDIX IV (cont.)

Public Act 173

Special education monies—investment
(Senate Bill 1052)

Allows the county board of education to authorize the county treasurer to invest special education funds of the county in a) bonds, bills or notes of the United States, or obligations, the principal and interest of which are fully guaranteed by the United States, or obligations of the state; and b) certificates of deposit issued by any state or national bank organized and authorized to operate in this state.

Public Act 181

School board—majority
(House Bill 11)

Provides that no act of the board of education of any school district shall be valid unless voted at a meeting of the board by a majority vote of the members-elect of the board.

Public Act 188

Appropriations for various state institutions, departments, commissions, boards and other purposes relating to education (immediate effect)
(Senate Bill 1095)

Includes an appropriation of $4,382,490.00 for junior and community college operation to be distributed by the superintendent of public instruction to public school districts maintaining an approved college upon the basis of their enrollments in junior and community college credit courses. Included, also, are operating budgets for the Department of Public Instruction, state colleges and universities, Michigan School for the Blind, Michigan School for the Deaf, State Board of Control for Vocational Education, Veterans' Vocational School and the Michigan Public School Employees' Retirement System.

Public Act 203

Application to vote—30-day clause
(House Bill 236)

Requires that in all school elections, except elections for board members in primary school districts, electors shall identify themselves by executing an application to vote, and prohibits the holding of a regular or special school election within 30 days before or after any regular state general election.

Public Act 207

Registration—school elections
(House Bill 237)

Allows the board of education of any registration school district to contract with the city or township for general or special school elections; to change the last day for registration from the second Friday preceding to the thirtieth day preceding a general or special school election; and to prohibit registration for school elections at any time city or township registrations are closed.

Public Act 209

Retirement law—amendment
(House Bill 210)

Provides clarification in regard to administration of the law; and to include all employees of the Michigan College of Mining and Technology rather than only members of the faculty.

Public Act 218

Nomination petitions
(House Bill 235)

Brings certain school election procedures and nomination petition forms into conformity with general election laws.

APPENDIX IV (*cont.*)

School districts of the third class—pay tuition
(House Bill 292)

Public Act
219

Allows the board of any school district of the third class to use money in the general fund or funds received from state appropriations for aid to school districts for the purpose of paying tuition and transportation to another district of resident pupils, even though the grades in which the pupils may be enrolled are maintained with the district.

APPENDIX V

Methodological Note

This study uses a variety of methods to explore broad questions about the variables involved in education decision-making in three separate state political systems. However, the limitations of time, resources, and skill made it necessary on the whole to sacrifice precision of technique in favor of less rigorous methods. Our analysis is a tentative one relying more on impression and judgment than on measurement or proof. We hope that these shortcomings, if so they are, are compensated for by the effort to show in broad and comparative perspective the interactions of the major elements of whole political systems as they apply to a particular substantive policy area. If this effort has succeeded, it prepares the way for greater precision in subsequent research than might otherwise have been possible.

AN EXAMINATION OF CONSTITUTIONAL AND STATUTORY ARRANGEMENTS

Our first task was to examine carefully the constitutions and school codes of the three states in order to determine the functions and responsibilities of various state agencies for formulating and administering public school policies. This involved cataloguing the relevant provisions, but the range and complexity of these provisions made the cataloguing a sizable preliminary to our main concern.

INTERVIEW TECHNIQUE

We obtained the information on education decision-making in the legislatures and the pressures on them primarily from unstructured interviews with recognized political leaders who held official and unofficial positions of power. Despite their obvious disadvantages, the interviews were unstructured in order to allow respondents to give as comprehensive a view of the manner in which policies were formulated as their respective knowledge, experience, and willingness would permit. In Illinois, we interviewed the following people: members of the Illinois School Problems Commission; the leaders of each party in both the House and Senate; the members of Senate and House Education Committees; the registered lobbyists and leaders of the public school organized interests; representatives of the state Chamber of Commerce and organized labor unions; reporters who cover Springfield for leading metropolitan newspapers; and a number of politically active and informed observors of Illinois state government who do not fall into any of the above classifications. In several cases, we interviewed particular individuals more than once. For example, we interviewed some members of the School Problems Commission on three separate occasions. Lester Grimm, research director and chief lobbyist for the Illinois Education Association, was interviewed four different times concerning past and present educational developments at the state level.

In Michigan, we took a substantially different approach to the problem of data collection. Here in order to facilitate access to decision-makers, the principal researcher served as an administrative aid to Governor John B. Swainson. In this capacity, he was able to participate first-hand in the formulation of the governor's position on pending educational matters in the 1961 session of the Michigan legislature. He was also able to play an active role in the meetings of the state Educational Council, a group composed of representatives of the state department of education and education interests active in the state. We also interviewed political and legislative leaders in Michigan, as well as representatives of the various education and other groups, the press, and other politically active and informed people.

There were certain disadvantages to the procedure we followed in Michigan. Direct participation in a partisan environment may involve emotional commitments and introduce biases which distort the researcher's perceptions of the realities of a situation. In an attempt at least partially to offset this, other individuals conducted interviews at a later date with a number of the more prominent political and educational leaders and compared the results of these interviews carefully with results based on direct participation.

Finally, in Missouri, we followed the same general patterns we used in Illinois. Two members of the research staff made weekly trips to Jefferson City during the 1961 session of the legislature to interview legislators and other political officials. Officials of the Missouri State Teachers Association provided virtually a step by step account of current educational developments and strategies their organization followed during the 1961 session, as well as recollections of earlier developments.

OTHER DATA

In the course of a study this broadly conceived, we had to rely on secondary sources for data bearing on particular points. For example, a number of secondary sources dealing with the development of public education in America and in the states under consideration proved invaluable in preparing the introductory material. Existing studies of aspects of the political systems of Illinois, Michigan, and Missouri were extremely useful for analyzing the arenas of conflict and compromise in which education decisions and policies are formulated. In addition, the elaborate data compiled by the Bureau of Census, congressional committees, and the United States Office of Education in the Department of Health, Education, and Welfare, and the National Education Association (NEA) were used to prepare the tables.

Bibliographical Essay

In recent years, the increasing volume of publications dealing with the support and control of public school education in the United States has reflected a growing concern and controversy over its diverse aspects. To do justice to these materials would require a major bibliographical volume, a monumental work in itself which is not within the scope of this study. Touching, therefore, only the surface of the wide-ranging topics encompassed by the term "public education," the following titles offer to the reader a selective list of book-length works in the educational field. A few references to journal articles are indicated; but, in the main, we have not attempted to review the literature in periodicals. We have tried to include materials concerned with the various levels of the educational and the governmental process.

As the reader will note, not all of the works cited are up-to-the-minute commentaries. Thus, in some areas, a pioneering essay written three decades ago may overshadow more recent works and, in other fields, there may be no such classic. For example, the field of concentration in this volume, state politics and public education, pursues a topic subjected only recently to the researcher's scrutiny. Clearly, in the relatively new and growing literature on education and politics, state politics in particular is a meaningful and long neglected phase of research.

We still await a major study of politics and education. Its potential public grows steadily larger and more aware of the public school system as a focal point in American life. Philosophies and methods, beliefs, conflicts, and compromises with respect to both the learning process and the political process meet in the American public school classroom.

Some of the books chosen for this bibliography were written for a specialized, professional audience; some are polemical and controversial; and some are journalistic reports of recent episodes. We included all because we wished to provide a brief list, illustrating the general categories of studies coming off the presses in the effort to inspire and meet the interest of our communities in the evolving American school systems.

PUBLIC CONTROLS AND EDUCATION

One of the few historical efforts in the field of American public education which traces the evolution of the progressive movement in the broader social and intellectual context of American society is *The Transformation of the School* by Lawrence A. Cremin (New York: Knopf, 1961). The volume supplies valuable insight into the operating ideals of our school systems, covering a period from 1876 to 1957. Older but still useful is George Counts' *School and Society in Chicago* (Chicago: University of Chicago Press, 1928).

For studies of special aspects of educational control, such as the role of school boards and voter participation, see also Counts' *The Social Composition of Boards of Education* (Chicago: University of Chicago Press, 1927). Follow-up works have contributed further evidence of Counts' thesis that school boards are dominated by those individuals who control the nation's economic resources. Conclusions of a similar nature have been drawn about higher education by Hubert P. Beck, *Men Who Control Our Universities* (New York: King's Crown Press, 1947). For a detailed study of the institutional controls determined by constitutions, legislatures, governors, and administrative agencies over colleges and universities, see Malcolm Moos, *et al., The Campus and the State* (Baltimore: Johns Hopkins Press, 1959).

Stanford University has done some research in voter interest and participation in school affairs for the U. S. Office of Education. The apparent willingness of the public to leave school matters to professionals is indicated in *Voters and Their Schools* by Richard Carter (Stanford: School of Education, Institute for Communication Research, 1960).

COMPARATIVE EDUCATION

Comparisons of the educational systems of the United States and other countries open up fruitful areas of discussion. Serving as background preparation are such works as Robert Ulich's *The Education of Nations* (Cambridge: Harvard University Press, 1961) and Kurt London's *Backgrounds of Conflict: Ideas and*

Forms in World Politics (New York: Macmillan, 1946). Ulich's volume emphasizes the continuity of Western educational thought and systems, tracing development from antiquity to the modern age of science and technology. The London study is excellent for its placement of the education process in an interdependent network of political, economic, religious, and educational factors making up a nation. Other leading works in the field include: Nicholas Hans, *Comparative Education* (London: Routledge, 3rd ed., 1961); Vernon Mallison, *An Introduction to the Study of Comparative Education* (New York: Macmillan, 2nd ed., 1960); Friedrick Schneider, *Vergleichende Erziehungswissenschaft: Geschichte, Forschung, Lehre* (Heidelberg: Quelleund Meyer, 1961).

For an example of comparative study brought to bear on concrete issues in curriculum and school organization, see James B. Conant's *Education and Liberty* (Cambridge: Harvard University Press, 1953). Accompanying his report on secondary education in Great Britain, Australia, New Zealand, and the United States, Conant calls for a revamping of our values and implementing procedures with regard to general education and the recognition of special talents and worth.

CHURCH, STATE, AND EDUCATION

The role of the schools in the church-state controversy is an area of continuing argument. The well-grounded reader will want to familiarize himself with the most comprehensive work in this field, *Church, State, and Freedom*, by Leo Pfeffer (Boston: Beacon, 1953). Also valuable are *The American Tradition in Religion and Education*, R. Freeman Butts (Boston: Beacon, 1950); and *Religion and Education Under the Constitution*, James M. O'Neill (New York: Harper, 1949). Butts' secular viewpoint contrasts with O'Neill's theistic analysis of the meaning of the First Amendment. For an excellent summation of the leading U. S. Supreme Court decisions on education in the past four decades, we turn to Professor David Fellman, *The Supreme Court and Education* (New York: Teachers College, Columbia University, 1960).

More specialized but useful in their approach are several recent publications on various aspects of church-state arguments and the schools. A timely study of the Bible-reading controversy can be found in *The Bible, Religion, and the Public Schools* by

Donald E. Boles (Ames, Iowa: Iowa State College Press, 1961). An excellent case study of one state's legislation regarding parochial school pupils appears in Theodore Powell's *The School Bus Law* (Middletown: Wesleyan University Press, 1960). The arguments of the supporters and opponents of a recent school bus law in Connecticut are examined and the roles of various interest groups, the political parties, newspapers, the PTA, and others are defined in this step by step analysis of the legislation. *Render Unto Caesar: The Flag Salute Controversy*, David Manwaring (Chicago: University of Chicago Press, 1962) examines the legal efforts of a religious group to express its views on the context of the public schools. No bibliography of the church, state, and education issues, however brief, can overlook comment on the parochial school question. An authoritative statement on the parochial school system comes from the Jesuit, Neil G. McCluskey, *The Catholic Viewpoint on Education* (Garden City: Hanover House, 1959).

RACE, CLASS, AND EDUCATION

The turmoil following in the wake of the U. S. Supreme Court's historic desegregation decision evoked a dispassionate discussion of the legal, sociological, and psychological aspects of the decision by Albert Blaustein and Clarence Ferguson, *Desegregation and the Law* (New Brunswick: Rutgers University Press, 1957). This work traces the development of the court's reasoning regarding school facilities from "separate but equal" to "separate is essentially unequal." Accounts of some of the major events of post-1954 school integration history appear in former Little Rock School Superintendent Virgil Blossom's *It Has Happened Here* (New York: Harper, 1959). *Virginia's Massive Resistance*, Benjamin Muse (Bloomington: Indiana University Press, 1961) and *With All Deliberate Speed*, Don Shoemaker, ed. (New York: Harper, 1957), merit close examination.

The school problems of the South have served as only one focus for current educational commentary. Patricia C. Sexton's *Education and Income* sounds a plea for reform of educational inequalities in our major cities. The author cites evidence of the physical and mental deprivations of low-income neighborhood schools. Expanding this field of investigation and recommending specific reforms is James B. Conant's *Slums and Suburbs* (New York:

McGraw-Hill, 1961). Documentation of the wide divergency in American high school education in this and an earlier volume, *The American High School Today* (New York: McGraw-Hill, 1959) supports Conant's conclusions in an outstanding interpretation of national school needs.

THE FEDERAL GOVERNMENT AND EDUCATION

An inventory of the federal government's role in education from the elementary school to the college and university level is contained in *The Federal Government and Education* by Hollis P. Allen (New York: McGraw-Hill, 1950). Although published a decade ago, this volume is still useful, especially if supplemented by current material in, for example, *Federal Interest in Education,* Homer D. Babbidge and Robert M. Rosenzweig (New York: McGraw-Hill, 1962). The authors of the latter volume, one an officer of the American Council on Education, the other a high-ranking official of the U. S. Office of Education, consider the relations between the federal government and higher education as a vital issue of public policy. Along the same lines is a recent collection of essays from an American Assembly Conference edited by Douglas Knight, *The Federal Government and Higher Education* (Englewood Cliffs, New Jersey: Prentice-Hall, 1960). The contributors launch into issues such as government control of research, local versus federal administration of education, and segregation.

EDUCATION AND POLITICS

For an introductory reading in the area of education and politics, we turn to another title by James B. Conant, *The Child, the Parent, and the State* (Cambridge: Harvard University Press, 1959). A call for further research into the political ramifications of lay-professional interaction in the schools appears in "Toward an Understanding of Public School Politics," by Thomas H. Eliot, in *American Political Science Review* (LIII, December, 1959, pp. 1032-1051).

Who Runs Our Schools? is an analysis of educational policy-making based on interviews of school board members and school superintendents by Neal Gross (New York: Wiley, 1959). Somewhat polemical in tone but providing incisive criticisms is Myron

Lieberman's *The Future of Public Education* (Chicago: University of Chicago Press, 1960). Among Lieberman's contentions is the view that national professional education associations should assume the decision-making role now in the hands of local school boards. Another approach to the establishment of school policy can be found in *The Politics of Education* by Frank MacKinnon (Toronto: University of Toronto Press, 1960). MacKinnon, fearful of the "politicalization" of school administrators, calls for the creation of procedures insuring the autonomy of teacher control.

The perennial question of civil liberties and the teaching profession is treated in Lawrence Chamberlain's *Loyalty and Legislative Action* (Ithaca: Cornell University Press, 1951). For some insight into the picture academicians have of themselves, Paul Lazarsfeld and Wagner Thielens present *The Academic Mind* (Glencoe: The Free Press, 1958).

More valuable material on educational policy and the political process can be found in *Community Leadership for Public Education* by Truman Pierce (New York: Prentice-Hall, 1955). Bruce Raup's *Education and Organized Interest in America* (New York: G. P. Putnam, 1936); and "Education and the American Political System" by York Willburn in the *Teacher's College Record* (LIX, February, 1958, pp. 292-298).

An increasing number of local and regional political studies devote some attention to the public schools. We might cite as a brief sampling: Robert Dahl's *Who Governs? Democracy and Power in an American City* (New Haven: Yale University Press, 1961); V. O. Key's outstanding *Southern Politics in State and Nation* (New York: Knopf, 1950); *New England State Politics* by Duane Lockard (Princeton: Princeton University Press, 1959); *Political Influence* by Edward Banfield (Glencoe: The Free Press, 1961); and John H. Fenton's *Politics in the Border States* (New Orleans: The Hauser Press, 1957).

First in a projected series of studies of the economics and politics of public education from the Maxwell School of Public Administration is *Schoolmen and Politics: A Study of State Aid to Education in the Northeast,* by Stephen K. Bailey, *et al.* (Syracuse: Syracuse University Press, 1962). Twelve monographs in the series examine the governmental process and its consequences for the fiscal support of public education.

SCHOOL ADMINISTRATION AND FINANCE

There are numerous works available on public school finance; however, we have singled out *The Economics of Public Education* by Charles S. Benson (Boston: Houghton, Mifflin, 1961). This is an outstanding study—not only of the management of school finances, but especially of the underlying structure and growth potential of economic resources in public education. For example, it considers such topics as national income, tax structure at all levels, and measures of productivity in education.

Typical of other volumes in educational finance are W. Montfort Barr, *American Public School Finance* (New York: American Book Company, 1960) or Paul Mort, *et al.*, *Public School Finance* (New York: McGraw-Hill, 1960, 3rd ed.), or *Budgeting for Better Schools* by Leon Ovsiew and William Castetter (Englewood Cliffs, New Jersey: Prentice-Hall, 1960).

Some noteworthy titles in school administration are *Administration and Policy-making in Education* by T. Walten (Baltimore: Johns Hopkins Press, 1959), and Leon Ovsiew, *Emerging Practices in School Administration* (New York: Metropolitan School Study Council and Cooperative Program in Educational Administration, 1953). A text by Harlan Hagman, *The Administration of American Public Schools* (New York: McGraw-Hill, 1951) is particularly useful in regard to the relationship of federal and state agencies to local school administrators.

ORIGINAL SOURCES

Those readers who may be interested in original source materials will want to turn to several organizations, both governmental and nongovernmental. The U. S. Office of Education publishes numerous bulletins, circulars, and pamphlets. The *Education Directory* contains information on the local governments and the states, county, and city school systems, higher education, and educational associations. Best known of the U. S. Office of Education efforts is the *Biennial Survey of Education*. A partial list of topical inclusions cites data on state school systems, city school systems, vocational education, enrollments, receipts and expenditures, personnel, schools and services provided, and administrative units.

A free list of U. S. Office of Education and Other Publications

Relating to Education may be secured from the Superintendent of Documents (Government Printing Office, Washington, D.C., revised annually).

Another governmental source is the U. S. Bureau of the Census. To locate census publications, such as, for example, the *1962 Census of Government's Preliminary Report, No. 1, Public School Systems* in 1961-1962, see the Bureau's *Catalog and Subject Guide*, which is a cumulative index to census publications.

The National Education Association is a ready source of material. Its *Research Bulletin* (published four times yearly) and the *Review of Educational Research* (five times a year) are particularly useful. The association publishes a *NEA Publications List* and its publications can also be located under topical headings in the *Education Index* and *Public Affairs Information Service*.

The American Council on Education should be noted for its *Studies*. Seven series in the *Studies* include School Plant Research; Student Personnel Work; Council Staff Reports; and the Financial Advisory Bulletin.

At the state level, the reader should note the Council of State Governments. Basic, statistical data can be found in its publication, *The Book of the States*. State departments of education usually publish annual or biennial reports and other bulletins. State professional education associations frequently have research departments. The titles of the publications of both state education departments and state professional education associations can be located under the name of the state in the *Education Index*.

Index

A NOTE ON THE TYPE

THE TEXT of this book is set in *Caledonia*, a Linotype face designed by W. A. DWIGGINS, the man responsible for so much that is good in contemporary book design and typography. Caledonia belongs to the family of printing types called "modern face" by printers—a term used to mark the change in style of type-letters that occurred about 1800. Caledonia borders on the general design of Scotch Modern but is more freely drawn than that letter.

Composed, printed, and bound by
H. Wolff, Inc., New York
Typography and binding design by
VINCENT TORRE